# *ASD Tugs:*
# *Thrust and Azimuth*

## Learning to Drive a Z-drive

Captain Jeffrey Slesinger

2nd Edition

CORNELL
MARITIME
PRESS

Edited by Ian Robertson
Designed by Jack Chappell
Type set in Serpentine/Zurich

ISBN: 978-0-7643-5682-7
Printed in the United States of America

Published by Schiffer Publishing, Ltd.
4880 Lower Valley Road
Atglen, PA 19310
Phone: (610) 593-1777; Fax: (610) 593-2002
E-mail: Info@schifferbooks.com
Web: www.schifferbooks.com

For our complete selection of fine books on this and related subjects, please visit our website at www.schifferbooks.com. You may also write for a free catalog.

Schiffer Publishing's titles are available at special discounts for bulk purchases for sales promotions or premiums. Special editions, including personalized covers, corporate imprints, and excerpts, can be created in large quantities for special needs. For more information, contact the publisher.

We are always looking for people to write books on new and related subjects. If you have an idea for a book, please contact us at proposals@schifferbooks.com.

*This edition is dedicated to Cynthia Wold,*

*whose light has guided me through many voyages.*

# Contents

# Preface

The first edition of this book was published in 2010, when Z-drive technology was well on its way to becoming the predominant propulsion system for new-build tugs and towboats. Today, Z-drives can be found worldwide and engaged in all types of towing applications: ship assist, escort, and inland, river, and coastal towing. The ability to handle a Z-drive-propelled tug or towboat has become a staple of any professional tugmaster's skill set.

This second edition is an evolution of the first, incorporating the recommendations of those who have used it as a training tool in simulators and onboard their vessels. As in the previous edition, the impetus for this book is to provide a systematic learning sequence for instructors and operators to use in acquiring the skill sets specific to handling an azimuthing stern drive (ASD) tug or towboat safely and competently. Readers are encouraged to use this book as a reference tool to assist in their individual paths of learning, practicing, and polishing the skill sets required to drive these fabulous vessels.

# Acknowledgments

I am deeply grateful to those who have helped in the production of this book. The pages that follow embody the collective expertise and wisdom of many individuals and institutions. I am particularly grateful to those ship pilots and tug and towboat captains who willingly shared their experience handling Azimuthing Stern Drive tugs and towboats and openly shared their expertise to benefit the larger maritime community.

I would like to thank my son, Nathan Slesinger, Cameron Falkenburg, and Kyle Knudson—whose illustrations lend clarity to the text—and also Professor Edward Wellin for his editorial insight and encouragement.

# Foreword

Capt. Jeff Slesinger is a breath of fresh air to tug captains, mates, and future crew members just starting their careers on tugs. Jeff walks tall and carries a big stick but is a gentle giant when dealing with trainees. As we say in the industry, Jeff came up through the hawsepipe, which gives him a unique insight into the many levels of training and abilities required to be a successful ASD tug captain. He has a special way of imparting his knowledge and experience to the people he trains. This makes it very easy to engage in the training. In this day and age, with the use of computer simulation, Jeff takes it one step further and adds the reality of the real world to training. This comes from years of experience, which he gladly shares with his trainees. He presents it in such a way that it does not look like physics—but it is. As well, he adds the risk analysis to the equation, drawing the two aspects together to give the captain a sense of competence when he makes those split-second decisions that are absolutely necessary in today's high-tech world with high-powered tugs.

Having used Jeff's first book, *ASD Tugs: Thrust and Azimuth*, in my training classes, I make it a prerequisite for my trainees to read the book before we get started, and to understand the maneuvers that are referenced. This cuts the training time down immensely and gives them confidence in making the transition from regular tugs to the new ASD tugs. The knowledge Jeff has incorporated in his book explains all the basics of the new "tugnology" and removes the fear factor, which in turn accelerates the training and gives them confidence to move forward. In going forward, this will help future captains develop their own techniques on the basis of Jeff's tried-and-true basics. Jeff has walked the walk and now he can talk the talk—the results speak for themselves!

Capt. Ron Burchett

# *Chapter One*
## Before We Begin

## Introduction

One can't learn to drive a Z-drive by reading a book. Z-drive maneuvering is a hands-on skill; true competence can come only from "learning by doing." However, a book can be a helpful learning tool along the journey to competence. The purpose of this book is to use language and illustrations to paint mental pictures of an efficient learning process, the principles of Z-drive maneuvering, and the effect of various thrust configurations. It should serve as a reference during the process of learning to drive a Z-drive-propelled vessel. Before undertaking that voyage of learning, we all must speak the same language and agree on the terminology.

This is particularly true with Z-drives, because many technical and colloquial terms thrown about in reference to Z-drives can be confusing. Tractor tug, reverse tractor, azimuthing stern drive (ASD), azimuthing tractor drive (ATD), Rotortug®, Z-drive tug, or towboat all are terms associated with Z-drive propulsion. In addition, Z-drive control systems have evolved and include terms such as combi-lever, master pilot system, and slipping or speed modulating clutches. This book will focus on the most common Z-drive configuration and control system: two Z-drive propulsion units mounted athwartships in the stern of the vessel and controlled by two independent control handles, allowing the operator to manipulate the azimuth and RPM of each drive unit independently.

Here is an explanation of those terms and a description of the terms that will be used in this book.

## Explanation of Terms

### Z-drive

Z-drive refers to a type of propulsion system. It does not refer to the number or location of Z-drive units in a vessel. Z-drive units may be forward, aft, or in both locations on a vessel. Outside the US, Z-drive propulsion may also be referred to as Zed drive.

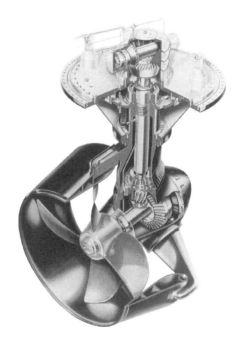

Fig. 1-1
Z-drive propulsion unit
*Courtesy of Schottel GmbH*

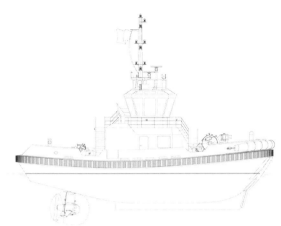

Fig. 1-2
ASD (azimuthing stern drive)
configuration
RApport 2400
*Courtesy of Robert Allan, LTD.*

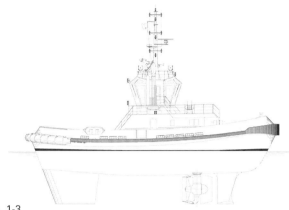

Fig. 1-3
ATD (azimuthing tractor drive)
configuration
Z-drive propulsion
TRAktor-Z
*Courtesy of Robert Allan, Ltd.*

Fig. 1-4
Tractor tug configuration
VSP propulsion
TRAktor-V
*Courtesy of Robert Allan, Ltd.*

Fig. 1-5
Rotortug®
ART 70-30
*Courtesy of Robert Allan, Ltd.*

### ASD

ASD is the initialism for Azimuthing Stern Drive and refers to a vessel that has two [2] Z-drive units positioned athwartships near the stern of the vessel. This is the most common configuration of towing vessels that utilize Z-drive propulsion.

### ATD

ATD is the initialism for Azimuthing Tractor Drive and generally refers to a vessel that has two [2] Z-drive units positioned athwartships, forward of amidships of the vessel. The most common application of this configuration is in Z-drive-propelled towing vessels dedicated to ship assist work.

### Tractor Tug

Tractor tug is one of the most misused and misunderstood terms used in reference to Z-drives.

A tractor tug is a vessel that has its propulsion system forward of amidships, and the term refers to the location of the propulsion units in a vessel—not the type of propulsion. The propulsion can be either Z-drive or VSP (Voith Schneider Propeller). In the US, this term is broadly used to describe all types of tugs that are equipped with omnidirectional thrust propulsion, regardless of the type or location of the propulsion units. Although this may be useful as a marketing term, it has led to confusion as to what the vessel looks like under water and its capability in towing applications.

### Rotortug®

A Rotortug® is a term used to describe a vessel that has three [3] Z-drive units, with two [2] Z-drive units forward—similar to a tractor configuration—and one [1] Z-drive unit aft.

### Double-Ended Z-drives

There are several tug designs that place one Z-drive propulsion unit forward and one aft, creating a double-ended vessel.

This book focuses on the Azimuthing Stern Drive configuration: two Z-drive propulsion units side by side in the stern of the vessel.

# Terms Used in This Book

Using a book as a learning reference requires a clear understanding of the book's terminology. It is difficult enough to paint a mental image of the cause and effect of two independently controlled Z-drive units while your hands are turning the controls. We do not need to complicate the learning process by using confusing terms to describe the principles, equipment, and techniques required to drive these vessels proficiently and safely. With clarity as the goal, the following terms and definitions will be used throughout this book.

• ASD: Refers to a tug or towboat that has two Z-drive drive units positioned side by side near the stern of the vessel.
• azimuth: Refers to the angle the drive unit is positioned in reference to a horizontal plane.
• controls: Refers to two independent Z-drive control handles mounted in the vessel's pilothouse.
• drive unit: Refers to the individual (port or starboard) Z-drive mounted in the stern of the vessel.
• propeller wash: Refers to the direction and magnitude of the water flow created by the rotating propeller.
• thrust: Refers to the directional effect of the propeller wash. In other words, the direction of thrust is *opposite* the direction of the propeller wash.
• towboat: Refers to a towing vessel that operates primarily on inland rivers in a push towing mode.
• tug: Refers to a towing vessel that operates primarily in harbors, coastwise, and ocean towing and may operate towing astern, alongside, pushing ahead, or in shipwork.
• Z-drive: In this book a Z-drive refers specifically to a tug or towboat that has two Z-drive units positioned side by side near the stern of the vessel. *It does not refer to a Z-drive vessel configured with drive units side by side in the forward part of the vessel (ATD), or with one drive unit forward and one drive unit aft.*

The terms "Z-drive" and "ASD" will be used interchangeably in this book. Both terms refer to a vessel (either a tug or towboat) that has two [2] Z-drive units positioned athwartships near the stern of the vessel.

Z-drive propulsion represents an evolution in the towing industry. In that context, we should also acknowledge the increasing role of women operators on tugs and towboats. While recognizing the maritime roles of men and women, for the sake of simplicity, "he" will be used as an all-inclusive pronoun that replaces "he/she" throughout this book.

Now that we have established a common language to describe the equipment, principles, and techniques of maneuvering a Z-drive-propelled tug or towboat, we can begin the learning process.

# Notes

_____

_____

_____

_____

_____

_____

_____

_____

_____

_____

_____

_____

_____

_____

_____

_____

_____

_____

_____

_____

_____

_____

_____

_____

_____

_____

_____

# Chapter Two
## The Learning Process

An ASD tug or towboat is a high-performance vessel—responsive, quick to maneuver, and extremely powerful. It is the "Formula 1" race car of the waterfront—a nimble, powerful machine with tremendous maneuvering potential. But like a Formula 1 race car, it requires a skilled hand at the wheel. An ASD tug or towboat needs to be "driven" almost all the time and does not forgive a lapse in concentration or an error in judgment. If your hands and mind cannot keep up with the vessel, you will not be driving the vessel—it will be driving you. The design aspects that make these vessels so quick and nimble under skilled hands are the same ones that can put a Z-drive rapidly out of control under those of a novice.

Initially, the learning process can be frustrating. Your instincts and experience that have served you so well on a conventionally propelled vessel may betray you when your hands are on the controls of a Z-drive tug or towboat. An operator of a conventional tug with years of experience and expertise may suddenly feel that all the traditional rules have been changed when he first steps onto the bridge of a Z-drive-propelled vessel. The vessel behaves erratically and unpredictably under his hands. He may feel incompetent and may struggle to operate with the finesse he has developed over the years.

Many professional mariners comment that learning to drive a Z-drive was one of the most challenging but most rewarding experiences of their career. Part of the difficulty in learning to drive a Z-drive is that most operators will need to reprogram both their minds and hands. For those who have extensive experience in twin-screw conventional vessels, the first step in the learning process is to forget what they know. It may sound contrary—to temporarily take all the knowledge, experience, and skills acquired over the years and place them off to the side, but that is a necessary step in the learning process for the conventional tug or towboat operator. An ASD tug or towboat may look like a conventional tug, but a Z-drive-propelled vessel maneuvers and performs differently. It is similar to the difference between a fixed-wing airplane and a helicopter.

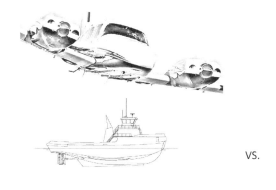

VS.

Fig. 2-1
Twin engine versus helicopter

Both fly through the air, and both obey the laws of aerodynamics, but the controls and performance of each are completely different. One would never climb into the passenger seat of a helicopter with a pilot who has flown only conventional fixed-wing aircraft. It is the same with a Z-drive—throwing the keys of a Z-drive to a conventional tug operator without retraining invites disastrous consequences.

The conceptual picture of how a conventional tug maneuvers simply does not apply in the context of a vessel propelled by Z-drives. Similarly, the movement of one's hands on the controls, and the tug's response, does not mimic a conventional tug. Many of the hand movements on Z-drive controls are in direct conflict with the instincts of the twin-screw operator. This contrariness can create the "twin-screw twilight zone"—a nebulous operating atmosphere in which intellect and instinct fight each other over who has control of the hands, and ultimately the vessel. It takes practice, repetition, and a bit of "letting go" to clear the haze and embed a new, instinctual way of handling the vessel. Mastering a Z-drive-propelled vessel requires you to temporarily let go of your previous maneuvering instincts and experience. To begin the Z-drive learning process, both your mind and your hands require a clean slate.

Learning to drive a Z-drive vessel is a hands-on process, but it is not hands alone. Two simultaneous processes occur as you learn. One is a remapping of your brain so that new, specific control movements are intuitively associated with responses from the tug or towboat. The other is to train your mind's eye so that it can reliably explain the vessel's behavior in the present and predict it in the future.

Re-mapping the pathway between your brain and hand movements requires repetition and time. Multiple repetitions of maneuvers are required to put muscle memory in your hands so that they may react intuitively, without conscious thought. A common training principle in many martial arts is that it takes at least one thousand repetitions of a technique before the movement becomes embedded in muscle memory and neurological pathways, and as many as 10,000 repetitions until the movement becomes instinctual. Learning to handle an ASD vessel is not different. The same maneuver will have to be replicated multiple times before the vessel's response feels natural and predictable.

And you will make mistakes! This, too, is part of the learning process. Learning the new hand movements is in large part a process of continual trial and error. Both success and mistake are equally valuable if they can be placed in a mental context that explains why one technique works and another fails. This is where the second learning process comes into play: training your mind's eye so that it "sees" the cause and effect of the vessel's behavior.

As you acquire the skills to maneuver an ASD tug or towboat, you will also begin to construct a mental picture of the drive unit configuration and the effect it has on the vessel's motion.

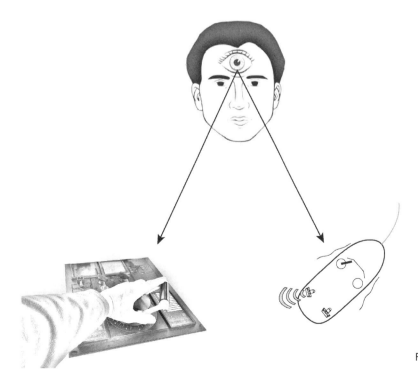

Fig. 2-2
Retraining your "mind's eye"

A clear and accurate picture allows your mind to catalog, in an organized fashion, the experience acquired through your hands, and corroborate that the vessel's behavior makes sense both in your head and your hands.

# Learning Phases

There are four [4] phases of learning Z-drive maneuvering techniques:

1. It is all in your head.
2. Your hands develop a "feel."
3. Your hands drive while your mind is ahead of the boat.
4. You learn to juggle.

It is not only the new Z-drive operator who goes through these phases; an experienced operator will go through the same sequence when acquiring a new maneuvering technique. Awareness of these learning phases is important not only for efficient learning, but also for the safe management of the vessel. The time interval between recognition and response is different for the four [4] phases and will have to be accounted for in managing the speed and complexity of the maneuver.

## Phase 1: It's All in Your Head

A new Z-drive tug or towboat operator begins the learning process in his head. Each maneuvering sequence consists of a chain of conscious decisions. In the early stages of learning, the tug operator "thinks" his way through each maneuver. He engages in a repeating cycle of

- identifying the maneuvering objective,
- determining the method,
- taking action, and
- evaluating the results.

This thought process typically creates a "bird's-eye" image of the drive units. This perspective is also used in many of this book's illustrations. These illustrations use a common set of drawing symbols to represent the drive unit's azimuth, direction, amount of thrust, and controls, and the tug's motion (fig. 2-3).

A simple example of an operator thinking his way through a maneuver would be advancing and turning the vessel to starboard from a stopped position (fig. 2-4).

Fig. 2-3
Drawing symbols

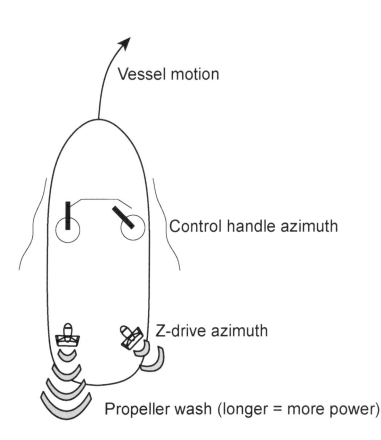

Vessel motion

Control handle azimuth

Z-drive azimuth

Propeller wash (longer = more power)

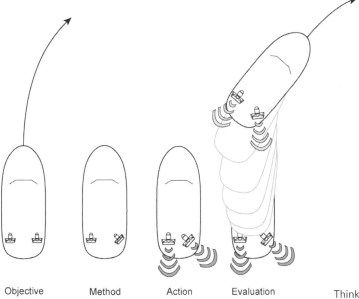

Fig. 2-4
Thinking your way through a maneuver

Objective          Method          Action          Evaluation

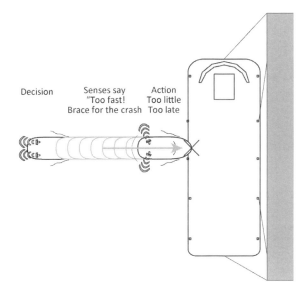

Decision          Senses say          Action
                  "Too fast!          Too little
                  Brace for the crash  Too late

Fig. 2-5
Vessel speed faster than thinking speed.
Watch the bump!

The sequence begins with the operator visualizing a bird's-eye view of the drive unit's configuration. The next step is to make a "best guess" as to a drive unit configuration that will produce the desired motion of the tug. The operator moves his hands, clutches in, and observes the motion of his vessel. In this example, the tug or towboat reacts as expected and turns to starboard. The operator immediately repeats the cycle for the next step—in this example, controlling the rate of turn. In the early learning stages, this cycle repeats itself throughout all aspects of a maneuver.

This phase can be mentally exhausting because your mind is trying to filter, prioritize, and organize a continuous stream of sensory information. Your eyes will be picking up a constant flow of visual cues and will be taking rapid snapshots of the horizon and other reference points, such as docks, buoys, or vessels in your vicinity. Your sense of balance will engage as your vessel heels one way or the other in response to the drive unit's thrust. Your ears will pick up the sounds of the engines as they spool up or down in response to throttle commands. As you change drive unit configurations, you will sense these changes—sometimes subtle, sometimes dramatic—in the way your vessel shakes and vibrates. All these sensory cues can be correlated with the tug's or towboat's behavior. In the early learning stages the correlations are not clear, and your head will be inundated with confusing sensory information. In the midst of trying to make sense of what your eyes and ears perceive, you will be consciously attempting to achieve your maneuvering objective by sorting through choices of method, taking trial actions, and evaluating.

Take the example of a tug advancing bow first to push on a barge (fig. 2-5). A few tug lengths from the barge this novice Z-drive operator begins his thought process as to which drive unit configuration will be effective in bringing the tug to a stop. While he mentally processes his options, the tug continues to advance toward the barge. A few boat lengths from the barge he is bombarded with sensory warnings—the rate of closure to the barge is too fast and the heading of the vessel is yawing back and forth! The tug is not responding and becomes hard to keep on course. He physically braces for impact, instinctively rises up on his toes, tenses his muscles, holds his breath, and leans back, hoping body English will stop the tug. Finally his mind clicks in and he starts to move the controls, but his mental processing speed is slower than the tug's speed and he leaves his mark on the barge.

#### Phase 2: Your Hands Develop a "Feel"

Over time, the results of multiple repetitions of maneuvers and of conscious trial and error begin to become embedded in your hands. A point arrives when you realize your hands are beginning to move without thinking. You will have programmed them to act intuitively on what your mind's eye sees. Conscious thought will drop out of the pathway between perception and action. You will no longer have to think about what to do; you will just do it.

You can tell you have begun to move into this phase when you can multitask while maneuvering the vessel. When your hands are doing the "thinking," your mind will be free to engage in tasks other than figuring out how to keep the vessel under control. The hands will be making constant, subtle movements at the controls while your mind effortlessly accommodates radio conversations, winch operation, and wheelhouse conversation.

The second phase marks the beginning of feeling that *you're driving the Z-drive*, not the other way around.

#### Phase 3: Your Hands Drive While Your Mind Is Ahead of the Boat

Although you may feel as if your hands alone can drive a Z-drive, it is important to keep your mind engaged in the tug's or towboat's maneuvering sequence. One pitfall in handling a Z-drive is the difficulty in recovering from a situation in which the drive units are grossly out of position. When in the correct drive unit configuration, the tug or towboat will feel nimble and respond immediately to subtle hand movements on the controls. As the maneuver evolves, if the operator has not thought ahead, he may suddenly discover the drive units are 90° or 180° out of position and the tug or towboat is on its own. In other words, if your mind is not leading the vessel, the vessel will be in command of you.

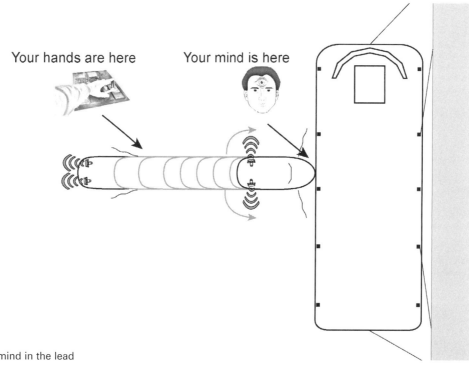

Your hands are here   Your mind is here

Fig. 2-6
Hands in the present, mind in the lead

A tug advancing bow first to push on a barge illustrates this principle (fig. 2-6). As the tug approaches the barge, the skilled operator's hands make subtle control adjustments to keep the tug on course and control the rate of closure. While the operator's hands control the tug's advance, his mind has already projected itself into the future and is at the point of contact on the barge. He draws a mental picture of the drive unit configuration required to have the tug stopped, but in position. The ideal is to think both with your mind and your hands. Your hands should be in the current moment, reacting to the tug's subtle changes in direction and speed, while your mind assesses the maneuvering sequence and the required drive unit's positions two to three boat lengths ahead.

### Phase 4: Learning to Juggle

Juggling is an activity that requires constant refocusing and prioritizing of one's attention from an overall goal to multiple subsidiary tasks. Learning to operate an ASD tug is similar to becoming a professional juggler. Instead of keeping multiple balls suspended in the air, you will be juggling the factors required to maneuver your multimillion-dollar Z-drive around ships and barges:

• Drive unit azimuth
• Power
• Speed
• Rate of turn
• Rate of closure
• Space restrictions
• Time restrictions
• Hydrodynamic effects

Handling a Z-drive competently requires being proficient in multiple, stand-alone maneuvering skills. Most practical maneuvers require using these skills in combination—sometimes in rapid succession, sometimes simultaneously. An operator new to a Z-drive will focus on mastering these individual skills one at a time, but he must also acquire the ability to shift rapidly from one skill set to another with appropriate timing and application.

The feeling for the new Z-drive operator may be similar to the novice juggler, who is comfortable tossing one ball in the air but stresses and struggles to keep multiple balls airborne. Steering a Z-drive in open water is a one-ball juggling act. But bringing a Z-drive tug alongside a moving ship or downstreaming a Z-drive towboat to face up on a barge are much more demanding performances.

The new Z-drive operator may feel overwhelmed by the number of skill sets required for a complex maneuver, but he can acquire the ability to appropriately select, shift, and apply these skills through a systematic learning process. There are two keys to the process. One is to vary the complexity of practice maneuvers in an organized manner. The other is to become aware of whether the Z-drive operator is thinking in his hands or his head.

# Varying Complexity

There are six (6) basic Z-drive maneuvering skills (fig. 2-7):

• Steering
• Managing speed
• Stopping
• Moving laterally
• Hovering
• Operating stern first

**steering:** Ability to change or hold the tug's heading and manage its rate of rotation as it moves through the water.
**managing speed:** Ability to hold, retard, or increase a rate of advance.
**stopping:** Ability to bring the tug to a zero rate of advance.
**moving laterally:** Ability to control lateral movement.
**hovering:** Ability to hold the vessel in position with no fore/aft, lateral, or yawing motion.
**stern-first operations:** Ability to operate the stern (propulsion end) first.

Once having mastered them as individual skills, the new operator must learn to apply them in combination under restrictive conditions that fall into the following (4) four categories (fig. 2-8):

• Space restrictions
• Time restrictions
• Transitions
• Relative motion

**space limit:** Constricted maneuvering space due to the presence of fixed or moving objects.
**time limit:** Limited time to complete a maneuver, as in maneuvering to pick up a man overboard.
**transitions:** Changing or reversing the tug's primary direction of motion. For example, transitioning from forward to lateral motion, or from running bow first to stern first.
**relative motion:** Maneuvering within the context of other moving objects or in current.

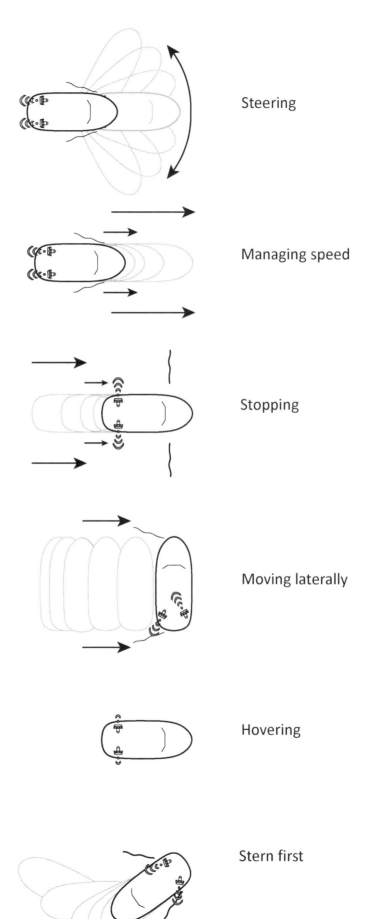

Steering

Managing speed

Stopping

Moving laterally

Hovering

Stern first

Fig. 2-7
Z-drive basic maneuvering skills

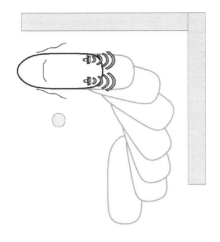

**Restricted Space-**
Limited space due to the presence of fixed or moving objects

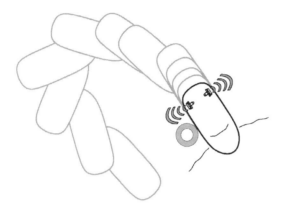

**Restricted Time-**
Limited time to complete a maneuver

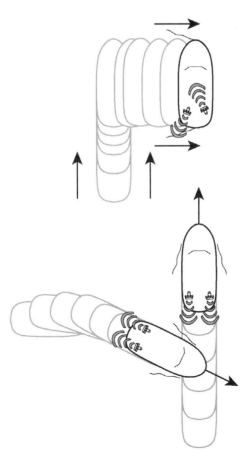

**Transitions-**
Changing or reversing the tug's primary direction of motion--e.g. forward to lateral motion

**Relative motion-**
Maneuvering with the context of other moving vessels or in current

Fig. 2-8
Layers of complexity

The complexity of a maneuver is determined by the combination of skill sets and conditions associated with the maneuver. For learning purposes, the complexity can be controlled by choosing practice maneuvers that gradually require more skill sets to be employed under an increasing number of restrictive conditions.

In a book or in simple training exercises, it is easy to view these skills and conditions as separate entities, but the reality on the water is that they are commonly interrelated. A good example of this interrelation is a tug coming alongside a moving ship or a towboat facing up to a barge.

In the case of the tug coming alongside the ship, the operator will use two basic skills: steering and managing speed. However, he must apply these in the context of the relative motion and rates of closure between ship and tug (fig. 2-9).

He must be able to

- steer the tug,
- adjust his speed of advance,
- adjust his course relative to the ship's heading,
- regulate the tug's rate of turn to gently come alongside the ship,
- maneuver within the context of the relative motion between ship and tug, and
- manage the hydrodynamic effects of the ship's pressure and suction zones.

In the example of a towboat facing up to a barge, the operator is steering and managing speed. However, he must do so within the context of controlling his speed and direction over the ground and his position relative to the barge, and maneuver with precision to spot the bow of the towboat at a specific location on the barge (fig. 2-10).

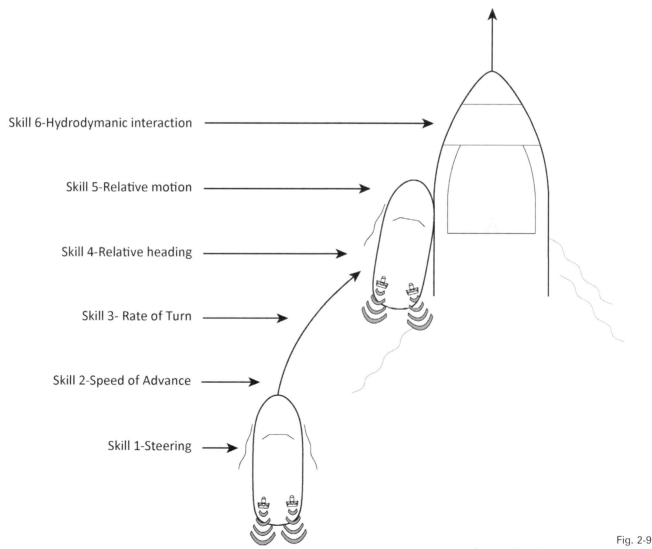

Skill 6-Hydrodymanic interaction

Skill 5-Relative motion

Skill 4-Relative heading

Skill 3- Rate of Turn

Skill 2-Speed of Advance

Skill 1-Steering

Fig. 2-9
Tug coming alongside a moving ship

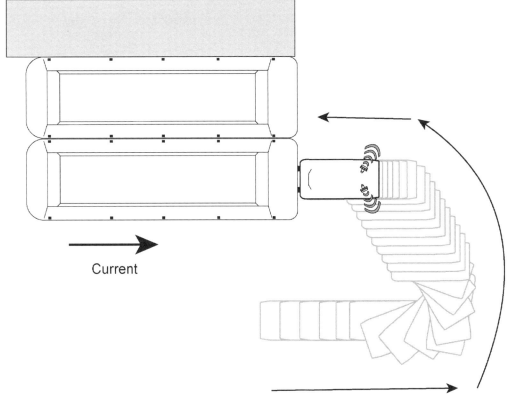

Current

Fig. 2-10
Towboat facing up

He must be able to

- steer the tug relative to the ground and fixed obstructions,
- adjust his course relative to the barge's fixed position,
- adjust his speed over the ground,
- adjust his rate of closure to the barge to touch up gently,
- manage the yaw of the towboat so that it remains perpendicular to the end of the barge, and
- manage the hydrodynamic effects of water flowing around and under the barge and off the bank.

The experienced operator may make this maneuver look seamless and graceful, but he is in fact rapidly selecting and shifting between appropriate maneuvering skills in the moment.

An operator's ability to manage multiple skill sets depends on the amount of maneuvering skills embedded in his hands. Knowledgeable hands, reacting intuitively to the cues one's senses pick up, are much more efficient than a conscious thought process. In addition, the hands can transition between skill sets much more rapidly than can the mind. The key to becoming an expert Z-drive operator is to hone your ability to "think" with your hands. The more skills that lie in your hands, the more comfortable you will be in complex maneuvering situations.

## Operator Awareness

When an operator is intuitively handling the tug, his mind is free to tackle other tasks. An operator's awareness of which mode he is in—hands or head—is a personal sign that he is or is not ready to add another ball to his juggling act, or to move on to a more complex maneuver. For example, say you have become comfortable steering the tug or towboat and managing its speed of advance in open water. If you are driving the vessel in those circumstances and find your mind wandering—chatting in the wheelhouse, thinking about what's for lunch, making plans for your time off—this is a sign that you are ready to focus your mind on additional maneuvering skills. For instance, it could be adding a space restriction, such as steering through a series of buoys (fig 2-11).

Fig. 2-11
Turning practice with space restrictions
*Courtesy of the Pacific Maritime Institute, Seattle, WA*

Your hands are maneuvering the tug around the buoy close aboard while your head is in front of the tug, calculating the adjustments in speed and turn rate required to round the next buoy.

During the learning process, it is essential for the operator to maintain self-awareness of how much of his driving is in his hands versus his head. This is the measure of an operator's ability to take on the conscious process of learning an additional skill set. Even those with years of experience and a wealth of hands-on Z-drive knowledge will occasionally find themselves in new and unique conditions. Under those circumstances, they will literally be in the same boat as the new Z-drive operator—consciously thinking their way through a maneuvering sequence step by step, embedding new knowledge in the hands and adding another skill set to their repertoire.

# Learning Safely and Efficiently

There are many aspects to learning to drive a Z-drive-propelled tug or towboat, but they all are linked by one common, simple learning principle—*repetition*. Mastering a maneuvering skill requires practice—not just once or twice, but multiple times. The single biggest factor in effective and safe practice is maneuvering speed. The tug's or towboat's maneuvering speed should be slow enough to allow the operator to make a mistake, recognize the error, and implement a successful corrective action without causing damage to equipment or property. A safe maneuvering speed for a specific practice exercise may vary quite a bit from one operator to another. In general, "thinking with your head" requires much more time than "thinking with the hands" when practicing a maneuvering sequence. The maneuvering speed should be appropriate to the operator's learning phase.

While this book can expedite the learning process, it is not a substitute for hours of practice under the watchful eye of a mentor. Mastering a Z-drive requires hands-on skills.

Take every opportunity to get your hands on the controls and practice, practice, practice. Hours of systematic and organized repetition will transform practice into proficiency and experience into expertise.

# Notes

# *Chapter Three*
## How to Use This Book

This book is designed to facilitate learning through two pathways: intellectual and hands-on. The first is to help you develop a clear understanding of Z-drive maneuvering principles; the second is to assist you in acquiring the intuitive feel for handling the tug or towboat. Text and illustrations are designed to help build intellectual understanding; recommended simulator or live-tug practice exercises are included to embed hands-on knowledge.

## Organization

The remaining chapters in this workbook cover basic elements of maneuvering a Z-drive tug or towboat:

- Z-drive mechanical systems
- ASD maneuvering principles
- Balance of thrust
- Stepping up to the controls
- Steering
- Managing speed
- Stopping and hovering
- Moving laterally
- Transitions
- Basic light tug/towboat maneuvers
- Barge work maneuvers
- Shipwork maneuvers
- Staying out of trouble

Each chapter includes one or more of the following subsections:

- Overview
- Topic synopsis or practical exercise
- Why this is important
- What it looks like in your mind
- What it feels like in your hands

Although the chapters are laid out in a linear learning sequence, instructors and operators should feel free to follow an order appropriate to the individual. We all step into the wheelhouse of a Z-drive with varying amounts of experience and individual strengths and weaknesses, and we all have different learning paths. Some of the maneuvering skills will come easy to one person and with difficulty to others. All of us will encounter learning speed bumps—those times when a particular maneuver seems a confusing and unsolvable puzzle. That is when we can neither get our mind wrapped around the principles involved, nor get our hands to make the right movements. Those situations require extra focus and practice and may also require reviewing some of the basic skills.

A good example of this is the skill required to walk or make the tug move laterally. The relative ease with which this maneuver can be done in a Z-drive tug or towboat is one characteristic that sets it apart from a conventional tug. It may look easy, but the Z-drive's lateral movement is a result of the operator's skillful manipulation of the balance between fore and aft (speed) and rotational thrust (steering). If the operator struggles with this maneuver, it may be due to a lack of proficiency in one or both of these separate skill sets. In other words, if you can't manage the vessel's fore and aft speed and steer as stand-alone skills, you may stumble when you try to walk.

This book is a learning tool. Feel free to move to the chapter that matches best with your learning sequence, but avoid prematurely moving into complex maneuvers before becoming well versed in the fundamentals.

# Notes

_____

_____

_____

_____

_____

_____

_____

_____

_____

_____

_____

_____

_____

_____

_____

_____

_____

_____

_____

_____

_____

_____

_____

_____

_____

_____

# *Chapter Four*
## Know Your Tug

## Overview

Driving a Z-drive tug or towboat is more than a matter of knowing which way to twist the control handles. It also requires an understanding of the Z-drive propulsion system and how its components interrelate.

At times, Z-drive operators will find themselves in situations in which they have made a boat-handling mistake or misjudgment. Extricating oneself from those types of situations might undoubtedly involve anxious turning of the control handles in hope of an instantaneous response from the tug. Under these circumstances, correctly manipulating the control handles is only half the story. The outcome is dependent both on the operator's choice of an appropriate corrective action and on the reliability and performance limits of the vessel's propulsion system. Assuming that the correct choice of azimuth and throttle have been made, there is a long journey between the electrical signal associated with the anxious twisting of the handle and the propeller wash in the right amount and direction. It is a path that leads through delicate circuit boards and wiring, as well as through robust gears and steel- or carbon-fiber shafts linking mechanical, electrical, and hydraulic machinery.

An understanding of these components is essential to verify that the Z-drive systems are functioning and integrated properly, and to appreciate their capabilities and limits. If you want a Z-drive tug or towboat to work for you, you must understand how it works (fig. 4-1).

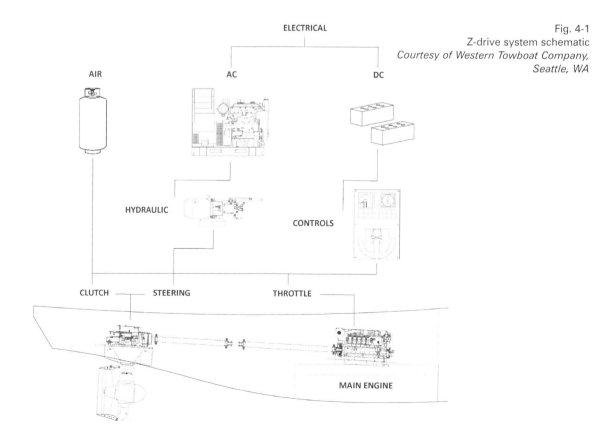

Fig. 4-1
Z-drive system schematic
*Courtesy of Western Towboat Company,*
*Seattle, WA*

# Why This Is Important

A basic understanding of the tug's or towboat's propulsion system enables the operator to

- verify that the propulsion system is fully functional,
- troubleshoot propulsion system malfunctions, and
- operate within the propulsion system limits.

Many Z-drive maneuvers require intense focus on the tasks immediately at hand: looking out the window, tracking the tug's or towboat's motion, and moving the controls appropriately. If there are interruptions or distractions, it may be difficult to maintain or recapture the necessary level of concentration. One source of distraction can be mechanical mysteries that we suspect may be affecting the vessel's behavior.

For example, take the situation of an ASD tug coming alongside a bulk carrier's bow. If the tug suddenly becomes unresponsive and dives toward the ship, there is little time to identify and rectify the cause. Is the cause environmental (e.g., the ship has an unusual pressure wave at the bow)? Is it mechanical (e.g., the port drive unit has a split hydraulic hose)? Or is it human (e.g., the operator turned the handle the wrong way)? At this point, the operator's instinct is to move the control handles while mentally running through a list of causes and effects. Any unessential items on the list only delay his reaction. This is not the time to learn how the tug's mechanical, electric, and hydraulic systems work. In fact, at this juncture, the application of the three knowledge tools—verification, troubleshooting, and operating within performance limits—might have prevented or resolved the tug's errant turn toward the ship.

### Verification

It is a standard practice in aviation to verify that an airplane's critical equipment is functional *before* taking off—instruments, engine, ailerons, flaps, rudder, etc. We would do well to follow the practice of our aviation brethren, particularly on a Z-drive tug. The new Z-drive operator should get into the habit of going through a "preflight" check every time he steps up to the controls. He should ensure that the engines, drive units, controls, and their electrical and mechanical links are functioning properly. One can't do that without a fundamental understanding of how these component systems interrelate.

The system verification check should also be done prior to beginning a maneuvering sequence that will require complete focus. This will ensure that you are not inadvertently complicating the maneuver by dragging a system malfunction into the fray, and it will also free your mind to focus on critical tasks at hand.

Let us go back to our ASD tug that suddenly veered toward the bulk carrier. Our operator found himself in command of an ASD tug rapidly closing the distance between tug and ship, but he had done his verification check prior to commencing his maneuver to come alongside. He confirmed that all components of the propulsion system were online and functional. His mind is not cluttered with questions as to whether he remembered to turn on the correct steering pump or checked to make sure the controls had proper voltage and were responsive. He knows he started this maneuver with a fully functional tug. His mind is free to move on quickly to the next phase of preventing what appears to be an imminent collision with the ship: troubleshooting.

### Troubleshooting

Knowledge of the vessel's propulsion system enables a rapid and systematic status check of the system's components. It allows one to quickly rule in or rule out mechanical or electrical glitches as factors contributing to a maneuvering problem. If there is a system malfunction, this knowledge enables the operator to quickly isolate and neutralize the problem.

In the case of our tug heading for the bulker's bow, there is no system problem. Our operator takes a quick glance down and confirms that both drive units are responsive, and that all the instruments, gauges, and indicator lights are alive and well. He knows that his success in extricating himself from hard contact with the looming bow of the ship is dependent on his skill and the operating limits of the tug.

### Operating within System Limits

ASD tugs are remarkably maneuverable, but like all vessels, they have limits that are, in great part, determined by the performance characteristics of the steering and propulsion machinery. For instance, a common mistake made by a new ASD tug operator is to move the control handle more quickly than the steering system can physically turn the propeller nozzle. His hands may be taking the correct action, but the drive units may not immediately catch up with the command from the controls. If the tug does not immediately respond, it can create uncertainty and self-doubt in the mind of the new ASD operator. Rather than be patient, he may quickly try another control position. While an anxious apprentice rapidly moves the control handle back and forth and wonders why the tug is not responding, the nozzle heading lags behind, still laboring to catch up to the first of a series of taxing electrical commands. If you want the tug to work for you, you have to work within the tug's limits.

Our operator in command of the ASD tug coming alongside the ship is well versed in the system limits of his tug. He knows how long it takes a main engine to increase or decrease RPM in response to his throttle adjustments, he knows the time delay between clutching in and out, and he is well aware of how many degrees per second the drive unit turns in response to his hands turning the control handles. At this point in the maneuver, he realizes that the unexpected turn toward the ship was caused by the ship's pressure wave at the bow. He has come alongside many ships, but this is his first bulk ship. The pressure wave effect is unexpected but manageable. He knows how his tug responds to changes in RPM or azimuth and the limits of both. His hands manipulate the controls with expertise, finding the balance between power and azimuth that propels the tug away from the ship. He feels as if he reacted instinctively, but his instinct was shaped by his understanding of the tug's propulsion system. He knows his tug.

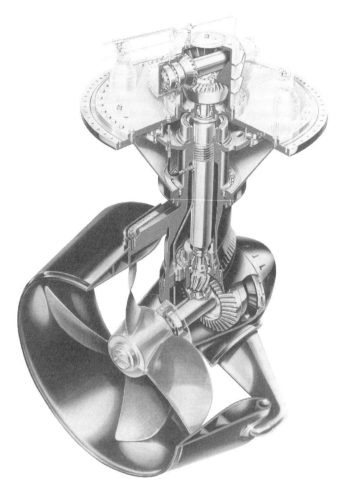

Fig. 4-2
Z-drive
*Courtesy of Schottel GmbH & Co.*

## Synopsis

Engine power is transmitted through a shaft to the upper casing of the drive unit housed inside the tug. A pneumatic or hydraulic clutch regulates the connection between this output shaft of the engine and the input shaft of the drive unit. A series of shafts and right-angled gears convert the horizontal rotation of the engine output shaft into vertical rotation, then the horizontal rotation of the propeller shaft (fig. 4-2). This pattern of gears and shafts roughly resembles a "Z"; hence the name "Z-drive" or "Zed drive" is used when referring to the drive unit. The upper Z-drive gear casing resides inside the tug and houses the upper right-angle gear set, one end of the vertical transmission shaft, clutch, steering motors, and lubrication pumps. The vertical transmission shaft extends into the lower drive leg to another set of right-angle gears that rotate the propeller shaft and propeller. The lower drive leg can be rotated through 360° by hydraulic or electric motors.

Controlling the amount and direction of thrust is dependent on three [3] critical systems:

• Power system
• Electrical system
• Hydraulic system

These three [3] systems are present on all Z-drive tugs. A fourth system—compressed air—may also be an integral part of a Z-drive system. Compressed air is used in some but not all Z-drive systems. Z-drive systems vary depending on the tug designer, manufacturer, and operating niche. Each operator should become familiar with the machinery specific to his tug or towboat.

# Power

The propeller requires a power source to generate thrust in water. Traditionally, a diesel-fueled main engine provides the source of propelling power. New Z-drive designs may also use LNG-fueled main engines, auxiliary batteries or engines, or both to augment the power created by a main engine. Regardless of the source of power, the purpose is to transfer energy into the rotational power of an output shaft (fig. 4-3). This rotational energy is transferred through a series of gears and shafts to the propeller. In addition, the power source may also drive a hydraulic pump that provides steering power.

Fig. 4-3
Typical diesel engine power source

### Why This Is Important

It is obvious that a source of power is required to turn the propeller. While this concept is clear when you read it, it can sometimes be lost in the context of Z-drive machinery that combines both steering and propulsion. Part of every Z-drive operator's rite of passage is the experience of turning the control handles but wondering why the tug or towboat is not reacting in response to his command. When this happens, we instinctively try to figure out which function is lacking: steering or propulsion. It is not unusual for an operator to focus on the steering function first and sometimes overlook the most obvious cause: a failure of the transfer of power from the main engine to the propeller. This failure can be as simple as having unintentionally lost the connection between the main engine and the Z-drive unit (e.g., the operator nudged the control handle and inadvertently clutched out), or, less frequently, a mechanical malfunction that stopped the main engine. In either case, the drive unit may be rotating, but the propeller is not.

# Electrical

### Direct Current

Twenty-four-volt direct current is the life blood of a Z-drive control system (fig. 4-4). Z-drive controls are powered by DC current. Some are set up to run off battery banks and some on AC-to-DC converters, while many have redundant systems that employ both. The purpose of using direct current is to have a source of power (batteries) independent of the tug's or towboat's auxiliary generator. Even if the auxiliary generator fails, the controls will remain energized. In other words, you may still be able to steer if the lights go out.

Fig. 4-4
24-volt Z-drive control system

### Why This Is Important

Z-drive controls are extremely sensitive to variations in voltage. A drop in DC voltage could render the controls useless or induce random, erratic, or unpredictable responses from the drive unit. The drive unit may thrust while continuously rotating through a full 360° circle, it may be impossible to get out of gear (declutch), the main engine may be completely unresponsive to any throttle commands, and the azimuth indicator may not move or be aligned with the drive unit's direction of thrust. To someone experiencing these conditions for the first time, the tug or towboat may seem possessed by a demonic spirit. The vessel refuses to respond to the controls in any rational or predictable manner. The vessel's other Z-drive steering and propulsion systems may be fully functional but rendered inoperative without 24 volts streaming through the control system. A fully charged 24-volt system is as important to the controls as the skilled hands that manipulate them.

### Alternating Current

Auxiliary generators supply alternating current to a number of domestic and mechanical systems throughout the tug or towboat. One Z-drive component that relies on AC current may be the electric motor that supplies power to the Z-drive's steering motors (fig. 4-5).

### Why This Is Important

On some Z-drive systems, an AC electric motor may be the sole source of power for the steering pump. On these vessels, an interruption in the AC current supply will disable the motor that rotates the drive unit. In other words, you can turn the control handles but you can't steer. The root of this problem is obvious if the tug's or towboat's entire auxiliary generating system goes down (e.g., the lights go out), but typically the cause is much more subtle. Some common causes are a tripped breaker, a wheelhouse selector switch in the wrong position, or an electric motor's thermal reset switch that has overheated. These are just a few examples of the mechanical malfunctions or human errors that can interrupt a critical AC energy supply.

## Hydraulic

Most Z-drive units utilize the fluid power of high-pressure hydraulics to steer. Z-drive systems employ hydraulic motors (fig. 4-6) to rotate the lower drive leg that houses the propeller.

Fig. 4-5
Electric AC steering pump

Fig. 4-6
Rolls Royce and Schottel hydraulic steering motors

These hydraulic motors receive their power either from an electrically driven or mechanically driven hydraulic pump. Electrically driven pumps utilize the AC power discussed previously. Mechanically energized pumps are typically driven by the main power source. The pump may be attached to the main engine, belt driven off the power source output shaft, or attached to the upper Z-drive unit. Regardless of location, mechanically driven steering motors must have the main power source on to steer. In other words—no main engine on, no steering.

### Why This Is Important

The machinery components that physically rotate the lower drive leg are dependent on the integrity of the hydraulic system. Worn hydraulic motors or broken hoses or fittings will negatively affect or disable the Z-drive steering system. The equation is simple: no hydraulics equals no steering.

## Air System

A number of Z-drive manufacturers make use of air pressure as an actuating force. Some utilize a pneumatic clutch to connect the main engine output shaft to the Z-drive input shaft. In addition, some manufacturers utilize air-actuated solenoids to engage or disengage the clutch, select one steering system over another, or regulate the main engine's RPM.

### Why This Is Important

If air pressure is a component of your tug's or towboat's Z-drive system, inadequate pressure will affect its performance. For instance, a pneumatic clutch might engage but still slip with low air pressure, control solenoids may not shift fully or at all, or the main engine may respond sluggishly to control signals for more power. Since Z-drive air systems depend on compressors and air tanks that are part of the vessel's common air system, leaks in any part of the Z-drive systems, or those that are induced by other auxiliary machinery, could also jeopardize the Z-drive system. A low-air alarm may be a warning that a loss of clutch or RPM control is imminent. It should be taken as a signal to get the tug in a safe position if the cause cannot be found and fixed quickly.

## You and Your Z-drive

Handling a Z-drive tug with expertise requires not only hands-on skill, but also a clear understanding of the interrelationships among Z-drive machinery components. It also demands an appreciation of the capability and complexity of a Z-drive system. Main engine, shafting, clutches, and hydraulic motors are robust components but are dependent on a delicate array of circuit boards, relays, potentiometers, and nests of tiny wires (fig. 4-7).

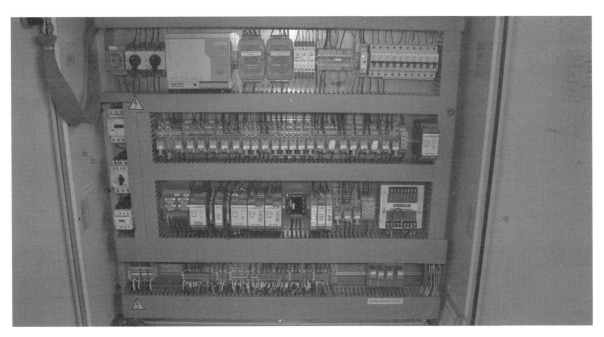

Fig. 4-7
Z-drive control wires

Fig. 4-7
Z-drive control wires

A Z-drive operator's reputation—even his career—depends on all those tiny wires remaining connected. If vibration, chafing, or heat degrade those connections to the point that they are weak or broken, the Z-drive operator may find himself with a sudden loss of azimuth, throttle, or clutch control. If the event is ill timed—making a lock or going bow to bow with a moving ship—the results can range from embarrassment to disastrous. Be wary of excess cavitation or vibration, inspect critical components regularly, and verify that all systems are functional before a critical maneuver.

Take care of your Z-drive system and it will take care of you.

# Notes

# *Chapter Five*
## ASD Maneuvering Principles

## Overview

Four basic principles govern the behavior of an ASD tug or towboat:

- The stern drives the tug.
- Steering and speed are inextricably linked.
- The balance of thrust propels the tug.
- There is a one-to-many relationship between drive unit azimuth and vessel response.

## Why This Is Important

These four principles form the framework of the understanding required to handle an ASD tug or towboat competently. This understanding translates into a picture in your head that serves as the reference point for your actions. It makes it possible for your mind to stay ahead of the tug or towboat and facilitates your hands' skillful translation of principle into action during a maneuvering sequence. If you find a Z-drive's behavior confusing and unpredictable, the source of the ambiguity can usually be traced to an incomplete understanding or application of one or more of these principles.

## Synopsis:

## The Stern Drives the Tug

An ASD tug or towboat can move easily bow first or stern first. Regardless of the direction of movement, the vessel is controlled by the position, thrust, and movement of the stern. When operating bow first, the stern must swing around and push the bow in the desired direction; when operating stern first, the stern leads the way and the bow follows (fig. 5-1).

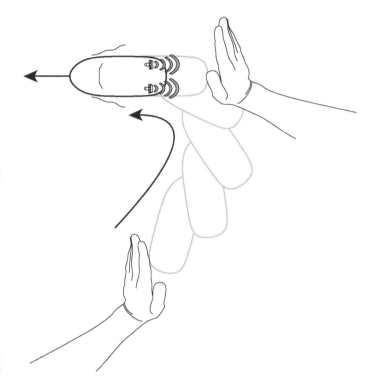

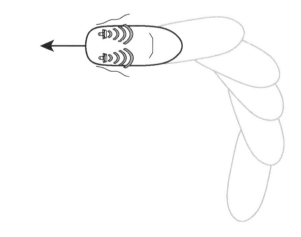

Fig. 5-1
Stern drives the tug

## Why This Is Important

Losing control of an ASD tug or towboat almost invariably means losing control of the stern. If you control the stern you control the vessel. Conventionally propelled tugs are subject to this same principle, but in an ASD vessel this characteristic is exaggerated due to its omnidirectional thrust capability.

The stern of an ASD tug or towboat reacts almost immediately to any changes in thrust, regardless of whether that thrust was correctly or incorrectly applied. If applied incorrectly, a Z-drive can be unforgiving. It may obey the erroneous command with surprising speed and immediacy, leaving little time to correct and recover.

As you go through the learning process, strive to develop a keen and constant sense of the location and direction of the tug's stern.

# Steering and Speed Are Inextricably Linked

When the tug is viewed in dry dock, it is obvious that each drive unit of an ASD tug or towboat houses both the steering and propulsion functions. There is no rudder. Instead, the propeller turns inside a nozzle attached to a drive leg that rotates 360° (fig. 5-2). Steering and speed are inextricably linked. You can't change one without affecting the other.

## Why This Is Important

In a dry dock, the relationship between steering and propulsion is visually clear, but in the water, this relationship may appear murky to the new operator. He is more prone to prioritize one function over the other and lose his awareness of the impact that steering has on speed and vice versa (fig. 5-3).

Fig. 5-2
All in one—steering and propulsion
*Courtesy of Schottel GmbH & Co.*

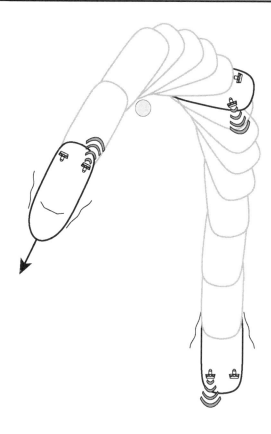

Fig. 5-3
Steering affecting speed

In this example, the Z-drive operator uses one drive unit to round a buoy that lies close aboard a dock, but as he approaches the buoy, he is concerned about the proximity of the dock. He increases the azimuth angle but misjudges how much headway will be lost. As the thrust angle approaches 90° to the tug's centerline, the tug turns more sharply and rapidly, losing its speed of advance. This action brings the buoy unexpectedly close aboard the tug's port side.

The link between steering and speed is constant. As you gain more experience, you will use this principle to your advantage. You will learn to manipulate the drive unit configuration so that changes in speed and steering work in unison toward, and not in opposition to, your maneuvering objectives.

# The Balance of Thrust Propels the Tug

*Balance of thrust* is a term used to describe the resultant force on the tug generated by two drive units. Regardless of their configuration, the two drive units create one force that affects the tug. This concept may seem counterintuitive. After all, we have two hands on the controls, moving independently of each other, affecting the drive units as separate entities. When we move one hand and not the other, the tug responds. From a tactile perspective, the control of the tug lies in the one hand. From a hydrodynamic perspective, the tug's response is due to the changing *relationship* between the thrusts of the two drive units, not the movement of one hand.

Viewing the drive units as two separate entities is strictly a learning tool used to help create an intellectual understanding of their relationship to each other. Below the waterline, in the physicality of the fluid realm, the two drive units are always working in conjunction with each other. The *balance of thrust* is a conceptual tool to help us link these two perspectives.

## Why This Is Important

As you develop your skills as a Z-drive operator, you will learn to manipulate the drive units with a variety of hand movements on the controls. There will be times when your hands may move one at a time in unison, or other times simultaneously but with independent motions. Regardless of the hand movements, it is important to retain your awareness of the interrelationship between the two drive units' thrust. The tug responds to your manipulation of the balance of thrust.

The term *balance of thrust* is more than just a concept; it is also a term that describes a type of feel you will have when the tug is in complete control under your hands. Effective use of the balance of thrust creates the "sweet spot" you feel in your hands. The sweet spot is the drive unit control position in which you can control the tug with very small, subtle hand movements and have it respond instantly. An understanding of the balance of thrust and a tactile feel for the "sweet spot" creates the bridge between being a Z-drive boat handler who is simply functional and one who handles it with finesse.

The balance of thrust is such an important topic that an entire chapter will be devoted to describing it in more detail.

# One-to-Many Relationships

There are two (2) factors that define each drive unit's contribution to the balance of thrust:

• Direction of thrust (azimuth)
• Amount of thrust

The direction of thrust can be any point along the 360° circle of potential azimuth positions. The amount of thrust is dependent on the velocity of propeller rotations, varying from zero to the designed maximum. When these variable factors are combined into two drive units, possible drive unit configurations are almost infinite.

At first, the new Z-drive operator may find this confusing and difficult to grasp, particularly if he has had experience handling conventionally propelled tugs. A conventional tug has several one-to-one steering and propulsion relationships. On a conventional tug advancing ahead, when the helm is put over to starboard, the tug turns to starboard. On a Z-drive there are multiple drive unit configurations that will turn the tug to starboard. And even when one azimuth position is chosen, it can still create multiple responses from the tug or towboat (fig. 5-4).

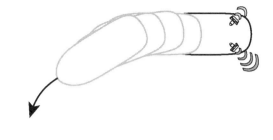

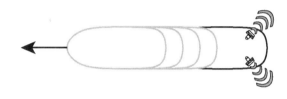

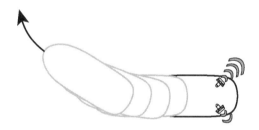

Fig. 5-4
One-to-many maneuvering principle

In this example the azimuth remains the same, but the differing amounts of power are applied by the port and starboard Z-drives. The vessel motion is dependent on how each unit's azimuth and RPM contribute to the balance of thrust at that particular moment. Different balances result in different results, even though the azimuth remains constant.

### Why This Is Important

As a new Z-drive operator manipulates the controls, he searches for hand positions that will reliably and repeatedly produce the same movement of the tug. That is not the nature of Z-drive. The same hand position may produce multiple outcomes.

It is important for the new Z-drive operator to embrace rather than fight this characteristic. While the new operator may be frustrated that the same hand position produces a variety of results, this trait can be a powerful tool once he becomes an expert. The expert learns to use the maneuvering potential held in a particular hand position to his advantage. That is what allows him to nimbly handle the tug, swiftly and smoothly changing directions with minimal hand motion.

Leveraging the maneuvering potential held in the one-to-many principle in combination with an understanding of the balance of thrust and a feel for the sweet spot opens the doorway for the Z-drive operator to elevate his boat handling to high art.

## Conclusion

An understanding of the four ASD maneuvering principles should accompany you into the wheelhouse each time you get your hands on the controls. It is not that you should constantly think about them; rather, view them as a library of reference books. When the tug's or towboat's behavior is puzzling, or you need to get your head out farther in front of the tug, pull these principles off the shelf and apply them to the maneuver at hand.

# Notes

# *Chapter Six*
## Balance of Thrust

## Overview

Driving a Z-drive tug or towboat is all about controlling the amount and direction of thrust. First, we must define thrust before we can discuss thrust in the context of learning. The definition of thrust must create a clear mental picture both of the direction of the propeller wash and its resultant effect on the tug or towboat. This can become a chicken-versus-egg discussion: Does thrusting to starboard mean the propeller wash is going to starboard, or is the effect of the wash propelling the drive unit to starboard? It is not important to use one definition over another. What is important is to use the term consistently within the context of maneuvering a Z-drive. For current purposes, thrust refers to the directional effect of the propeller wash.

In other words, the direction of thrust is opposite to the direction of propeller wash.

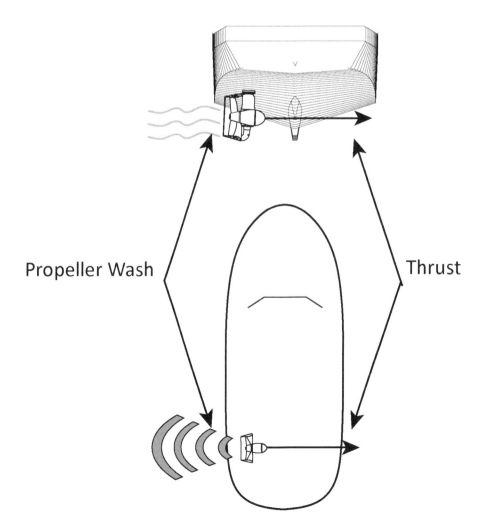

Propeller Wash

Thrust

Fig. 6-1
Propeller wash and thrust

This is easily visualized when only one drive unit is thrusting. In fig. 6-1, the drive unit of the tug is thrusting to starboard and the propeller wash is going to port, with the result that the drive unit, and subsequently the stern of the tug, are pushed to starboard. It gets more complicated when two drive units are thrusting. Each drive unit's thrust becomes a component of the overall propulsion force acting on the tug or towboat.

In chapter 5, the balance of thrust was defined as the resultant force on the vessel generated by two drive units. While it is important to have a picture of this principle in your head, its practical use lies in how it feels in application. When the two drive units are in a balanced configuration and working together, they create a feeling—the "sweet spot." This feeling is one in which you feel that the tug or towboat is alive under your hands, and you have pinpoint control of the tug's or towboat's movement. It is the "I got this!" feeling of confidence in yourself and your hands that you are in control with precision, finesse, and absolute command.

Maneuvering a Z-drive is an exercise in deftly and subtly manipulating the balance of thrust. As you gain more time at the controls, your hands acquire the sensitivity to manipulate the balance of thrust intuitively. Acquiring this sensitivity requires a learning process that includes creating both an understanding in your mind and a feeling in your hands. This chapter will describe both.

First, accept the fact that individuals find their way to this understanding through a variety of pathways. Some need to construct the image of the balance of thrust in their minds before their hands can acquire the feel. Others have to "feel it" before they can picture the combination of the drive units' thrust. Both pathways lead to the same result—a feeling of absolute control in the hands and a clear picture in the mind—but they may take different routes. An individual does not have to follow the sequence set in this chapter; one might read about the feeling in the hands before constructing the picture in the mind, or vice versa.

## What It Looks Like in Your Mind

Many operators find that the image of two hands pushing on the stern of the tug creates an understanding in their mind. The simplest example is when both hands are pushing equally and in direct opposition to each other. This is similar to having both drive units aligned to thrust 90° toward the tug's centerline (fig. 6-2A). In this example, the two hands negate each other's effort. The stern and, consequently, the tug do not move. However, if one hand pushes less (fig. 6-2B), it will be overpowered by the other, and the stern will move toward the weaker hand. Similarly, the point is that if one hand pushes proportionately more, it will overpower the other.

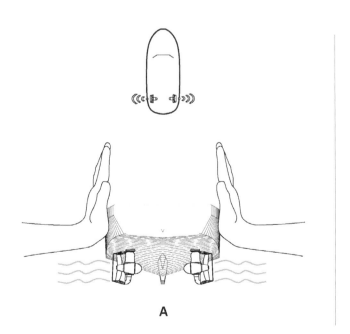

**A**

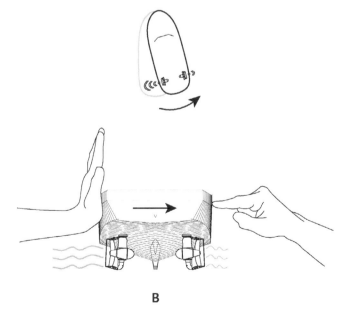

**B**

Fig. 6-2
Balance of thrust
Thrust at 90°

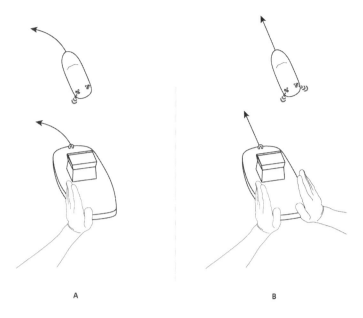

Fig. 6-3
Balance of thrust
Thrust at 45°

If one hand pushes 45° on the corner of the port stern, the tug will move ahead and rotate (fig. 6-3A). However, if both hands push at 45° on the corner of the tug's stern, the rotational aspects of the two hands are canceled out by each other. The tug moves straight ahead (fig. 6-3B).

If one hand or thrust is weaker than the other, the stern will rotate toward the weak side as it moves ahead.

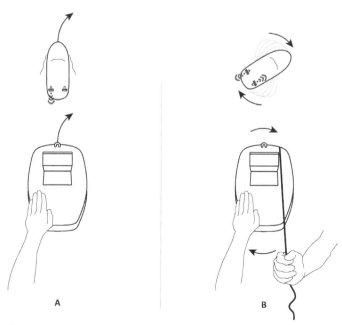

Fig. 6-4
Balance of thrust
Effect of offset thrust

As the two hands shift directions and push at a position parallel to the tug's centerline, the effect of their offset location comes into play (fig. 6-4A). The port Z-drive is attempting to push the stern forward, but its offset position also creates a turning force to starboard. The starboard drive unit has a similar effect, except that its turning force is to port. If both drive units are of equal RPM, the vessel moves straight ahead.

When the two drive units are in opposition to each other, but parallel to the centerline, the effect is similar to the twin-screw maneuver on a conventional tug. The hand on the side pushing ahead is attempting to push the stern forward and, because of its offset position, to rotate the tug around a point toward the bow. The hand on the side pushing astern is attempting to push the stern aft and, because of its offset position, rotate the tug in the same direction around a point toward the stern. The sensation is that one hand is pushing the stern around and the other is pulling the bow. If these two hands are of equal strength they will negate each other's fore and aft force, leaving only rotational force. The tug rotates without moving ahead (fig. 6-4B).

These may seem simplistic and obvious examples to the experienced conventional tug or towboat operator, but tracking the balance of thrust while maneuvering a Z-drive is more complicated. A Z-drive maneuver demands constant, subtle variations in azimuth (angle of thrust) and RPM (amount of thrust), sometimes in rapid succession. This can cause an operator to blur or lose the picture in his mind of the balance of thrust.

The image in your mind of the balance of thrust should serve as a reference point to evaluate the effectiveness of the current drive unit configuration, to plan the next configuration in a maneuvering sequence, and to troubleshoot maneuvering errors. You can't drive a Z-drive by the picture in your mind alone. Maneuvering accuracy and finesse require the other component of the balance of thrust: the feeling in your hands.

# What It Feels Like in Your Hands

The balance of thrust is more than an abstract concept. It also describes a sensation you will strive to acquire as you learn to drive a Z-drive. When the two units are closely balanced, the tug or towboat is highly responsive to slight changes in azimuth or amount of thrust. This is due to an aspect of one drive unit's thrust working against an aspect of the other. Because one is countering the other, one can quickly shift between opposing effects by using slight increases or decreases in the angle or amount of thrust, or both. Small changes in the amount or direction of thrust will result in very fine control of the vessel's motion.

When the two drive units are working together in balance, they create the "sweet spot." This is the feeling that the tug or towboat is alive under your hands. You will feel it instantly respond to small hand movements and to accentuate, retard, or change the vessel's direction at will. There will be little or no lag time between your hand motion and the tug's motion. This sensation is the mark of an operator who is in command of his Z-drive and not the other way around.

In the beginning of the learning process, the sweet spot can be elusive and easily lost. The trick is first to find it, and second, not to lose it while maneuvering. The previous section in this chapter describes a means of picturing the balance of thrust so that the drive units were close to a position that created the sweet spot. In other words, the picture in your mind creates a starting point for your hands to find the sweet spot. Creating mental images does not work for everyone. Some require starting from a drive unit configuration that can consistently produce the feeling of the sweet spot.

This is one of the roles of the "happy place." This term may seem out of place in the context of a powerful tug or towboat being controlled by a professional mariner. Nevertheless, you will hear many veteran Z-drive operators and trainers use this term. The happy place is created when both drive units are positioned at 90° to the vessel's centerline, propeller wash is going outboard, and thrust is going inboard, with both engines at equal RPM (fig. 6-5).

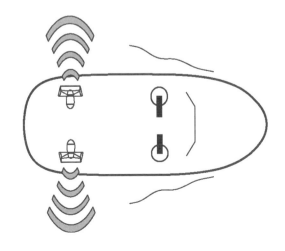

Fig. 6-5
Happy place

The term is derived from the feeling that accompanies this drive unit configuration. The vessel is stable, moving very little, and it consistently creates the feeling of the sweet spot. Some equate this feeling as being similar to holding a ball by pressing each hand in a horizontal direction (fig. 6-6).

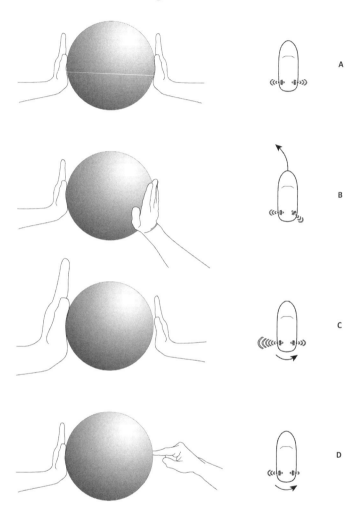

Fig. 6-6
Hands working together

If your hands are pushing in equally and directly in line with each other, the ball remains stationary (fig. 6-6A). If each hand pushes equally but one is angled, the ball rotates and moves forward (fig. 6-6B); if you want to move the ball with control to one side or the other, one hand pushes more (fig. 6-6C) or the other pushes less (fig. 6-6D), and the ball moves toward the weak side. The key to keep from dropping the ball is to create just enough counterpressure that the ball moves in the desired direction but does not drop to the floor. The hands must remain in a finely tuned balance. This is the

feeling of the sweet spot—both hands working together, subtly manipulating the drive units' thrust to create the desired vessel movement, but with just enough counterpressure to maneuver with control. The "happy place" drive unit configuration is the same as holding the ball stationary. It is a position that allows you to capture the feel of the sweet spot with minimal vessel movement and creates a starting point in which you can manipulate the balance of thrust to complete and control the desired maneuver.

## The Equations of Thrust

Remember, the vessel always moves as a result of the combination of the two drive units' thrust. A simple conceptual equation is always at work:

Port Drive Unit Thrust + Starboard Drive Unit Thrust = Vessel Motion

This holds true regardless of each drive unit's azimuth, the amount of RPM, or whether one unit is clutched out; the boat always responds to the combination of the two drive units. A simple example illustrating this concept is a tug turning to starboard (fig. 6-7). In all four scenarios, one drive unit is set with its azimuth aligned straight ahead and the other drive unit at 45°. The effects of each configuration result from the combination of thrust, drag, and offset position of the drive units in relation to the tug's centerline. In fig. 6-7A, the drag force of the port drive unit retards the turning effect of the starboard thruster, and the rate of turn is decreased. In fig. 6-7B, the drag force is neutralized by clutching in the port drive unit, and the turn rate increases. In figs. 6-7C and D the situation is reversed: the drag of the clutched-out unit (starboard) increases the turn rate, and when clutched in retards the turn rate. This is just one example of how a Z-drive's one-to-many relationship in combination with the balance of thrust can create a variety of techniques to accomplish the same maneuvering objective.

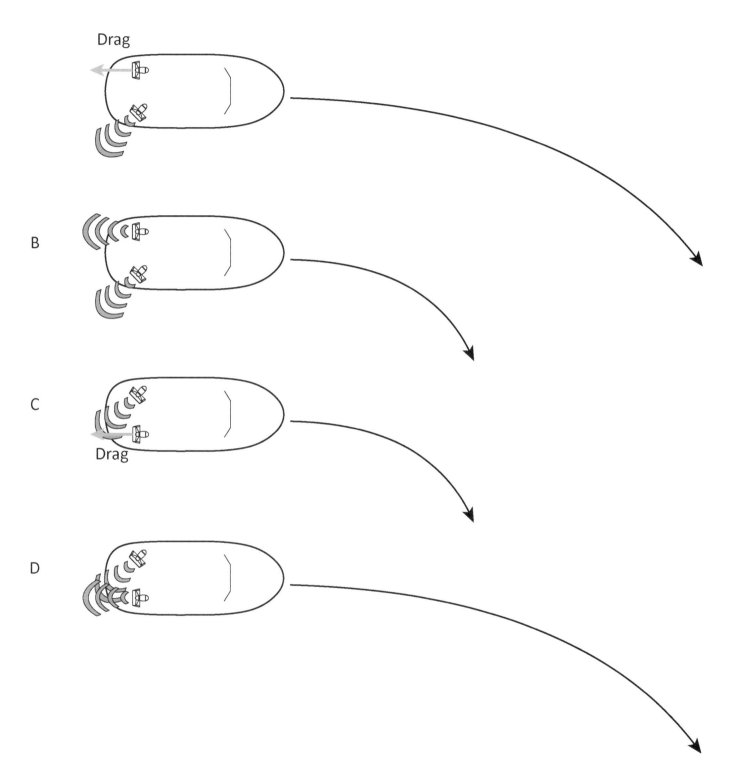

Fig. 6-7
Balance-of-thrust combinations

# Sweet Spot and the Balance of Thrust

The next series of illustrations and text will take you from simple to more-complex applications of finding and working around the sweet spot and the resultant changes in the balance of thrust. For the sake of simplicity, the following examples will illustrate only changes in azimuth. The RPM of each drive unit will remain constant. The starting point is to understand that each drive unit's thrust can be broken down into three principal force components (fig. 6-8):

- Headway
- Turning
- Sternway

The sweet spot is attained when these forces are working together in finely tuned balance, so that the tug or towboat responds quickly to subtle adjustments to any or all of the three components. This is the configuration that enables you to maneuver with precision by using your hands and mind to subtly manipulate the controls and subsequently the balance of thrust. In other words, the Z-drive operator changes this thrust equation with deft hands and clarity of mind to produce the desired vessel movement.

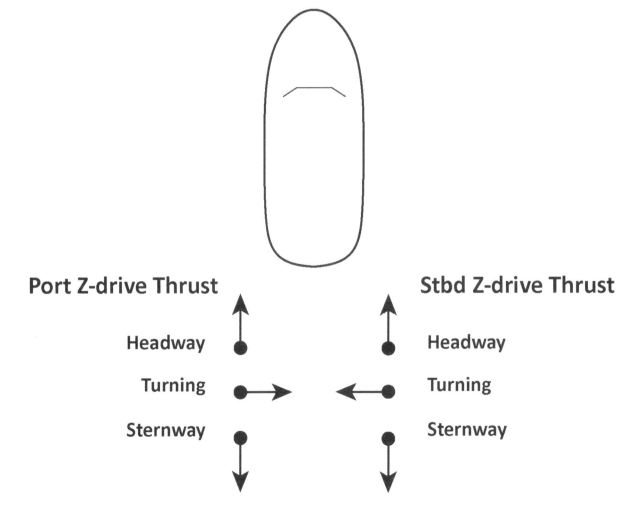

Fig. 6-8
Balance of thrust
Vector equation

## Happy Place

As a starting example, take the happy-place config-uration (fig. 6-9). In this configuration the three com-ponents of one hand negate the three components of the other. The headway and sternway components of both drive units are zero, and the turning components are of equal amount, but in opposite directions. Thus, the vessel remains stationary.

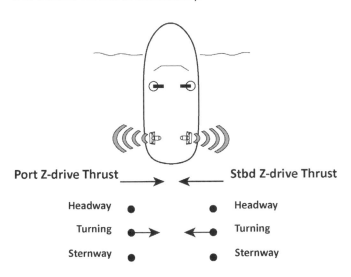

Fig. 6-9
Happy-place equation of thrust

## Headway in a Straight Line

The next step in the series is to move the control handles slightly forward and maintain the same RPM. This changes the balance-of-thrust equation by adding the same headway component equally to each drive unit's thrust. The turning components remain the same and cancel each other out. As a result the vessel moves straight ahead (fig. 6-10).

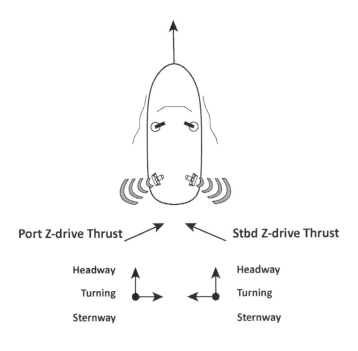

Fig. 6-10
Changing the equation
Add headway with no turning

## Headway and a Turn to Starboard

If the port drive unit azimuth moves slightly more ahead, the headway component increases and the turning component changes (fig. 6-11)—the vessel picks up headway and turns to starboard.

Note that the change in only one drive unit—the port unit—causes three things to occur simultaneously:

- Headway increases
- Stern moves to port
- Vessel turns to starboard

The starboard drive unit remained unchanged, but because the turning force of the port drive unit lessened, a slight imbalance in the overall turning force is created and the stern moved to port. In other words, the starboard turn was not due to an increase in thrusting to starboard; it was caused by a reduction in the thrust component to port by changing the azimuth of the port drive unit. In addition, it is important to note that the changes in azimuth represented in the illustration are exaggerated for illustration. In practice, the turn to starboard could be initiated with much-smaller control movements, albeit in the same direction as in the illustration.

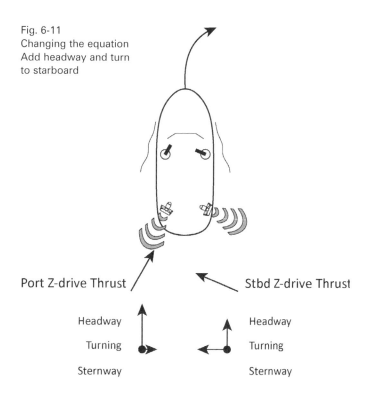

Fig. 6-11
Changing the equation
Add headway and turn
to starboard

Port Z-drive Thrust        Stbd Z-drive Thrust

Headway          Headway

Turning          Turning

Sternway         Sternway

# Checking the Swing and Steadying Up on the New Course

This is where the balance-of-thrust equation gets interesting and can be confusing. The vessel has gained headway and has started turning to starboard. To stop the swing to starboard and steady up on the new course, the drive units have to be adjusted. Of the multiple drive unit configurations to accomplish this, we will look at three. All three will check the swing and steady up on the new course, but one choice *increases* headway, one *reduces* headway, and one *maintains* headway.

If the starboard drive unit is adjusted to mirror the port, the result is that more headway force is added to the starboard, and the turning forces are opposed and equalized. As a result, the vessel accelerates ahead and steadies up on the new course (fig. 6-12). Moving just the right hand alone results in three simultaneous occurrences:

• Headway increases
• Stern stops swinging to port
• Vessel steadies up and runs straight

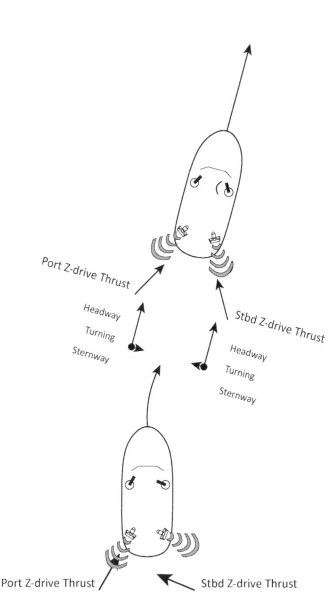

Port Z-drive Thrust

Headway

Turning

Sternway

Stbd Z-drive Thrust

Headway

Turning

Sternway

Port Z-drive Thrust        Stbd Z-drive Thrust

Starboard turn with headway

Fig. 6-12
Steadying up and
*increasing* headway

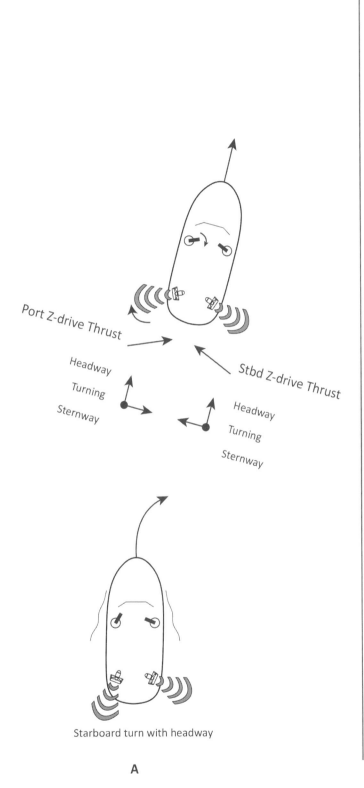

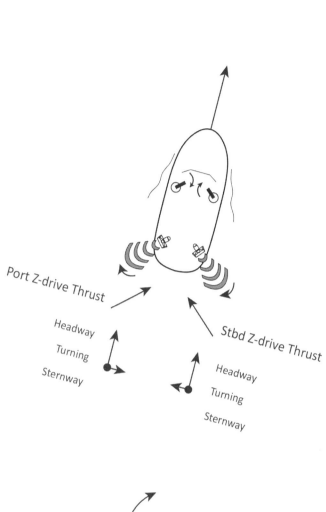

Port Z-drive Thrust

Stbd Z-drive Thrust

Headway
Turning
Sternway

Headway
Turning
Sternway

Starboard turn with headway

**A**

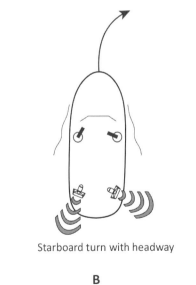

Starboard turn with headway

**B**

Fig. 6-13
A: Steadying up and *decreasing* headway
B: Steading up and *maintain*ing headway

If the port drive unit is brought back to its position prior to starting the turn (mirroring the starboard), headway force is reduced and the turning forces are opposed and equalized. As a result, the vessel reduces headway and steadies up on the new course (fig. 6-13A). Moving just the left hand alone results in three simultaneous occurrences:

- Headway decreases
- Stern stops swinging to port
- Vessel steadies up and runs straight

If the port and starboard drive unit are moved simultaneously, with the port thrust angling in toward the centerline and the starboard angling more forward, the result is that the vessel maintains the same amount of headway and steadies up on the new course (fig. 6-13B). Moving both hands in opposite directions—left hand slightly more aft and the right hand slightly more forward—results in three simultaneous occurrences:

- Headway stays the same
- Stern stops swinging to port
- Vessel steadies up and runs straight

These three choices all are equally valid. It is not that one is right or wrong, but rather which one is the best choice in the context of the maneuver at hand. Turning to starboard and accelerating may be best if departing a berth and heading to open water. Turning to starboard and reducing headway may be best if it is in the context of lining up to face up on a barge or push on a ship.

These examples focus on changing the thrust equation by azimuth only, but the equation can also be manipulated by changes in RPM, or combinations of azimuth and RPM. This is why solving the balance-of-thrust equation can become confusing and complex.

### Why This Is Important

The text in this chapter may seem complicated and confusing at first, but remember, this is an explanation of the balance of thrust—it is not the process you are expected to go through every time you want to maneuver your tug or towboat. Once you understand the balance-of-thrust equation, variables, and how to manipulate them, you will gain insight into six essential maneuvering maxims of handling a Z-drive tug or towboat:

- The sweet spot equals command of the balance of thrust.

- Stay close to the sweet spot.
- All control changes affect steering and speed simultaneously.
- 1 = 2 and 2 = 1.
- The hands always work together.
- Less is more.

# Stay Close to the Sweet Spot

The sweet spot can be elusive to find and hang on to. When you watch an experienced Z-drive operator, you will notice his hands are moving in small increments; sometimes in rapid succession, sometimes with periods of no movement. What you are witnessing is the operator working around the sweet spot, staying close to the drive unit configuration that allows him to easily control the variables of headway, sternway, and turning. Keeping your hands close to the sweet-spot configuration facilitates two things. One is that you can easily induce, accelerate, retard, or counter the vessel's motion with small hand movements. The other is that should you make a mistake or become confused (and you will; we all do), you can quickly return to the configuration that enables you to recapture the sweet spot and command of the vessel.

Losing the sweet spot means losing track of the interrelationship between the two drive units' thrust during a maneuvering sequence. A key effect of independently controlled drive units is the capability of one drive unit to quickly counter the thrust of the other. This is critical in close-quarters maneuvering. If you allow the drive units to get too far out of balance, you may be caught in situations in which the drive units are grossly out of position and unable to retard or change the vessel's unwanted motion toward an object.

In fig. 6-14, the operator has both drive units thrusting the tug's stern toward the dock. In this configuration, he has no means of checking or retarding the swing and will strike the dock. This is readily apparent in the diagram. It is easy to end up in this type of situation if you have lost the feel of the sweet spot.

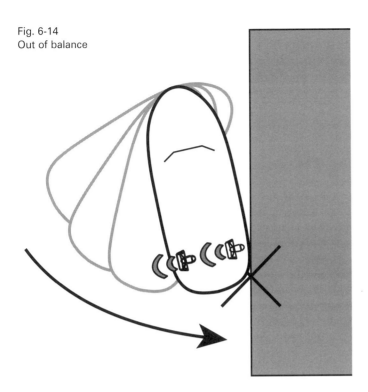

Fig. 6-14
Out of balance

# All Control Changes Affect Steering and Speed Simultaneously

This concept sounds simple but can be easily lost. This is a fundamental difference between a conventionally propelled vessel and a Z-drive. Every time you adjust the controls—azimuth, RPM, or both—both steering and speed are affected. It does not matter whether it is one hand or two hands moving—it is just a fact of Z-drive life that can't be escaped. A new operator may shift the controls to steer but not account for the effect on speed, or vice versa. Our brains like to make one-to-one associations. If we move one hand and the vessel turns, we tend to associate it with only that—turning the vessel. But hidden in that hand movement is also a manipulation of speed—to either increase, decrease, or maintain it while turning. It takes time for a new operator to embed in his mind and hands that the variables of steering and speed must always be solved in any change to the balance-of-thrust equation. Every change in the controls, every nuanced shift in azimuth or RPM, must always take into account both steering and speed.

# One Equals Two, Two Equals One

Two equations are axioms of the balance-of-thrust formula: $1 = 2$ and $2 = 1$. These may appear contradictory but can be understood through an appreciation of the fact that steering and speed are always linked. Any single control change in azimuth or power will affect both steering and speed simultaneously. The result of *one control* change is that both the vessel's heading and speed will change. In other words, one control change equals two effects on the boat.

The reverse equation is also true. If only one change is desired in vessel speed or direction (e.g., turn but maintain speed, or maintain course and reduce speed), it will always require two control changes. The *two control* changes can be within one control (e.g., azimuth and power) or a combination between controls (e.g., azimuth change both on port and starboard).

Most maneuvers require a rapid sequence of manipulating the Z-drive's heading and speed. The mind is constantly manipulating the two equations by the timing and sequence of control adjustments. The hands follow the mind's directives, making a series of coordinated control changes—some subtle, some large—but always with the hands appearing to work together.

# Your Hands Always Work Together

The tug or towboat moves in response to the propulsion force that results from the combination of the two drive units' thrust components. The effect of one or more of these components may be countered or accentuated by the other drive unit's thrust. When you turn the controls, you are selectively emphasizing or diminishing specific thrust components of each individual drive unit. The effect on the tug's motion is always a result of the interrelationship between the two drive units. Even if only one drive unit is moved or clutched out, you alter the effect of the other and the relationship between the two. You can't move one hand without it affecting the other. Your hands are always working together, directing the tug's or towboat's motion by constantly manipulating the interrelationship between the two drive units. There is a constant give and take between the hands or, as one experienced Z-drive operator put it, "what one hand giveth, the other taketh away."

As the positions of the hands become more varied, one or more aspects of their efforts may negate or enhance the other. You will learn to manipulate the balance of thrust and begin to associate a clear cause and effect between specific balance configurations and the vessel's response.

It is important to emphasize that the concept of the hands always working together does not mean they always move at the same time. As you become more experienced, you will learn that timing of hand movements is as important as the actual change in azimuth or RPM. There will be scenarios in which moving one hand alone may be appropriate, or the better choice may be moving both hands simultaneously, or moving them in a staggered sequence. This will be described in detail in later chapters.

## Using Less Is More

The less-is-more concept applies both to hand movement and amount of thrust. Moving the hands in small, incremental movements on the controls yields much-better results than large changes, and a reduction in thrust of one drive unit can be just as effective as an increase in thrust in the other.

The balance of thrust that results in a successful maneuver lives in a very narrow range. It does not take too-much change in thrust of either drive unit to lose the sweet spot, the balance of thrust, and control of the vessel. Once the sweet spot is attained, precision in maneuvering depends on small, incremental control changes. The difference between a large change in azimuth or RPM and a small one is usually control. Both may produce the desired change in the vessel's motion, but the small change keeps the vessel under control, while the large one launches the boat in a direction that can't be stopped. Even when a large change in azimuth or RPM is required, it is usually far better to make the transition in small, incremental steps. Less hand movement on the controls is better and more effective than large hand movements.

The less-is-more concept also applies to the amount of thrust. A reduction in thrust may be as effective as an increase in thrust to control the vessel's motion. There are many drive unit configurations in which a thrust aspect of one drive unit cancels out an aspect of the other. If the desired tug motion requires reducing or eliminating this canceling effect, a reduction in one side may have the same effect as an increase in the other.

A common tug-handling instinct is to apply more power to accentuate the desired motion in the tug. However, there are many situations in which a "less-is-more" approach is as effective and may be more appropriate. In fig. 6-15, the objective is to swing the stern toward the dock. Rather than increasing power on the port engine to create a favorable balance of thrust, the operator reduces the power on the starboard.

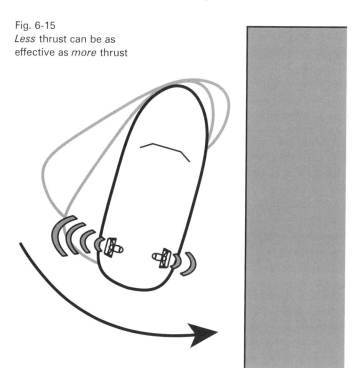

Fig. 6-15
*Less* thrust can be as effective as *more* thrust

## Summary

The balance of thrust is both a tactile and conceptual tool. Acquiring the sensation of the balance of thrust—the sweet spot—is the first step toward being able to trust your hands to intuitively drive the tug or towboat. When the concept is clear in your mind it facilitates thinking ahead; anticipating the appropriate drive unit positions that will be required several boat lengths into the future.

Although this chapter uses terms such as "equation" and "balance," it is important to emphasize that a proficient Z-drive operator does not require a degree in mathematics or physics. What is required is enough training, practice, and repetition so that his mind and hands solve the balance-of-thrust equation intuitively, without conscious thought.

When you observe an experienced operator handle a Z-drive, you are also witness to the manifestation of a split-second solution to the balance-of-thrust equation. The hand movement you observe and the vessel's response is a result of the operator instantly processing data, solving the equation, and delivering the solution to the hands. His eyes and inner ears have taken in the data that accurately assess the direction and momentum of the vessel. His mind matches those data with the desired maneuvering effect and calculates the required change to the thrust equation. His brain sends the appropriate electrical pulses down to his hands to adjust the controls. This all happens instantly and without conscious thought— this is the behind-the-scenes activity of "thinking with the hands."

Solving the balance-of-thrust equation is not a one-time occurrence. It is not static. It is dynamic and constantly changing, requiring manipulation of the variables and adjustment of the controls as the maneuver unfolds. This is why you may see an experienced operator moving his hands in frequent, small increments when required to maneuver with precision. His hands and mind are effortlessly processing a constant stream of new data and the required changes to the balance of thrust.

You do not have to be a Nobel Prize winner to attain this level of competency; it just takes practice and repetition to find the genius in your hands.

# *Chapter Seven*
## Stepping Up to the Controls

## Overview

Previous chapters have focused on conceptual learning about the principles and machinery that propel a Z-drive tug. It is now time to apply this knowledge and begin the hands-on learning process. When you step up to the controls, your first task is to verify that the Z-drive machinery is fully operational and that your mind and hands are oriented correctly to the tug or towboat. In other words, both man and machine must be fully functional. You should develop a personal premaneuvering routine that fulfills both functions.

## Develop a Routine

A consistent and accurate routine is a key factor in ensuring that both you and the Z-drive are ready to work. This routine has multiple applications. You will use it prior to leaving the dock, before you enter into complex maneuvers (e.g., coming alongside a moving ship), and to troubleshoot steering and propulsion malfunctions.

Z-drive operators and aviators share the necessity of utilizing a "preflight" routine—both operate high-performance machinery that depends on the reliable function of critical machinery components. You can create an effective routine for Z-drives by borrowing some of the principles used by our aviation brethren. Aviators use a standardized checklist format to verify that critical system components are fully operational and in good order. This extensive preflight checklist is required by regulation in the aviation world. Z-drive operators have no such requirement, but you can use the principles of the aviator's preflight routine as a guide to develop a written or mental checklist that works for you; one you will follow every time you step up to the controls.

The routine described in this chapter contains three elements that constitute a good Z-drive premaneuvering checklist:

- Visual scan
- Function test
- Hand orientation

These three elements are the building blocks of a good routine and should be incorporated in the development of your personal checklist.

## Visual Scan

The first task is to visually scrutinize the Z-drive control panels. Your eyes will inspect the indicator lights and selector switches on the panel to confirm that the following system components are "live":

- Control handle
- Azimuth indicator
- Main propulsion
- Steering
- 24 volts
- Clutch

It is important that you develop a systematic and consistent scan pattern. You will use the scan dockside in a relaxed atmosphere before getting underway during normal maneuvering, as well as in the heat of the moment, when you are closing rapidly on a dock or ship and have experienced an equipment failure. The purpose of the scan may vary, but the routine is the same. The technique should be consistent and habitual, so that your eyes automatically assess the instrument panel and quickly absorb critical information.

Aviators use a technique called the *selective radial scan* to make an organized visual assessment of their instruments. The scan begins at the primary instrument and moves to the secondary supportive dials and switches, depending on the purpose. The same principle can be applied to the Z-drive control panel (fig. 7-1).

The hub of the Z-drive control panel is the azimuth indicator; it is the primary reference instrument. When you glance down at the instrument panel, your eyes should go first to the azimuth indicator. Then, depending on purpose, shift back and forth between the azimuth indicator and the other panel components. When you are maneuvering underway in normal conditions, your primary focus will switch between the azimuth indicator, control handle, and engine or shaft rpm. If you are about to take over the controls, you should do a full scan so that your mind has fully integrated the operating status of all the Z-drive systems.

Fig. 7-1
Z-drive radial scan

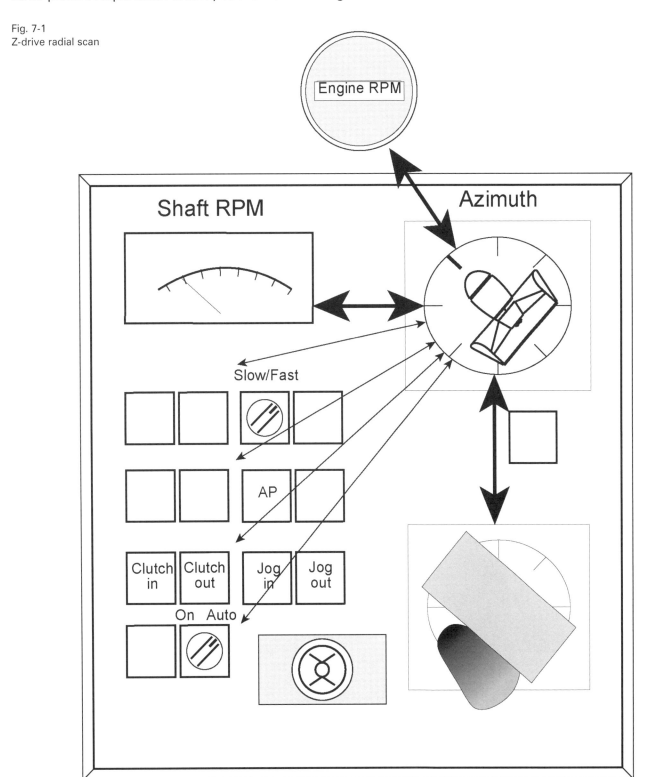

Fig. 7-2 depicts the information you will gather from your full scan. It uses a ZF control panel for illustrative purposes. In this example, a proper scan should immediately answer the following questions:

- Are the azimuth indicators and the position of the control handles synced?
- Is the main propulsion on, and what is the RPM?

- Is the steering pump on?
- Do I have the desired steering mode selected?
- Is the autopilot engaged?
- Are the Z-drives clutched in or out?

Other manufacturers' panels may differ in appearance but will convey the same information.

Fig. 7-2
System verification—ZF control panel

Engine RPM
(Main engine on or off?)

Control Mode
(Combi-lever, NFU or PIlot?)

Shaft RPM
(Propeller turning or not?)

Azimuth/Control Handle
(Positions synched?)

Clutch
(In or out?)

Fig. 7-3
Testing functionality—Schottel control panel

What you do

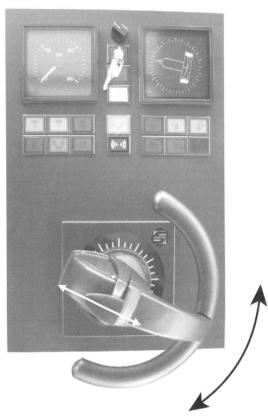

Clutch in and out
(*Verify drive unit clutches in/out and
main engine responds to rpm commands*)

Move the control handle back and forth a bit
(*Check to see azimuth indicator is moving and synchronized with the control handle*)

In addition to visual verification, you should also conduct a brief functionality test of the Z-drive system (fig. 7-3). Wiggle the control handle to see if the azimuth indicator follows. If you are underway and have room, change the RPM to see if the main propulsion system responds.

And there may be circumstances when it is appropriate to test clutch functionality by clutching in and out on each drive unit. Be wary of testing clutch or RPM functionality if you are secured to a dock. Docks and lines are no match to a Z-drive's ill-timed, misdirected, unbalanced, or high amount of thrust. Nothing is as demoralizing for a new operator than to leave the dock unexpectedly and prematurely, leaving broken lines and splintered piles in his wake.

Verification of Z-drive system functionality is not solely a visual process; you should listen as well as look. Once you have operated the same tug for a while, you will become accustomed to the sounds of your vessel's normal operation—the clicks, vibrations, whines, and whooshes as you clutch in

and turn the drive unit or raise the propeller RPMs. These should be your ears' benchmarks when you go through your system check.

These simple functionality tests are the final steps in verifying that the Z-drive machinery is responding correctly to control movements and that the tug or towboat is ready to work. The next step is to verify that you are ready to work.

## Hand Orientation

When you begin to maneuver a Z-drive tug or towboat, you will be processing both visual and tactile information that comes from your eyes and hands. This information builds the picture in your mind and the feel in your hands of the relationship between the thrust of the Z-drive units and the motion of the vessel. Mentally tracking this relationship is what allows you to "keep your head in front of the boat" and ensure that the drive units are properly configured. When first learning to handle a Z-drive, and as a maneuvering sequence unfolds, this mental picture can become complex. Before you begin to maneuver, it is important to start out with a clear picture in your head. Also, it is important that your hands feel solidly connected to the tug or towboat through the controls. To do that, you must make sure your eyes and hands are oriented correctly.

Once you begin maneuvering, your eyes will be quite active, searching for visual references to assess and predict the vessel's motion. In addition, new Z-drive operators will frequently look down at the instrument panel to orient themselves to the azimuth indicators. Both perspectives are essential. Tracking the azimuth while twisting handles tells you what *should be* happening; looking out the window tells you what *is* happening. It is best to track both simultaneously. A quick look out the pilothouse window gives you a sense of the vessel's motion; a quick glance down at the instrument panel gives you a picture of the drive unit's configuration. Make sure that both those snapshots make sense.

As you become more comfortable handling the Z-drive, your hands, rather than your eyes, will become the primary azimuth indicators. You will rely more and more on the position of your hands to tell you in which direction the drive units are thrusting, and your eyes will be free to take in other visual cues. This is the ideal to strive for—your eyes are focused primarily out the pilothouse window, maintaining a seamless vision of the vessel's motion and response to changes in thrust, while your hand position and tactile sensations convey the drive units' thrust configuration.

Do not underestimate the importance of consistent hand orientation on the controls. "Hand confusion" and a loss of azimuth awareness is a common cause of losing control of a Z-drive. For your hands to become useful azimuth indicators, you must develop sensitivity to two sensations: the first is proprioception, and the second is tactile familiarity with the control handle shape. Proprioception is the unconscious perception of movement and spatial orientation that comes from the body—you know how your hands are oriented without looking. As you develop your skills as a Z-drive operator, the sensation of knowing where your hands are positioned in space will become directly correlated with specific drive unit configurations. This correlation is accurate only if your hands hold the control handles in a consistent manner.

Your primary cue for hand orientation is the tactile sense of the control handle shape and feel. You should develop a consistent and systematic method of placing them on the controls. There are as many methods as individual Z-drive operators. Differing techniques share the same objective— providing tactile cues that allow you to know which way the drive units are thrusting without having to divert your eyes to the azimuth indicator. Each of these methods shares two common elements: some aspect of the hand is lined up with the drive unit's thrust, and the hand is in a position to orient itself to the shape and tactile feel of the control handle. The importance of hand position is not so much the actual physical arrangement of your palm and fingers; rather, it is that you trust your hands to give you an accurate and reliable sense of the direction and amount of thrust of each drive unit.

Fig. 7-4 illustrates a common hand position on a ZF control head. The handle is equipped with three tactile cues: the "T"-handle, steering stick, and round control base. The combination of these three aspects gives the handle an asymmetrical feel, offering the operator several hand orientation options. In this case, the operator has chosen to place his thumb on the T-handle so that it controls RPM and is pointed in the direction of thrust. His little finger rests on the steering stick, giving him a tactile cue as to the direction of wheel wash.

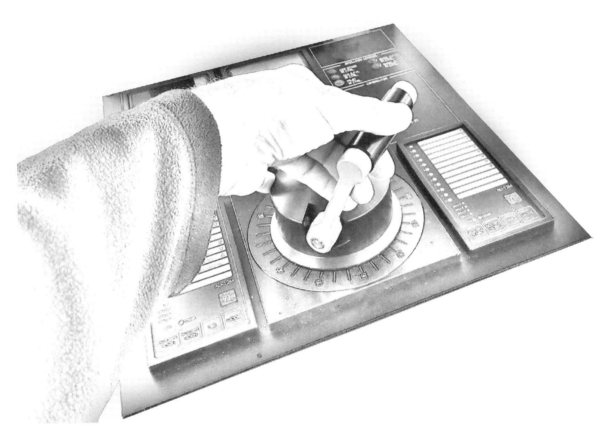

# The left hand paints this picture in your mind

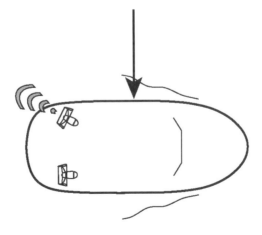

Fig. 7-4
Hand orientation—ZF control handle

The left hand paints this picture in your mind

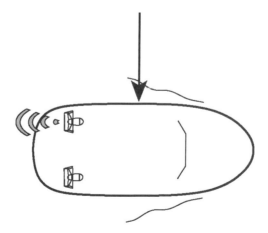

Fig. 7-5
Hand orientation—Schottel control handle

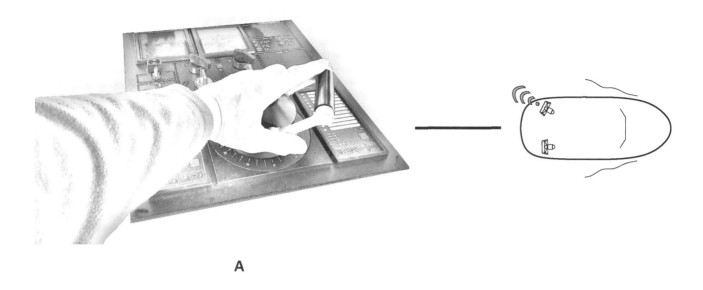

A

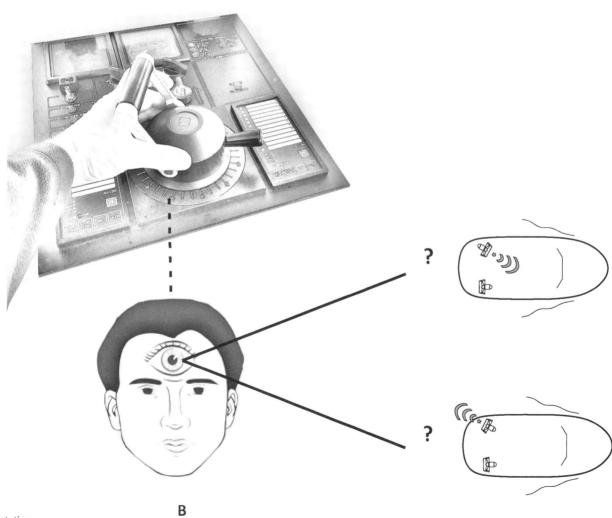

Fig. 7-6
Hand orientation
Hand confusion

B

Fig. 7-7
Hand orientation
Better hand orientation than in fig. 7-6B

Fig. 7-5 applies the same principles to a Schottel control head. The Schottel control handle is asymmetrical, with numerous tactile cues to help orient your hand. In this example, the operator uses his thumb as an azimuth indicator, as well as the means to manipulate and estimate the amount of throttle.

## Why This Is Important

Your hands should be your azimuth indicators. If they are not oriented correctly, your perception of drive unit alignment will be inaccurate, raising the potential for "hand confusion" and maneuvering mistakes. There are many maneuvers that require the drive units to be opposed—thrusting in opposite directions— to create an effective balance of thrust. If the operator is inconsistent in his hand orientation, it is easy to have both hands oriented the same way, even though the thrust is in opposite directions. This leads to the common mistakes of turning the azimuth the wrong way, increasing instead of reducing RPM,

and increasing thrust rather than clutching out. Consistent hand orientation helps prevent these types of errors and trains your hands to be accurate azimuth indicators.

Fig. 7-6 illustrates a classic hand orientation error. The hand position in fig. 7-6A is commonly used when the port drive unit is thrusting ahead at an angle. If the operator uses this hand orientation consistently in these circumstances, a correlation between the hand position and resultant thrust becomes embedded in his mind's eye. In fig. 7-6B, the operator is using a similar hand orientation to thrust at an aft angle with the port drive unit. The hand position is similar, but the drive unit azimuths are 180° apart. This disparity can lead to a puzzled look in the mind's eye and some common errors. If the operator moves his hand forward to call for more thrust, as he would when the drive unit is thrusting ahead, he will clutch out instead; if he thinks that angling his hand more toward the centerline of the vessel will thrust the stern to starboard, he will thrust to port instead.

Fig. 7-7 is one example of an alternative hand position for thrusting aft at an angle that lines up some aspect of the hand with the drive unit's thrust, is oriented to the shape and tactile feel of the control handle, and is distinct from the hand orientation used when the azimuth is 180° different.

These illustrations are only one of a set of hand positions you may utilize. An individual's hand and wrist range of motion and the ergonomics of the control layout are additional determining factors for an operator's hand orientation system. As you engage in more-complex maneuvers and begin to use the full 360° thrust capability of each drive unit, you will develop other hand positions.

These variations in control handle style and orientation serve to emphasize the importance of developing a premaneuvering routine. The Z-drive's machinery must be fully operational, your mind must have a clear bird's-eye view, and your hands must be connected to the tug.

Once you and the tug have achieved this state of preparedness, you are ready to "learn by doing"—to begin practicing the hands-on maneuvering exercises outlined in the following chapters. Learning the hand movements associated with each skill set requires much trial and error, and repetition. Trial and error identifies the successful technique; repetition embeds the correct technique in your hands. The text and pictures in the following chapters are designed to augment—not replace—your hands-on learning process. Once you gain proficiency in the basic maneuvering skills as separate entities, you will learn to apply them in combination as required by maneuvers that are more complex.

# *Chapter Eight*
## Turning

## Role of the Trainer

This chapter marks the beginning of our hands-on training. A word about the role of a trainer is appropriate before we take on the learning process aboard a live vessel. Hands-on training typically occurs on vessels worth millions of dollars, and during the time the vessel is either going about its revenue-producing business or is in-between jobs. Hands-on learning should be through a *controlled* process of trial and error, learning from mistakes and repetition. It is only by controlling these factors that the onboard training process can be completed effectively, safely, and without the high cost of "training" accidents. The role of the trainer is to guide the new operator through an effective learning sequence, demonstrate or verbalize the required skill sets, and be present to take control at the boundary between learning from mistakes and a training accident.

The practice maneuvers in this and the following chapters require an experienced trainer to be close at hand, ready to intervene if necessary to prevent damage to vessels or personnel. The trainer's role is to manage the learning scenario so that it allows the trainee to be challenged, make mistakes, and learn but also protect vessels and personnel. It is important that the trainer clearly set the boundary between the two both in his and the trainee's mind prior to beginning any training maneuver. These boundaries are the basis of the trainer-trainee ground rules. They should be communicated unequivocally to the trainee so that there is no debate if the trainer decides it is appropriate to intervene.

Establishing these ground rules is particularly important on a Z-drive tug or towboat. Z-drive wheelhouses are usually small and have only one set of controls. Unfortunately, they are not set up like the cockpit of an airplane with dual controls. The Z-drive trainer does not have the flight instructor's option to instantly grab the controls and abort a maneuver. The Z-drive instructor has two methods at his disposal: one is to give verbal instructions or commands, and the other is to physically displace the trainee's hands from the controls. This requires tactful positioning in the wheelhouse so that the trainer can reach the controls in a timely fashion without breathing down the trainee's neck. In short, the trainer must have set the stage with physical and mental parameters so that the situation and the controls are always within his reach.

In addition, it is important to communicate to other personnel that this is a training session, and that a trainee is at the controls. Deck personnel handling lines need to know who is at the helm. When they are working lines, their safety may depend on the skill of the operator. All parties will be reassured if they know the voice and skill of the trainer and are assured that the training session is under his supervision.

## Overview

We start our hands-on training with the first basic skill set: turning. It may seem simple, but this first step is essential in starting the process of remapping your brain to associate new hand movements with the Z-drive's response. This is a connection that leads to an intuitive "feel" for a Z-drive. Handling a Z-drive consists of many sensations, and turning requires that you bring four of them into play. The first is the sense that your hands are directly connected to the vessel, the second is a bodily awareness of changes in the vessel's speed of advance as the rate of turn increases or decreases, the third is an awareness of the vessel's pivot point, and the fourth is a constant perception of the location and movement of the vessel's stern. All four of these are essential to feeling "one with the boat."

# Why Is This Important?

### Hand Connection

To acquire the ability to "think with your hands," your hands must become the direct path of perception between changes in the direction and amount of thrust and the tug's or towboat's response. Once established, this feeling will give you confidence that when your hands move, you know how the vessel will move.

### Relationship between Rate of Turn and Speed of Advance

When you practice turning, you will notice that the sharper you turn, the more you slow down. This awareness is the first step in understanding the link between steering and propulsion.

### Pivot Point

When the tug or towboat turns, it rotates around a pivot point on the vessel as it moves through the water. The location of this pivot point depends on four primary factors: whether the vessel is moving bow first or stern first, speed through the water, rate of turn, and drive unit azimuth. Mathematically calculating the location of the pivot point is not important. What is important is that you develop an awareness of its location and how it shifts as you go through a maneuvering sequence. Practicing turns is the first step in acquiring that awareness.

### Location and Movement of the Stern

Remember that the stern drives the vessel. If you lose track of the stern, you lose one of your most valuable reference points: the propulsion end of the vessel. Without an awareness of the stern's location in the present, you can't anticipate where the stern—and the tug or towboat—will be two or three boat lengths in the future.

Practicing turns in open water is an ideal environment for the hands, body, and mind to associate sensory feedback with the vessel's response to twists of the control handle. There is room to learn and time to gain a feel for the Z-drive.

# Practical Exercises

The objectives of following practical exercises are to

1. begin programming the hands and remapping the brain,
2. build an awareness of the stern's location, and
3. manage the rate of turn.

It is best to follow the exercises below in sequence. They may appear simple, and indeed, you may find them quite easy. Great! However, the exercise sequence is designed to ensure that your brain is correctly linked to your hand movements. To do that effectively, you must start from the simple and build to the complex. You will know it is time to move on in the learning sequence when you execute the specific maneuver and can carry on a conversation at the same time; it is when you can do the maneuver without thinking.

# Learning Scenarios

1. S-Turns in open water
2. Slalom course, one drive unit only
3. Slalom course, two drive units in unison
4. Slalom course, two drive units with independent motion

# S-turns in Open Water

In a simulator or live tug, execute a series of S-turns: port and starboard, bow first and stern first. Attempt these first in open water with no obstructions. Strive for a smooth wake, rather than a series of chords (fig. 8-1). Once you feel comfortable in an open roadstead, create a practice course that contains reference points.

The ideal practice course is a slalom course set up with a line of buoys (fig. 8-2). Go through the practice course in the following configurations.

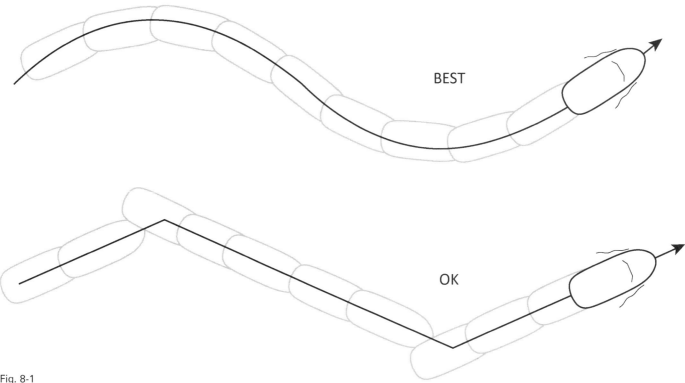

BEST

OK

Fig. 8-1
Smooth versus jagged turns

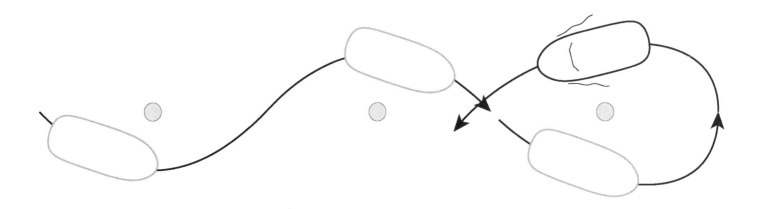

Fig. 8-2
Slalom course for training

# Slalom Course: One Drive Unit Only

The quickest way to begin programming your hands is to execute turns by using the thrust of one drive unit while the other is stopped in a fixed position. This eliminates possible confusion as to which drive unit is causing the tug or towboat to turn. It allows your hands and mind to readily associate a one-to-one relationship between hand position and the direction of thrust.

### What It Looks Like in Your Mind

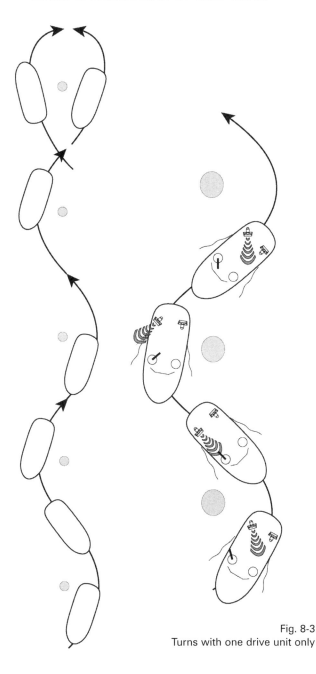

Fig. 8-3
Turns with one drive unit only

It is extremely important that you give equal time to maneuvering bow first and stern first. Both your hands and mind should become comfortable handling either drive unit, regardless of the direction that you are facing or that the vessel is moving. Most operators will face the leading end of the light vessel when it is in motion. This means facing the bow when running bow first, and facing the stern when running stern first. Many maneuvers require the operator to face away from the vessel's direction of advance.

In those cases most Z-drive operators face the working end of the vessel. For example, in shipwork, the operator will face the bow of the tug while moving stern first to work bow to bow with a moving ship (fig. 8-4A). The same circumstances apply to a towboat downstreaming (fig. 8-4B). The operator faces forward while the towboat is stern-up into the current. In both cases the vessel is moving through the water stern first. It is essential that your hands and mind become familiar with two operating orientations: facing toward the vessel's direction of motion or away from it.

### How It Feels in Your Hands

As you practice these turns, using just one hand and one drive unit, your hands should acquire an awareness of four sensations:

1. The relationship between the main engine's RPM and the vessel's responsiveness
2. The link between steering and propulsion
3. How azimuth and RPM can compensate for each other
4. The different feel between running bow first and stern first

**RPM and Responsiveness**

When the drive unit is clutched in and the main engine is at idle, a several-second delay usually occurs between the turn of the handle and the tug's or towboat's response. The vessel feels a bit sluggish to your hands, and it seems to require exaggerated hand movement to get it to respond. If you execute the same turn with maximum engine RPM, the vessel responds instantly to much less hand movement.

The relationship among RPM, speed, and the vessel's response is like a deal with the devil. Slower may be safer, but faster makes the tug or towboat more responsive. The trick is to use enough power to make the vessel responsive to your hands, but not so much that the speed of the maneuver exceeds the ability of your mind and hands to keep up with the boat. It is easy to be seduced into using large amounts of power due to the temptation of a vessel

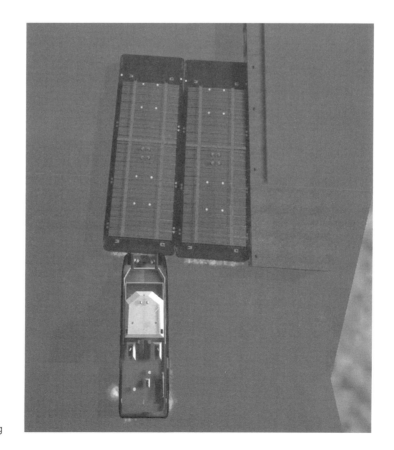

Fig. 8-4
A: Shipwork—bow-to-bow
operations
B: Towboat work—downstreaming

that is so sensitive it responds to the slightest movement of your hands. This is how a new operator can be enticed into using excessive power that he cannot control. It is important that you find a comfortable balance among power, control, and maneuvering speed. You will know you are in the right zone when there is enough RPM to make your hands feel that they are in sync with the vessel, but the maneuvering speed is slow enough that your mind is able to keep two or three maneuvering steps ahead.

## Linking Steering and Propulsion

This principle can be felt when rounding a buoy in the slalom course.

Rounding one buoy and setting up for the next requires the Z-drive operator to regulate the vessel's rate of turn and advance simultaneously. A typical occurrence for a new operator is to oversteer while guiding a Z-drive through a slalom course. Upon approach to a buoy ahead, he is required to change the azimuth to get the vessel to turn. A common error is to make too large a hand movement on the controls and increase the azimuth, causing the vessel to turn sharply, but also to slow down dramatically and pass too close to the buoy at hand. Upon sensing this, the new operator overcorrects. He swings the control handle the other way and decreases the azimuth, causing the vessel to accelerate, and sets up the symptoms of oversteering: the vessel gyrating and swinging from side to side.

One factor in setting up the oversteering cycle is that the operator is not fully aware of the relationship between angle of thrust and its simultaneous effect on steering and propulsion. As the azimuth and rate of turn increase, the advance through the water decreases.

The allocation of thrust to steering and propulsion varies with the azimuth and RPM of the drive unit. It would be nice if there were hard-and-fast rules that accurately predicted the effect of this allocation, but there are simply too-many combinations of magnitude and direction of thrust to make this possible. The importance to the Z-drive operator is to gain an awareness of the relationship between steering and propulsion, and to begin associating specific effects with physical sensations. You may sense that the vessel is accelerating but not turning fast enough. Or you may feel the vessel "bite" into the water and slow down as the drive unit's thrust angle approaches 90° to the tug's centerline. These sensations are the physical cues of the link between steering and propulsion. You will learn to use them to your advantage when you begin to simultaneously manage rate of turn and speed of advance.

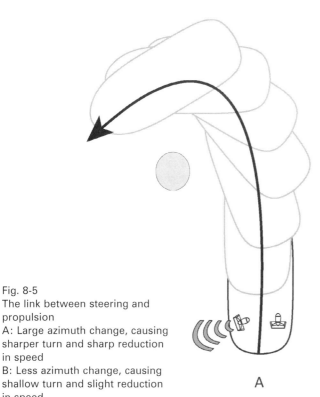

Fig. 8-5
The link between steering and propulsion
A: Large azimuth change, causing sharper turn and sharp reduction in speed
B: Less azimuth change, causing shallow turn and slight reduction in speed

A

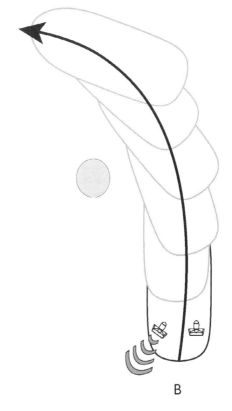

B

**Azimuth and RPM Compensate for Each Other**

Multiple options are at your disposal to direct both the direction and rate of the vessel's turn. One option is to utilize the relationship between azimuth and RPM. It is not just the *angle* of thrust that determines the turn rate—it is also the *amount* of thrust. The interplay between the two can produce the same rate of turn with different combinations of azimuth and RPM. Generally, more azimuth angle can compensate for lower engine RPM to produce the same rate of turn. Less azimuth angle can also compensate for higher engine RPM to produce the same results. This interplay is another tool the experienced operator utilizes to harness the maneuvering capability of a Z-drive.

**Bow First versus Stern First**

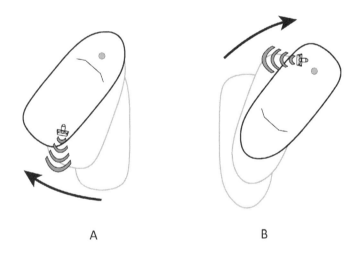

A                                    B

Fig. 8-6
ASD pivot points

When an ASD vessel is running bow first, the vessel's pivot point is toward the bow and away from the propulsion units (fig. 8-6A). To turn, the vessel's stern must rotate around the pivot point until the new heading is reached. The drive unit's thrust must be directed *away* from the direction of the intended turn. To turn to starboard, the thrust must push the stern to port. In addition, the turning effect of the Z-drive's thrust is magnified by the leverage created by the distance between the pivot point and the propulsion unit. It does not take much change in azimuth to change the vessel's heading. You should feel you can control the turn with relatively fine hand movements.

When running stern first, the pivot point is close to the propulsion units (fig. 8-6B). Due to the proximity of the propulsion units to the pivot point, there is little or no ability to change the vessel's direction by rotating around the pivot point. The stern must be moved toward the new heading, rather than pivoting around the bow. This requires that the drive unit's thrust be directed toward the direction of the turn. To turn to port, the drive unit's thrust must be to port, and its proximity to the pivot point gives it little leverage. You may feel you have to "muscle" the stern around by using greater azimuth angles, more thrust, or a combination of both.

Thrusting the stern toward or away from the direction of the turn is a source of confusion for many new Z-drive operators. Bow first, the drive unit rotates opposite to the direction of the desired turn; stern first, it rotates toward the direction of the turn. Use the simple, one-drive-unit turn to get your hands and mind programmed in the distinctions between the two modes. Remember that the stern drives the tug. When using only one drive unit, the stern moves in the same direction as the thrust, regardless of which way the tug is moving or you are facing. This is why it is so important to practice maneuvers both bow first and stern first. Becoming comfortable in these two modes with one hand may minimize confusion when you use two in more-complex maneuvers.

Once you acquire a feel for executing turns with one hand, both bow first and stern first, you are ready to add a second hand on the controls.

# Slalom Course, Two Drive Units in Unison

### What It Looks Like in Your Mind

Engaging the second drive unit will increase the vessel's speed and exponentially increase the amount of azimuth and throttle variables that your hands and head will need to process. In the early stages of learning, many new operators will use both hands in unison—using the same RPM and azimuth, as well as moving them simultaneously (fig. 8-7). In other words, one hand mirrors the other.

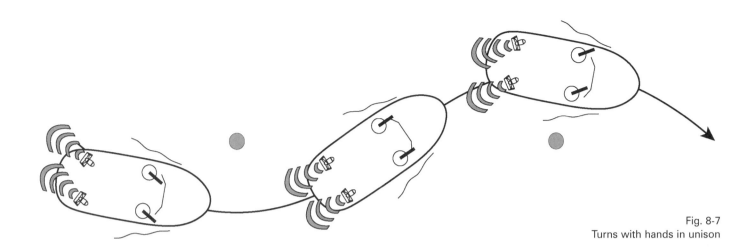

Fig. 8-7
Turns with hands in unison

### What It Feels Like in Your Hands

The use of both hands in unison is simply an extension of the brain-to-hand mapping when using one drive unit. Most new Z-drive operators have no trouble becoming comfortable with this steering mode; it feels simple. You twist the control handles, and if the vessel is turning the wrong way, you simply turn the control handles in the opposite direction. There is no worry about which hand might have induced the steering error. Both did, and both take the same action to correct. The trial-and-error process is quick and clear.

At some point during your practice you will notice that using the hands in unison makes it easy to oversteer. Using both drive units in unison creates powerful turning forces. The tug or towboat turns sharply and quickly but is difficult to control with finesse. A change in two drive units is too much; one may be all that is needed. This is the point that you may find your hands beginning to move independently in an instinctive or automatic manner.

They will no longer be exact mirror images. This typically occurs when the Z-drive operator is looking for finer control of the vessel's rate of turn.

When you reach this point, it is appropriate to move into the final turning practice—using two hands with independent movements.

# Two Drive Units Moving Independently

### What It Looks Like in Your Mind

When you turn the vessel by moving your hands independently, you delegate different amounts of steering and propulsion functions to each drive unit (fig. 8-8). Splitting steering and propulsion functions between two drive units is a particularly useful tool in the first phase of learning—thinking your way through maneuvers.

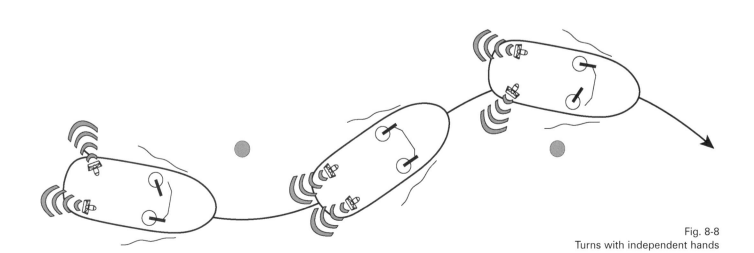

Fig. 8-8
Turns with independent hands

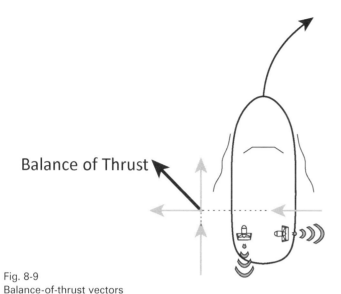

Balance of Thrust

Fig. 8-9
Balance-of-thrust vectors

Separating steering and propulsion functions enables you both physically and conceptually to break down the balance of thrust into its basic components (fig. 8-9). This may be easier on the mind, since it facilitates a one-to-one association between a function and a drive unit. It also simplifies the thought process of deciding which hand to move, because each hand has a primary function—steering or propelling. For example, some new Z-drive operators find it useful to use the saying "right turn, right hand; left turn, left hand" when they are running

bow first. This mnemonic device helps them keep the steering function assigned to one drive unit and clear both in their mind and hands as to which drive unit to use.

Utilizing independent hand movements does not mean that the steering and propulsion functions are separated completely between the two drive units; there is almost always an overlap (fig. 8-10). Some functions may be shared; some completely separate. As you become more adept at managing the balance of thrust, the boundary fades between the roles of each drive unit. The division of function becomes more fluid with practice and repetition. Your hands intuitively and automatically shift the role and purpose of each drive unit, emphasizing the appropriate steering or propulsion facet of each. Instead of being bound by a one-to-one relationship between hand movement and function, you will begin to realize a one-to-many relationship.

### What It Feels Like in Your Hands

At first, your hand movements may feel a bit robotic. This is a part of the learning sequence. Many new Z-drive operators move first one hand and then the other as they turn through the buoys. They are consciously directing their hand movements—thinking their way through the turns. For some it may be too difficult to problem solve the changing thrust requirements of both drive units simultaneously.

Fig. 8-10
Overlap of steering and propulsion functions

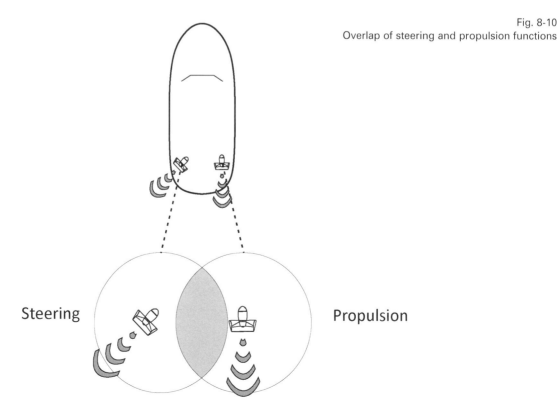

Steering

Propulsion

This one-at-a-time processing is reflected in their hand movements.

Part of learning to use two interrelated but independent hands is acquiring sensitivity to the tug's or towboat's physical cues. You will learn to associate changes in your vessel's vibration, lag between thrust and response, engine sounds, and heeling angle with specific aspects of the balance of thrust. These sensations will assist you in assessing the vessel's movement and processing the required changes in thrust configuration. You will be having a two-way conversation with your tug or towboat—listening to the vessel's physical signals while commanding it what to do. This marks the beginning of you driving the Z-drive and not the other way around.

Once you have become comfortable turning with two hands, you are ready to complete the following practice drill and move on to the next skill—managing speed.

## Practice Drills

### Buoy Circles

In a simulator or live tug or towboat, circle a reference point (buoy) and maintain a constant distance as you round the buoy. Steady up on a predesignated course or visual reference, execute a 180° turn, and circle the buoy in the opposite direction (fig. 8-11). Complete both maneuvers bow first and stern first.

The practice objectives are

- controlling the rate of turn,
- maintaining the same distance off a reference point while turning,
- steadying up on a new course without oversteering, and
- having no virtual collisions (in a simulator) or instructor intervention (live tug).

Fig. 8-11
Practice drill: rounding a buoy

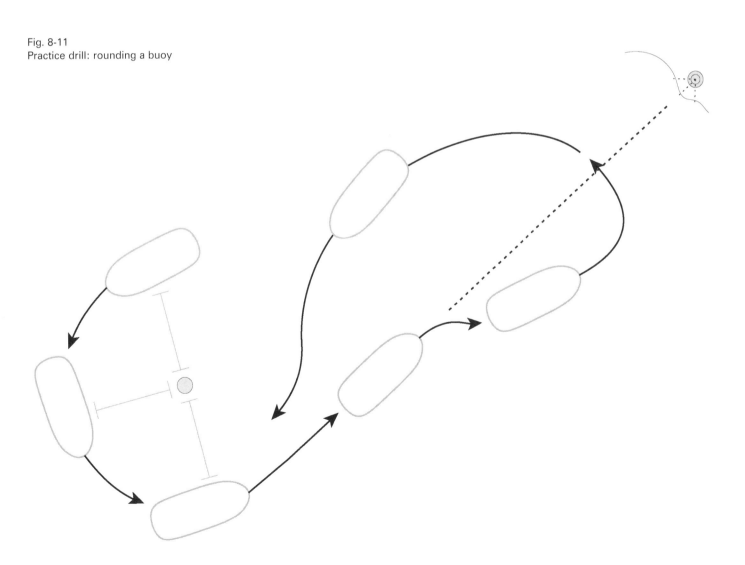

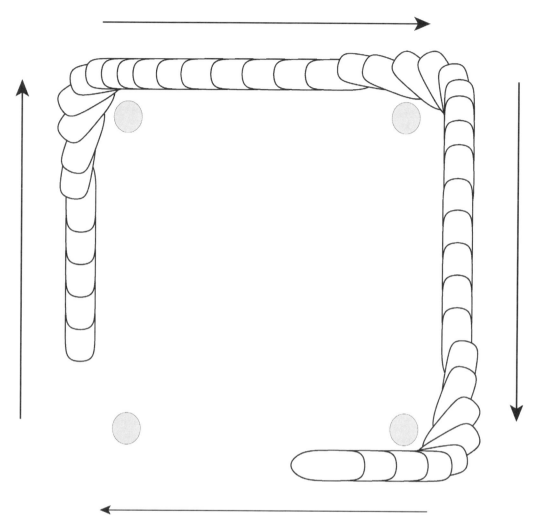

Fig. 8-12
Practice drill: scribing a rectangle

### Scribing a Rectangle

This course is to practice turns with precision. In a simulator or live tug or towboat, set up reference points that define a rectangular course. Follow the lines between the reference points, turn smartly at each corner, and then steady up on the next line with as little oversteering as possible. Complete the course bow first and stern first, as well as clockwise and counterclockwise.

The practice objectives are to

- control the rate of turn,
- execute a turn at a designated point,
- check the swing,
- steady up on a new course without oversteering, and
- have no virtual collisions (in a simulator) or instructor intervention (live tug).

The practical exercises in this chapter have focused on turning and establishing a positive connection among mind, hands, and vessel. Vessel speed was a secondary consequence. The next chapter focuses on building an awareness of how to manage speed to enable you to manage steering and speed simultaneously.

# Notes

# *Chapter Nine*
## Managing Speed

## Overview

Turning and managing speed are in separate chapters for the sake of discussion, but in practical application the two are inseparable. Changes in steering affect speed and changes in speed affect steering. Managing speed requires the Z-drive operator to focus both on the propulsion and steering component of the balance of thrust. These components are controlled by the drive unit's azimuth, the main engine RPM, or by a combination of the two. As in chapter 8 ("Turning"), propulsion and steering always affect each other. You can't simply slow down or speed up—you must also steer. Reducing or increasing the tug's or towboat's speed of advance is relatively easy; steering while manipulating speed requires a higher skill level.

Regardless of whether you use azimuth or RPM to control speed, the steering forces of the drive units should remain in balance and opposed to each other. This nullifies each drive unit's turning component, leaving only changes in the amount of propulsion. If azimuth is used to accelerate or retard speed, the change in drive unit angles must be equal and simultaneous (fig. 9-1A). Similarly, if a change in engine RPM is used, both engines must be increased or decreased equally and at the same time (fig. 9-1B).

On paper, these two methods appear simple and distinct. However, their boundary is not clear when applied in practical situations. Many maneuvers require a change in speed while maintaining directional control of the vessel, or a change in direction while maintaining speed. This may require constant and subtle changes both in azimuth and RPM. To manage speed effectively, you must develop the ability to simultaneously manage dual effects of the balance of thrust—speed of advance and turning.

Fig. 9-1
Managing speed
A: Azimuth only
B: RPM only

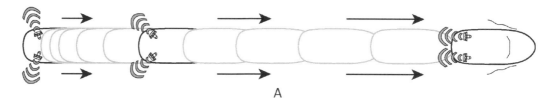

A

Slow                    Moderate                    Fast

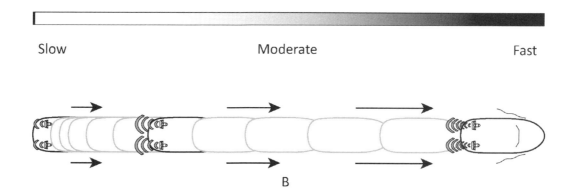

B

# Why This Is Important

Speed management is a key tool that enables you to keep your vessel under control. As noted, the ideal speed of advance is one in which your hands are in the current moment—reacting to the vessel's subtle changes in direction and speed—while your mind is two or three boat lengths ahead. This ideal speed varies depending on the complexity of the maneuver, the skill of the operator, and the Z-drive's capability. These three factors dictate how much time you may require to process incoming sensory information and translate that into the hand movements that meet your maneuvering objective. At times, you will undoubtedly find yourself in circumstances that exceed either your or the Z-drive's capabilities. Rather than you driving the Z-drive, you may feel the Z-drive is driving you. In these situations you need to create a cushion of time—time that allows your hands and mind to respond effectively to the physical cues picked up by your eyes and body. Speed management is a skill set that gives you the additional seconds or minutes you need to get the vessel back under control.

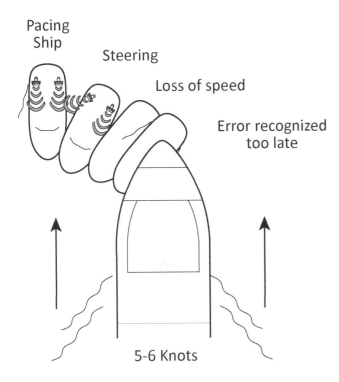

Fig. 9-2
Loss of steering and speed awareness

Pacing Ship

Steering

Loss of speed

Error recognized too late

5-6 Knots

In addition, an understanding of speed management helps identify the source of too-much or too-little speed. Steering and propulsion are inseparable, yet the effect of their inseparability may be lost in the heat of the moment. In fig. 9-2, the ASD operator is attempting to go bow to bow with an advancing ship to assist with a headline. At first, the operator is holding off the ship's bow, matching its speed of advance. However, he must subsequently maneuver the tug closer to pass a line. As the operator begins to steer by using the starboard drive unit, the tug immediately slows down relative to the ship. In this case, the operator neither compensates for the reduction in propulsion nor recognizes his error in time and finds himself in a precarious position under the ship's bow. The proportional relationship between steering and propulsion can easily be lost in the flurry of activity associated with close-quarters maneuvering. An understanding of this relationship is essential to the Z-drive operator's ability to control speed.

# Practical Exercises

The objectives of the following exercises are to practice

1. changing speed,
2. maintaining speed, and
3. maintaining a constant heading.

In a simulator or live tug, use the following scenarios to practice accelerating, slowing down, and maintaining speed while maintaining a steady course. You will need both open water and a reference point. Give equal time to maneuvering bow first and stern first. The following is a recommended learning sequence designed to program the mind-to-hand pathways that will allow you to control speed with a variety of appropriate hand movements. It progresses from the simple to the more complex. As noted previously, the clear sign that you are ready to move on in the sequence is the ability to carry on a conversation while successfully completing the practical exercise. You may find you quickly acquire the skill set to complete a particular exercise and can rapidly move on to the next, or you may find one particularly difficult. At the difficult junctures, it is important to spend an appropriate amount of time practicing until the mind-to-hand pathway feels intuitive or automatic.

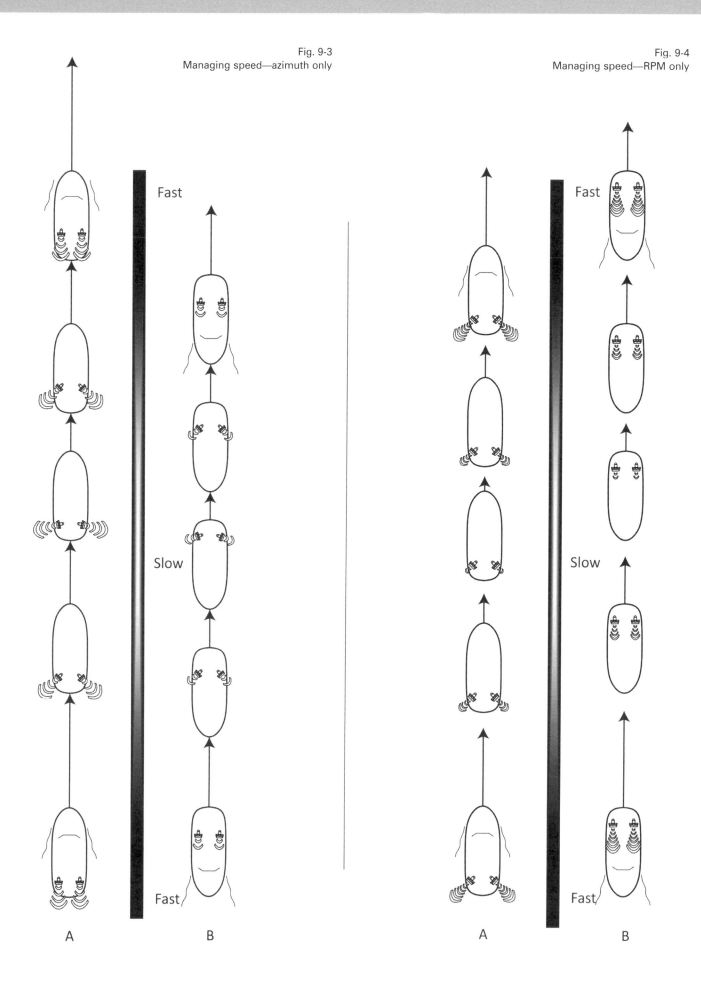

Fig. 9-3
Managing speed—azimuth only

Fig. 9-4
Managing speed—RPM only

Fast

Slow

Fast

A

B

Fast

Slow

Fast

A

B

# Learning Scenarios

The following scenarios are designed to practice the skills necessary to manage speed using combinations of azimuth and RPM. In all three scenarios the operator is to hold a steady course while using

1. azimuth only to control speed,
2. RPM only to control speed, and
3. azimuth of one drive unit and RPM of the other to maintain speed and steer.

# Speed Management— Azimuth Only

Utilizing a landmark or compass course as a reference, practice accelerating and slowing down by using changes in azimuth only. Attempt to hold a constant heading throughout the exercise. The objective of this exercise is to keep the engine's RPM matched and constant while managing speed. However, it is a good idea to practice with different but equal levels of power output. Experiment with the engines at idle, and at half and maximum power.

### What It Looks Like in Your Mind
Fig. 9-3 illustrates two examples of appropriate drive unit configurations utilized to control speed using only changes in azimuth: fig. 9-3A is bow first at high RPM; fig. 9-3B is stern first at a lower RPM. Experimenting with diverse levels of RPM exposes you to the different feel of each and will help you become comfortable throughout the Z-drive's entire power range.

# Speed Management —RPM Only

Using a landmark or compass course as a reference, practice accelerating and slowing down by using changes in RPM only. Attempt to hold a constant heading throughout the exercise. The objective of this exercise is to keep the azimuth constant and vary engine RPM. Practice using different but symmetrical azimuth angles, both bow first and stern first.

### What It Looks Like in Your Mind
Fig. 9-4 illustrates two examples of appropriate drive unit configurations utilized to control speed by using only changes in RPM: fig. 9-4A is bow first with the drive units aligned at approximately 45° to the tug's centerline; fig. 9-4B is stern first, with the drive units aligned parallel to the tug's centerline. Experimenting with different azimuth angles exposes you to the different feel of each and will help you become comfortable throughout the drive unit's 360° of available thrust.

# Speed Management— Azimuth and RPM

The next two practice scenarios have more educational value than practical application. They are designed to raise your awareness of the relationship between steering and speed. In both of the following scenarios, the objective is to *maintain* a constant speed. Attempt to hold a constant heading throughout the exercise. As in the previous exercises, practice bow first and stern first.

### Azimuth and RPM Combination No. 1
Using a landmark or compass course as a reference, practice maintaining speed while the azimuth of one drive unit changes and its effect on steering is compensated for by the RPM of the other drive unit.

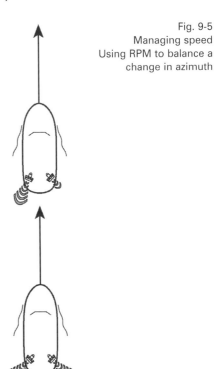

Fig. 9-5
Managing speed
Using RPM to balance a change in azimuth

### What It Looks Like in Your Mind

Fig. 9-5 illustrates an example of a configuration that will maintain speed and heading when the azimuth of the port drive unit changes and its effect on the vessel's heading is compensated by the RPM of the starboard drive unit. The port drive unit azimuth is shifted from 45° to approximately 20° to the vessel's centerline. This changes the balance-of-thrust equation so that the port side has increased its headway component and reduced its steering component. If no adjustment is made, the starboard unit's steering force will overpower the ports, and the vessel will increase speed and turn to starboard. If we wish to maintain the same heading and use only RPM on the starboard drive unit to counter this effect, we will have to *reduce* RPM on the starboard unit to balance the reduction in steering force of the port unit. This has the additional effect of reducing the headway component of the starboard unit. When all these effects are combined, the vessel maintains the same heading and speed, even though azimuth and RPM differ between the two drive units. Note that the illustration exaggerates these changes for the sake of clarity. In reality, the RPM adjustment is much more subtle.

### Azimuth and RPM Combination No. 2

Using a landmark or compass course as a reference, practice maintaining speed while the RPM of one drive unit changes and its effect on steering is compensated for by the azimuth of the other drive unit.

### What It Looks Like in Your Mind

Fig. 9-6 illustrates an example of a configuration that will maintain speed and heading when the RPM of the port drive unit changes and its effect on the vessel's heading is compensated by the azimuth of the starboard drive unit. Both drive units begin with equal RPM and thrusting at 45° toward the boat's centerline. The port drive unit RPM is then shifted from 1/2 to full. This changes the balance-of-thrust equation so that the port side has increased its headway and turning component. If no adjustment is made, the port unit's steering force will overpower the starboard's, and the vessel will increase speed and turn to port. If we wish to maintain the same heading and use only azimuth on the starboard drive unit to counter this effect, we will have to *increase* the thrust angle on the starboard unit toward the vessel's centerline to balance the increase in steering force of the port unit. This has the additional effect of reducing the headway component of the starboard unit. When all these effects are combined, the vessel maintains the same heading and speed, even though azimuth and RPM differ between the two drive units. Again, this illustration exaggerates these changes for the sake of clarity. The adjustments in RPM or azimuth in both these scenarios are based on feel, in which the hands figure out just the right amount of RPM or azimuth to apply.

### How It Feels in Your Hands

You will notice that the vessel feels more sensitive to your control movements when accelerating as opposed to decelerating. When speed is taken off, the controls may feel "mushy" or dead. This is particularly apparent when engine power is rapidly lowered to reduce the vessel's speed. In general, Z-drive tugs and towboats do not "dead stick" well. You will not sense the same inherent directional stability you do in a conventional tug when a Z-drive is being carried through water by its own momentum. In other words, a Z-drive likes to be "driven" and does not coast well.

Managing speed adds an additional layer of complexity to the simple task of steering. To successfully control the Z-drive's speed, the operator must be able to simultaneously manage two effects of the balance of thrust: steering and propulsion. The practice drills listed below draw on your ability to manipulate these two variables.

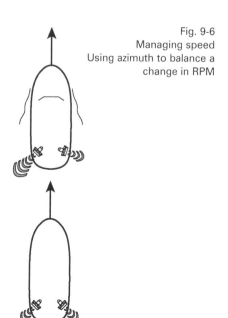

Fig. 9-6
Managing speed
Using azimuth to balance a
change in RPM

# Practice Drills

The following practice scenario requires two vessels. The role of the other vessel is to serve as a pace vessel—a moving reference point. Throughout the drill, the pace vessel should maintain a constant heading and a moderate speed (5–6 knots).

The objective of this drill is to practice varying speed while executing a 180° turn in reference to a moving object. In a simulator or live tug, start your vessel approximately 0.25 mile ahead of the pace vessel on a reciprocal course. Safely pass the pace vessel on one side, turn, and come up on the opposite side. Try not to fall more than 200 feet below the pace vessel while rounding its stern. Increase speed until abeam of the pace vessel and hold this position for one minute while matching the pace vessel's course and speed. After one minute, increase speed to pass the pace vessel while running parallel to its heading. Complete both maneuvers bow first and stern first. For further skill development, try to keep the same distance off while passing the vessel on a reciprocal course, rounding its stern and running parallel in the same direction.

The practice objectives are to

- vary speed relative to a moving vessel,
- control the rate of turn and speed simultaneously,
- steady up on a new course without oversteering,
- hold a consistent distance off a moving vessel, and
- have no virtual collisions (in a simulator) or instructor intervention (live tug).

Once your hands are adept at manipulating steering and speed simultaneously in open water, you are ready to apply the same skill sets to the everyday application described in chapter 10: "Stopping and Hovering."

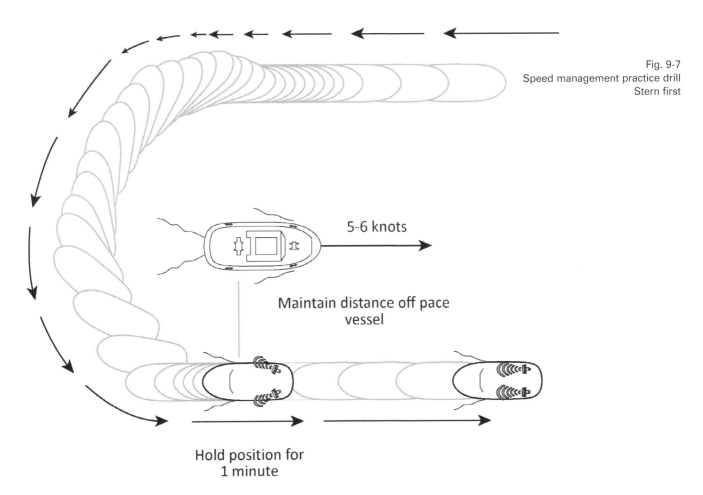

Fig. 9-7
Speed management practice drill
Stern first

5-6 knots

Maintain distance off pace vessel

Hold position for
1 minute

# *Chapter Ten*
## Stopping and Hovering

In this chapter you will learn to stop a Z-drive tug or towboat and hold it in a fixed position (hover).

## Overview: Stopping

A variety of techniques can be used to stop a Z-drive, but the origins of most stem from the principles either of a reverse arrest or a transverse arrest.

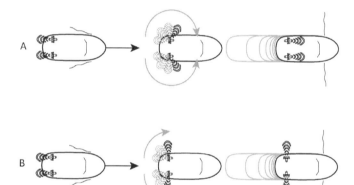

Fig. 10-1
A: Reverse arrest
B: Transverse arrest

## Reverse Arrest

A reverse arrest is similar to the technique utilized by a conventionally propelled vessel—the direction of the thrust is reversed. The conventional vessel accomplishes this by reversing the direction of the propeller's rotation. However, most Z-drives do not have a mechanism to reverse the propeller's rotation; rather, the drive unit must rotate 180° (fig. 10-1A).

## Transverse Arrest

A transverse arrest creates a braking effect by aligning the two drive units at 90° to the vessel's keel and thrusting in opposition to each other (fig. 10-1B). This creates sufficient drag to stop the vessel without actually thrusting in reverse. In fact, even at high speeds using full thrust, many Z-drives will stop within one or two boat lengths when utilizing a transverse arrest. Employed correctly, either technique will quickly bring the vessel to a stop. However, both are susceptible to failure if the operator has not thought ahead sufficiently and is caught with one or both drive units grossly out of position. In these cases, there may not be enough time to rotate them into position before the vessel reaches its required stopping point. To a Z-drive operator, the definition of eternity is the time it takes to rotate a drive unit 180° as the vessel rapidly closes on a dock or other unforgiving object. It is not uncommon for a Z-drive unit to take eleven to eighteen seconds to rotate a full 180°. If not anticipated, this can be a long and costly journey.

Stopping is part of a tug's or towboat's everyday life. It may seem like a relatively simple skill. There are circumstances when stopping the vessel can be as uncomplicated as taking all the way off immediately (crash stop), with no regard for the vessel's heading or rate of closure relative to other objects. Most stopping situations require more finesse. True competency in stopping requires proficiency in three skill sets: steering, managing the rate of closure (speed), and hovering. Good examples are the maneuvers required of a tug to put a working headline up to a ship preparing to depart its berth, or a towboat facing up to a barge. In both cases, you should be able to follow an approach path (steer), slow down (control the rate of closure), bring the vessel to a complete stop directly by the designated chock (tug) or barge (towboat), and hold position (hover) while the necessary lines are passed.

# Why This Is Important

Acquiring an ability to stop has two important applications. First, it has many practical uses in light-vessel, ship, and barge work—stopping before colliding with fixed or floating objects has long been a prerequisite for a good day at sea.

Second, it is a common abort maneuver employed to safely extricate the vessel and operator from situations in which the vessel is out of control. An essential principle of all vessel maneuvering is always to leave an "out," or a means to abort the maneuver. Stopping may prevent damage and may also build a cushion of space and time, enabling you to regain control and reassess the situation. Every Z-drive operator should be well versed in this technique.

# Practical Exercises

The objectives of the practical exercises that follow are to become proficient at

1. controlled stops and
2. steering while stopping.

In a simulator or live vessel you will need both open water and a fixed reference point (moored vessel or dock). The learning scenarios have two purposes. The first is to familiarize you with the performance limitations of your vessel in stopping situations. The second is to provide practice situations to build basic stopping skills—first as separate skills and then in combination. Give equal time to maneuvering bow first and stern first.

# Learning Scenarios

1. Stopping using one drive unit, reverse arrest
2. Stopping using two drive units

# Stopping—One Drive Unit, Reverse Arrest

This exercise is designed to sensitize you to the effects of rotating the drive unit 180°—both the time it takes and its impact on steering. It is not meant to teach you a practical stopping technique; rather, it is intended to sharpen your awareness of the forces at play when bringing the vessel to a stop.

You will need lots of open water for this exercise.

You will use only one drive unit to reverse arrest and to experiment with different hull speeds and engine RPMs, as well as bow-first and stern-first headings. Have fun with these experiments. This is an opportunity to safely gain a feel for the vessel's behavior when reversing thrust. Use it! The vessel will behave erratically and sometimes feel out of control; it will sheer off in one direction or the other or spin around in a circle while coming to a stop. This is all good! First, because it gives you a sense of how quickly and badly the vessel can get out of control, and second, it also gives you insight into some of the possible causes of a Z-drive's misbehavior.

This practice will also have practical application at some point in your Z-drive career. Unfortunately, almost all operators have had the experience of bringing their Z-drive-propelled vessel home on one drive unit due to a mechanical failure that rendered the other drive unit inoperative. As you will learn, the vessel handles quite differently when you have only one drive unit to turn, stop, and dock. This practice will help you prepare for that rare but inevitable occurrence.

### What It Looks Like in Your Mind

Fig. 10-2 illustrates two of many possible reverse-arrest trials with one drive unit. The first (fig. 10-2A) is a mind's-eye view of using one drive unit only, holding a steady course bow first, clutching out, rotating the drive unit 180°, and then clutching in, bringing the vessel to a stop. The second (fig. 10-2B) is stern first and leaves the drive unit clutched in for the entire 180° arc. There are many derivatives of these two examples. Try reversing thrust by using both possible 180° arcs of transition: one in which the drive unit's wash is directed away from the vessel's keel as it rotates, and one in which it is directed toward it. Be creative—use a variety of RPM, clutch sequencing, and stern- or bow-first headings.

### How It Feels in Your Hands

Attempting a reverse arrest with one hand feels awkward and unpredictable. As you rotate the control handle, you may or may not be able to predict which way the vessel will sheer. Once the drive unit has turned 180°, you will have taken the way off the vessel, but it may still have residual turning momentum rotating about its pivot point.

At this point in your training it should be taking some discipline to keep your unused hand off the other control handle. You should be feeling an impulse to grab the inactive control handle to counteract the

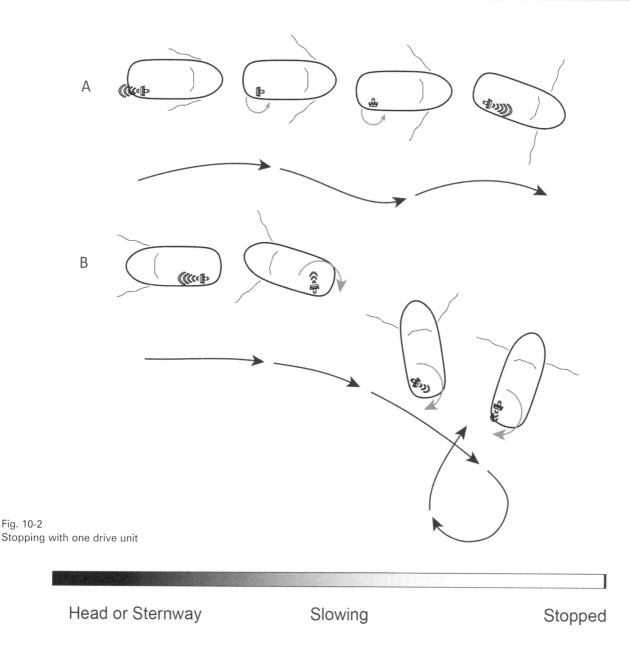

Fig. 10-2
Stopping with one drive unit

Head or Sternway          Slowing          Stopped

undesired changes in the vessel's heading. This is good. It indicates your instinctive reaction to an undesired offset in the balance of thrust. Your reach for the dormant control handle is an intuitive, corrective action, and a sign that your hands hold an understanding of the balance of thrust. For this practice, do not give in to temptation; just continue to control the vessel with one drive unit only.

## Stopping—Two Drive Units

This exercise is designed to train you in the skills required to stop and control the vessel by using two drive units. Use a moored vessel or dock as a reference and practice stopping and reversing direction within a defined space. Attempt to hold a constant heading and distance off the reference object throughout the exercise while alternating between headway and sternway. The operator of the vessel in fig. 10-3 is using the ship's transom and bow to define the limit of his fore and aft movement. He is trying to go no farther than abeam of each reference point and to hold the same distance off the ship as he goes back and forth. The objective of this exercise is to acquire the ability to steer while reversing the vessel's direction of advance. Practice with different levels of power output as you change the drive unit's azimuth. Experiment with the engines at idle, half power, and maximum power.

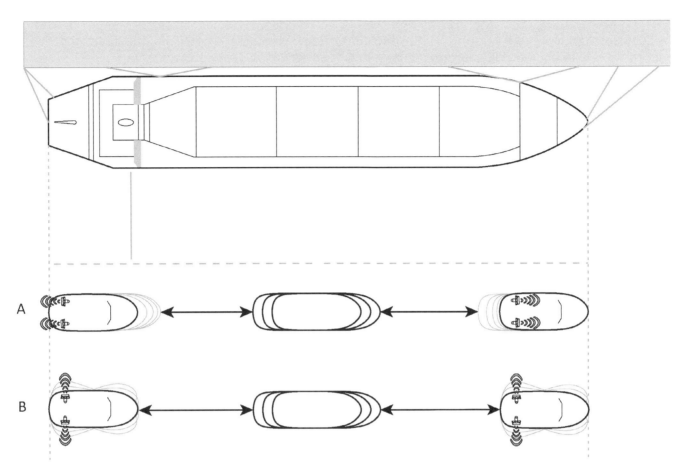

Fig. 10-3
Stopping and steering within a defined space

### What It Looks Like in Your Mind

As discussed, a reverse arrest and transverse arrest are terms used to describe two stopping techniques. On paper they appear clear and distinct (fig. 10-3). In practice, the two methods blend into each other, with the operator choosing a variation appropriate to the maneuvering circumstances.

A reverse arrest is a good technique to employ when the objective is to reverse the vessel's direction (fig. 10-3A), not just bring it to a stop and hold position. The point at which there is no way on the vessel is only a milepost on the path between the two directions. A transverse arrest is a good technique to employ when the objective is to stop and hold position (fig. 10-3B). Once the vessel's way is taken off, the transverse-arrest configuration transitions smoothly into a hovering technique.

### How It Feels in Your Hands

***Let your hands determine the stopping technique***
Stopping while simultaneously controlling the vessel's heading is a dynamic task; it is never the same two times in a row. There are always subtle—sometimes dramatic—differences in the required drive unit configuration. After a few passes back and forth, you will notice a relationship among the vessel's speed, its heading, the point at which you begin to take way off, and the drive unit configuration. For example, you may have decided in your mind to employ a reverse arrest to stop the vessel. However, if the vessel's speed is slow and you start rotating the drive units into a reverse-arrest position well before the designated stopping point, you will most likely take all the way off prematurely. The drive units will not pass the transverse-arrest position before the vessel comes to a halt. In other words, the vessel did not have enough momentum to *require* a reverse arrest.

Use the technique the vessel requires, not the one you think it requires. Bringing the vessel to a smooth stop requires that you constantly adjust to changing factors: how fast the vessel is decelerating; wind, current, or other environmental factors affecting the vessel's heading; and the relative position between the vessel and its stopping point. The drive unit position at any one point represents the solution to this evolving equation.

Let your hands do the figuring. With practice, your hands will begin naturally making adjustments in RPM and azimuth to control the vessel. At any given point during the stopping process, you will most likely find your hands in some variation of the transverse- or reverse-arrest positions. Let your hands decide which technique is most appropriate.

Use this exercise of going back and forth to expose your mind and hands to a wide spectrum of hull speed, engine RPM, and azimuth combinations. Go too fast, turn the drive units too early or late, and attempt to reverse direction at the last minute as fast as you can. This exercise is an opportunity to embed valuable experience and knowledge in your hands without the cost of an accident.

### The Dead Zone

You may have noticed a "dead zone"—a point during the vessel's transition from one direction to the other in which you feel disconnected from the vessel, or that the vessel's response is "loose" or sloppy. This is typically created when the drive units have been rotated rapidly while you still have moderate-to-high hull speed. This feeling is created by the propeller turning in turbulent, aerated water.

When you begin to rotate the control handle to reverse the vessel's direction, the nozzle diverges from the current created by the vessel's hull moving through the water. This may disrupt the water flow into the suction side of the nozzle and cause the propeller to cavitate (fig. 10-4). The propeller loses efficiency and the vessel feels less responsive or "dead." Bringing back the "live" sensation is a matter of restoring a smooth and uniform water flow to the nozzles. As the thrust becomes more solid and effective, the vessel regains its responsiveness.

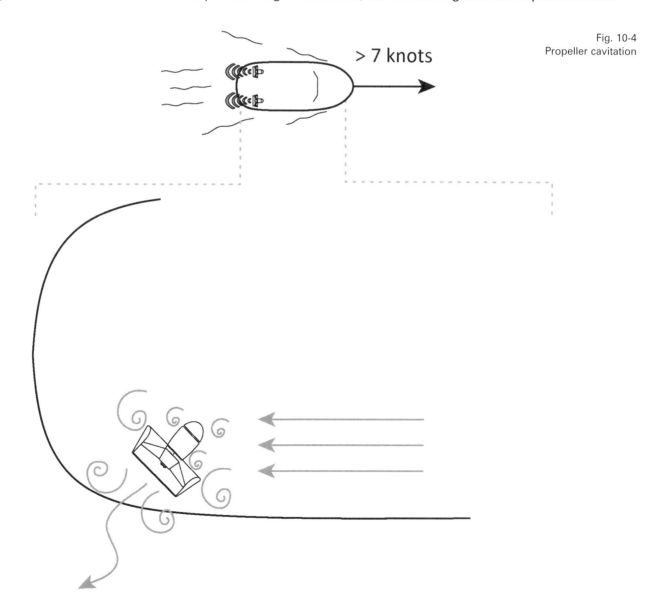

> 7 knots

Fig. 10-4
Propeller cavitation

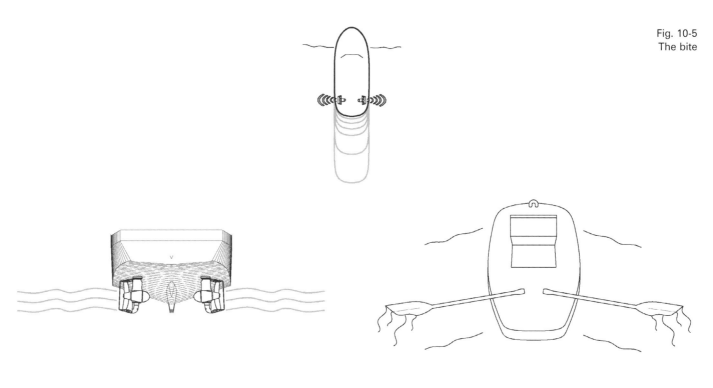

Fig. 10-5
The bite

### The Bite

You may have noticed the feeling of the vessel "biting" into the water as you bring it to a stop. This "bite" is a physical sense of the propeller wash and thrust applying the brakes to the vessel's motion. This is most apparent in a transverse arrest. Creating tunnels of opposing wheel wash at 90° to the vessel's centerline feels like dragging a set of oars in a rowboat (fig. 10-5). The longer and broader the oar blade, the greater the braking effect. In a Z-drive vessel, the length and breadth of the oar are determined by the rate of propeller revolutions and the amount of wash coming out of the nozzles.

These sensations—the dead zone and the bite—both are related to the quality of water flowing through the nozzles. This quality is a function of azimuth angle, propeller RPM, and the direction and velocity of the hull moving through the water. These variables can be influenced by your manipulation of the rate and direction of nozzle rotation and engine RPM. There is a "sweet spot" in which you can turn the nozzle in the direction you require, but do it in a manner that maintains the quality of water flow through the nozzle.

There are two keys to maintaining this sweet spot. The first is to turn the control handle at a rate that in combination with engine RPM provides sufficient suction to draw in good water. If the nozzle is turned too quickly or RPM is too low, the suction may not be adequate to pull in the water flowing by the nozzle. The flow is disrupted and breaks, and the propeller begins to cavitate.

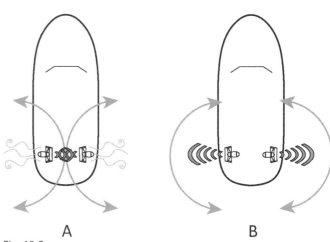

A                    B

Fig. 10-6
Creating and avoiding cavitation

The second key is to avoid drive unit configurations in which the two drive units' propeller wash will be pointed directly at each other. (fig. 10-6A). This is why most Z-drive operators have the drive units thrusting toward each other when they are in transition from one thrust direction to another (fig. 10-6B).

As you become more comfortable with these sensations, they will become one of the many sensory inputs you process as you maneuver the vessel. For instance, the propeller cavitation may cause extra vibration and noise. The sounds and the shaking are like an instrument measuring the propeller's efficiency and effectiveness. Cavitation is unavoidable in some maneuvers and will cause a dead zone, but with experience and practice you can predict the length of the dead zone and plan ahead for it.

# Overview: Hovering

Hovering is the term used to describe holding the vessel in a fixed position—stopped with no way on while simultaneously controlling the vessel's heading. It is one of the most mundane skills to practice, but also one of the most difficult. When a Z-drive is stopped with no way on, it is very sensitive to slight differences in azimuth or RPM. Even the most minor control adjustment in unskilled hands may cause the vessel to rotate, gain headway or sternway, walk laterally, or have these effects in combination. It requires a light touch and skilled hands to hold a Z-drive motionless, with no change in heading or movement over the ground or relative to another floating object. Hovering has many applications in shipwork and barge work, as well as light-vessel handling.

One of the most important applications of hovering is as a method of recovering lost control of the vessel. The drive unit configuration associated with hovering—two drive units thrusting equally toward each other at 90° to the vessel's centerline—is the equivalent of a safe house in Z-drive handling. It is where you go when you are struggling for control of the vessel, and enables both the vessel and operator to calm down. As the drive units are rotated into an equal and opposed 90° position, the tug's or towboat's turning motion dampens as the vessel slows and comes to a stop.

Three terms are commonly used to refer to the drive unit configuration in which two drive units are thrusting equally toward each other at 90° to the vessel's centerline.

1. Transverse Arrest
2. Happy Place
3. Feathered

These terms may seem odd and unnautical, but they make much more sense when linked to the context of their application.

*Transverse arrest* is used in the context of applying a braking effect. This term is utilized both in shipwork and light-vessel handling when referring to the 90° and equally opposed configuration as a method to retard or stop a vessel's advance. It is the most technically accurate term: the two drive units are thrusting transverse or crosswise to the vessel's centerline.

*Happy place* refers to the feeling that can be reliably created by the 90° and equally opposed configuration. Driving a Z-drive vessel requires a "feel" for the vessel, the sweet spot as described in the chapter on balance of thrust. Sometimes that feeling can be riddled with anxiety and doubt when a new operator senses he is on the verge of losing control of the vessel. In that context, the 90° and equally opposed configuration offers a reliable respite—indeed a happy place—from the anxiety and stress of a vessel out of control. Strange as it may seem, you will hear many veteran Z-drive operators and trainers use this term when they instruct you to "go to your happy place." It means go to the drive unit configuration that allows you to regroup, regain control of the vessel, and hover.

*Feathering* is a term commonly used in reference to controllable-pitch airplanes or ships' propellers. It is the position that allows the propeller to rotate but have a relatively neutral propulsion effect. The term has a similar connotation in handling a Z-drive, but not in a technical sense. Rather, it is used to describe the feeling of having both drive units thrusting but with each neutralizing the effect of the other—"feathered" in effect.

Even though these three terms refer to the same drive unit configuration, they differ in the context of their application. A simple translation of this Z-drive language is

- transverse arrest—apply the brakes,
- happy place—find the oasis that allows you and the vessel to settle down, and
- feather—keep the drive units thrusting but neutralize their effect on the vessel.

These three terms will be used in this context throughout the rest of this book.

# Practical Exercises

The objectives of the practical exercises that follow are to become proficient at

1. hovering and holding a steady heading, and
2. hovering but rotating about a central pivot point.

In a simulator or live vessel, you will need both open water and a fixed reference point (moored vessel or dock). The learning scenarios have two purposes. The first is to familiarize you with the hovering techniques. The second is to provide practice situations that combine basic stopping skills with hovering. Give equal time to maneuvering bow first and stern first.

# Learning Scenarios

1. Hovering and boxing the compass
2. Stopping and hovering at a predesignated point

### Hovering and Boxing the Compass

This exercise is designed to hone the skills required to hover—manipulating the vessel's rotation around its pivot point while keeping it from gaining headway or sternway. It is a simple exercise that requires a reference point. Using a moored vessel or dock as a reference, practice a variation of boxing the compass—hold position, rotate the vessel 90°, hold the new position for thirty seconds, rotate another 90°, hold, etc. (fig. 10-7). Practice rotating clockwise and counterclockwise. At first, try this at least two to three vessel lengths off your reference point. As you become more adept, move closer to the reference point until your bow and stern are only a few feet off the moored vessel or dock.

### What It Looks Like in Your Mind

Holding and rotating while having no headway or sternway requires subtle manipulation of the balance of thrust. Slight changes of azimuth or RPM will initiate or check the vessel's rotation.

When rotating while hovering, many Z-drive operators find it helpful to think in terms of the conventional vessel's "twin screw" technique. A conventional vessel can rotate in place by having one engine ahead and the other astern (fig. 10-8A). The Z-drive vessel can accomplish the same objective with a similar but much more subtle technique. To rotate to starboard, the Z-drive operator thinks about "twisting right"; the starboard drive unit is the backing engine and the port drive unit is the ahead engine. However, the Z-drive vessel does not have to fully align the drive units with the vessel's fore and aft axis to rotate. Rather, each drive unit has only to slightly tend toward the appropriate backing or ahead position and the vessel will begin to rotate (fig. 10-8B).

There is another technique to rotate about the vessel's vertical axis: have the drive units in the feathered position and vary the RPM so that one drive unit overpowers the other (fig. 10-8C). In theory, an imbalance in the amount of thrust in this configuration should result in the vessel rotating about its pivot point without any forward or aft movement, but it never quite works out that way in practice. You will find you must also make slight adjustments in azimuth to manage fore and aft and rotational movement simultaneously.

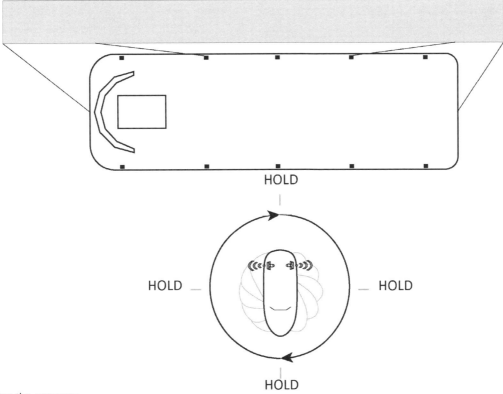

Fig. 10-7
Hovering and boxing the compass

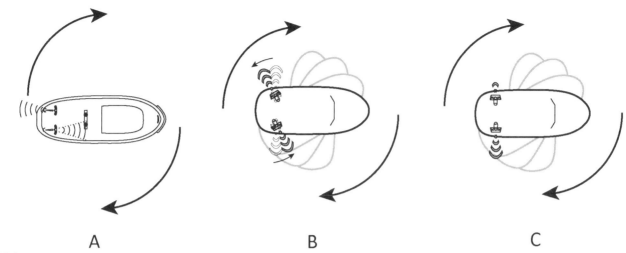

Fig. 10-8
Rotating while hovering

### How It Feels in Your Hands

Once the vessel has lost its headway or sternway, you should feel you have pinpoint control of the vessel. Hovering is usually one of the first maneuvers that gives a new Z-drive operator the feeling of being "one with the vessel." When the vessel is hovering it should feel stable, as if your hands and the drive units' thrust have a grip on the vessel, holding it in position. It should take slight but constant control adjustments to hold the vessel's heading or rotate as desired. These small hand movements make very fine adjustments to the balance of thrust. This is a prime example of the Z-drive handling maxim "less is more."

In the hovering state, the thrust of each drive unit works predominately against the other. It does not take much to tip the balance one way or the other to control the vessel. In fact, it is so sensitive in this state that a slight change in azimuth or thrust can make the vessel move in entirely different directions. For example, the drive unit configuration in fig. 10-8B may cause the vessel to rotate to starboard like a twin-screw vessel, but that is only one of several possible results from this general alignment. In fact, the vessel may rotate to port or starboard and move laterally, ahead, or astern. The motion of the vessel will be dictated by the nuance of your hands' motion. A subtle increase in RPM or twitch of the wrist can have markedly different results. This is a good example of the one-to-many relationship between drive unit configuration and the vessel's motion. When the vessel is in this highly sensitive state, you are driving predominately by feel.

You should feel connected to the vessel all the time. The vessel should respond almost instantaneously to your hand movements. There should be no feeling of a dead zone. If there is, it is a signal that you may be moving the drive units too fast or in too large an increment. When you are hovering and rotating, the rate of drive unit rotation and amount of thrust should be adequate to keep good-quality water flowing through the drive units and produce a solid sensory perception of control in your hands.

# Stopping at a Predesignated Point and Position

This exercise is designed to train you in the skills required to bring the vessel to a stop at a predesignated point and maintain a consistent angular aspect. The previous exercises had a built-in cushion of space between the vessel and the moored vessel or dock. That was to give you room to make mistakes while learning to stop, reverse direction, and hover. Once you feel comfortable in those three skills, it is time to practice stopping at a predesignated point while maintaining the vessel's angular aspect relative to a reference point. Simply stated, it is time to practice touching up and holding 90° to a vessel or dock.

Using a moored vessel or dock as a reference, pick a specific chock or cleat on the vessel as a landing point. First, approach bow first, maintaining a perpendicular aspect to the vessel or dock; slow the vessel, bringing it to a stop, and gently touch up on the vessel or dock. Back up until you are six to eight vessel lengths away from the vessel, stop and hover, rotate the vessel 180°, and then approach the landing point stern first. Repeat.

What It Looks Like in Your Mind

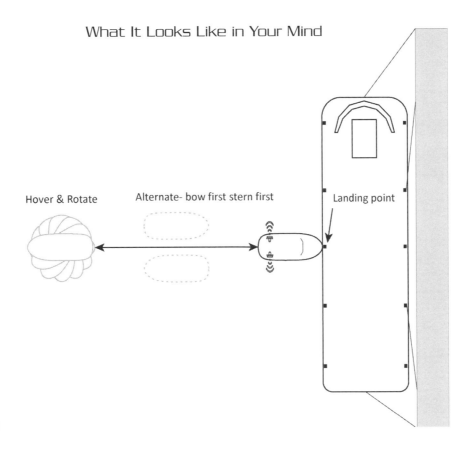

Hover & Rotate          Alternate- bow first stern first          Landing point

Fig. 10-9
Stopping at a specified point

How It Feels in Your Hands

### The 3-Foot Disaster Zone

This is the first exercise in which you intentionally bring the vessel to touch up on a stationary object. The 3-foot (or 1-meter) disaster zone is a phenomenon that frequently accompanies a new Z-drive operator. The operator has his Z-drive under exquisite control during the approach to a dock, ship, or barge, and all signs are that the maneuver will be finished with finesse. But when the operator slows the vessel to ease in the last few feet, he suddenly loses control, overcorrects, and causes damage. Once inside the 3-foot zone there can be a tendency for the new operator to get a little excited. The speed of advance and steering adjustments that appeared so slow a couple boat lengths away from the landing point may seem way too fast inside the 3-foot zone. The tendency of the new operator at this point is to overcorrect, using too-much change in azimuth or RPM. The vessel jumps a little in response, which only escalates both operator and vessel to a new level of excitement.

The key to maneuvering in close is to make sure you have positive control of the vessel prior to moving in the last few feet. When maneuvering close to an object, you will be maneuvering almost completely by instinct. In close quarters, the vessel requires your immediate reaction. Even at slow

speeds the vessel is so sensitive and the distances so close that there is simply not enough time to think your way in through those last few feet.

A common misconception is that the approach to the object and the final touch-up are variations of the same maneuver, and that the same drive unit configuration and technique is applicable to both. In reality they are two separate maneuvers. The approach is primarily a manage-speed-and-steer maneuver. The final touch-up is a variation on hovering. This is the common pitfall for a new Z-drive operator. He may not realize that he will need two separate skill sets to successfully complete this maneuver. Managing speed and steering is relatively easy in comparison to hovering inches off a fixed object.

A good learning technique is to incorporate a happy-place rest stop about 10 feet from the landing point. Bring the vessel to a complete stop and hover in a stationary position. In other words, go to your happy place before you close the last 10 feet. The 10-foot cushion of space leaves room to flounder a bit if that is what it takes to regain positive control of the vessel. If you can't bring the boat under control and hover at 10 feet, you certainly will not be able to do it during the last 3 feet of closure. Once you have dialed yourself back in and confirm you are driving the vessel and not the other way around, you are ready to cross the 3-foot threshold.

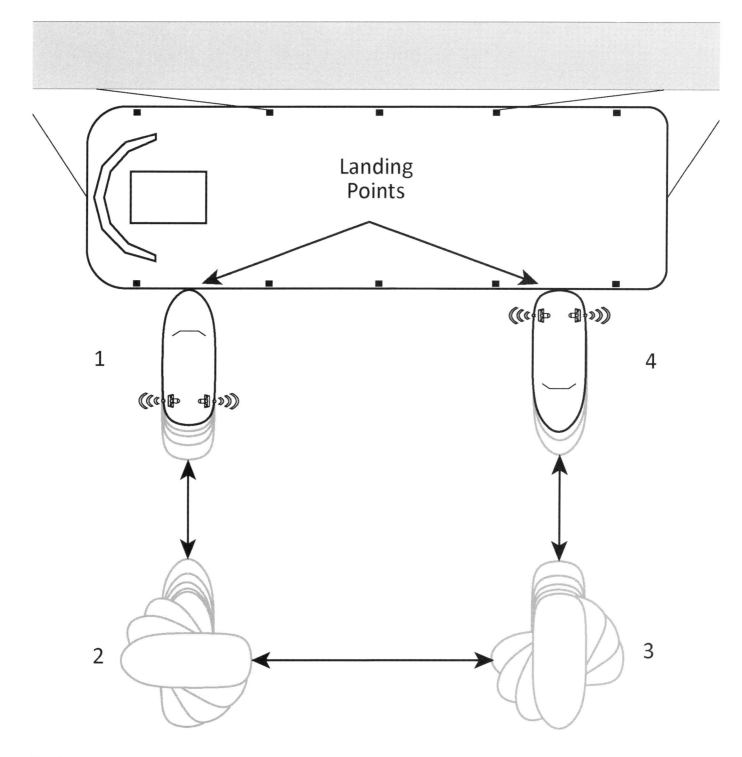

Fig. 10-10
Stop and hover drill

### Nervous Stern

A variety of words have been used to describe the behavior of an ASD's stern. A few of the more printable ones are nervous, active, squirrelly, and lively. The behavior of the ASD vessel's stern is like a double-edged sword. The design aspects that make it so lively and difficult to control are the same ones that make the vessel so maneuverable. In inexperienced hands, control of the stern can easily be lost. In the hands of a skilled operator, it is a powerful maneuvering tool. New ASD operators may be surprised at how sensitive the stern is to changes in azimuth or RPM. With all that thrust in the stern, it takes very little error to get the vessel moving rapidly in the wrong direction. This is particularly apparent when you are spotting either the bow or stern under a specific chock or cleat.

Feathering is a good technique to calm the nervous stern. If the stern is out of hand and swinging one way or the other, the feathered position is a good starting position to steady it up. It may take a fair amount of power to bring it back under control. Once stilled, you can continue in to touch up on the vessel or dock.

Stopping a Z-drive in a controlled manner is an essential skill set. To successfully bring the vessel to a stop, the operator must simultaneously juggle three maneuvering variables: steering, speed, and space limitations.

# Practice Drill

The objective of this drill (fig. 10-10) is to practice stopping the vessel at predesignated points, hover, and rotate as necessary. You will require a reference object (vessel or dock). In a simulator or live vessel, set up the drill by picking two landing points toward either end of a reference object (vessel or dock).

1. Approach the first landing point bow first.
2. Touch up on the landing point maintaining a 90° aspect (position #1).
3. Back away until approximately five boat lengths off the object.
4. Stop, hover, and rotate 90° (position #2).
5. Back up until abeam of the second landing point.
6. Stop, hover, and rotate 90° until the vessel's stern is pointed at the landing point (position #3).
7. Touch up on the landing point, maintaining a 90° aspect (position #4).
8. Reverse the process and repeat.

The practice objectives are

• touch down accurately at the designated landing points (± 1 foot),
• hover and rotate without advancing the vessel,
• hold a constant distance off the reference object vessel while transiting from one end to the other, and
• have no virtual collisions (in a simulator) or instructor intervention (live tug).

Once you can manage fore and aft speed and steering simultaneously, and feel confident holding in a stationary position, you are ready to tackle the skill set in chapter 11, lateral motion (walking).

# *Chapter Eleven*
## Lateral Movement

## Overview

Once you are comfortable turning, stopping, managing speed, and hovering, you are ready to combine aspects of these skills to produce lateral movement. Three of the more popular terms used to describe lateral movement are walking, flanking, and sidestepping. This book uses the term "walking."

Walking is defined as moving the tug or towboat sideways while simultaneously controlling fore and aft advance, and yaw (heading). It is as if the bow and the stern of the vessel are on parallel rails moving sideways (fig. 11-1).

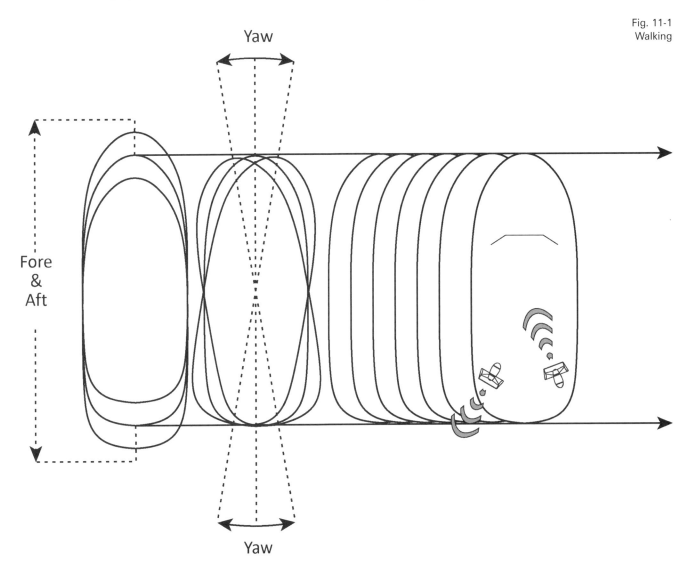

Fig. 11-1
Walking

Yaw

Fore & Aft

Yaw

Observing a Z-drive vessel sliding sideways at 3–4 knots gives the appearance that it is responding to direct, sideways thrust, but this is not the case. Rather, the force propelling the vessel sideways is the collective result of one Z-drive thrusting aft at an angle and the other thrusting ahead and at an angle. The drive unit thrusting aft produces forces that pull the bow or stern (or both) in the desired direction with sternway. The drive unit thrusting ahead produces forces that push the stern or bow (or both) in the desired direction with headway. The net result is the vessel moves laterally (fig. 11-2).

It would be wrong to assume that this is simple. Fig. 11-2 is a simplification and should be used only as a rudimentary understanding of how to walk. There is no one-size-fits-all configuration that works in all situations and on all ASD tugs or towboats. The actual drive unit configuration is more fluid and is adjusted continuously. Your hands must react instantly to constantly changing aspects of the vessel's motion: fore and aft movement, rotation about its pivot point (yaw), and the direction of lateral movement. You can't "think" your way through this maneuver. Simple pictures such as fig. 11-2 provide only the context for the initial configuration and may be helpful when large control corrections are required. But the success of this maneuver rests mostly on skilled hands—hands that grasp the finer points of the balance of thrust.

The balance of thrust that creates lateral motion varies both from vessel to vessel and from operator to operator. The variance from vessel to vessel is due to underwater hull shapes that differ in ASD designs.

The variation from one operator to another is a result of the operator's individual style—that is, how much power he is comfortable with, how quickly his hands respond to changes in the vessel's aspect, and how many maneuvering variables he can juggle at once.

The result is that a variety of related but different drive unit configurations may propel the ASD vessel sideways. Fig. 11-3 illustrates three of several possible configurations.

The balance of thrust that results in lateral motion can be elusive. Finding it is the mark of a Z-drive operator who is skilled at simultaneously managing three maneuvering aspects: fore and aft advance, yaw, and lateral direction.

# Why This Is Important

Of course, walking the vessel sideways has important practical applications. Three examples are docking the light vessel within a restricted space, shifting vessel positions in shipwork, and holding the vessel in against a barge or dock while lines are passed.

There is a more universal importance to mastering the art of walking a Z-drive. It is a demonstration that the operator has the ability to control all the fundamental motions of a Z-drive vessel—turning, speed, stopping, and lateral direction. He can control these motions singularly or in combination. And he "thinks" with his hands. Armed with this skill set, the Z-drive operator can take advantage of the vessel's tendency to walk one way or the other.

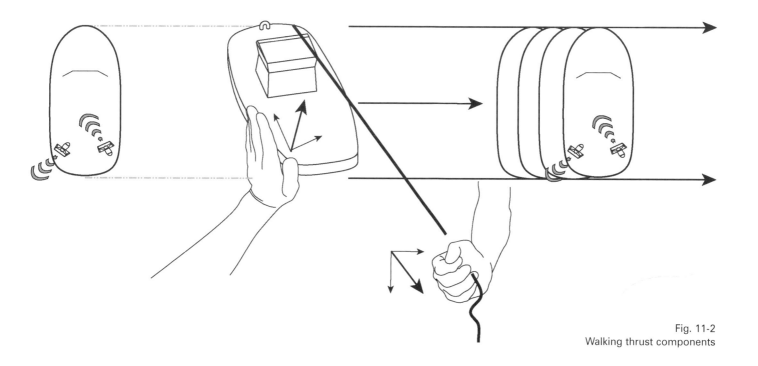

Fig. 11-2
Walking thrust components

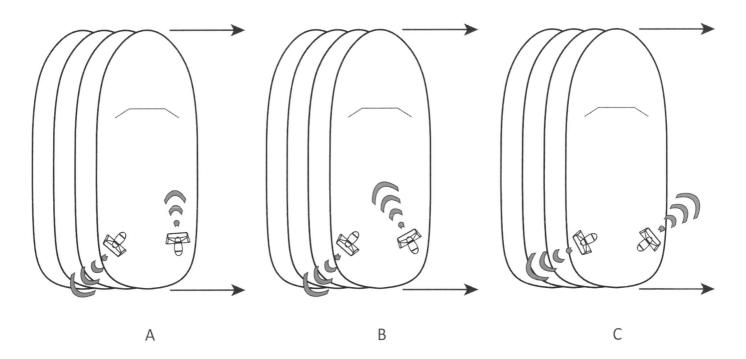

A              B              C

Fig. 11-3
Common walking configurations

Fig. 11-4
Walking away from the designated touchdown point

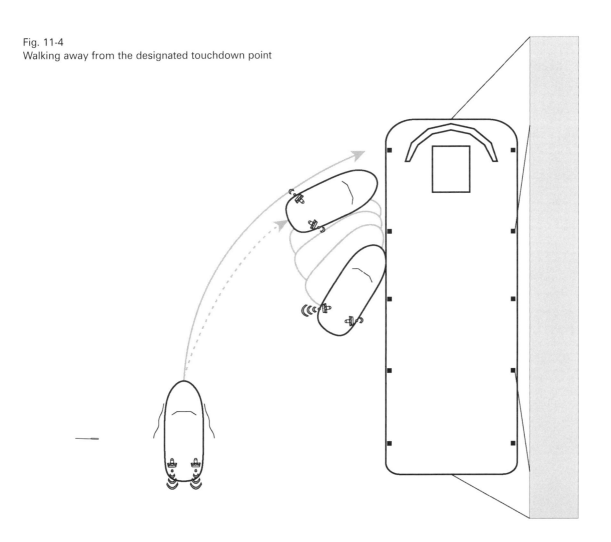

A Z-drive's tendency to walk can be the operator's friend or foe. A good example of this is the situation in which the operator undershoots his designated chock or cleat (fig. 11-4). In this diagram, the operator is offset to the right of his mark. He needs to bring the bow to port and shift toward the designated cleat. However, the drive unit configuration he used to stop the vessel has a residual effect of walking the vessel to starboard. This is due to the starboard drive unit having a backing component and the port having an ahead component. The operator can turn the vessel to port from this configuration or a close derivative. However, it has the secondary effect of walking the vessel away from the chock. This effect will continue until the starboard drive unit has an ahead component and the port a reverse component. An operator experienced in walking the vessel recognizes and corrects for this effect immediately. The less experienced may find himself turning in the right direction but becoming more distant from his destination. He may become a case of "so close, yet so far."

# Practical Exercises

The objectives of the practical exercises are to become proficient at

1. walking the vessel in a straight line, and
2. walking the vessel around a corner.

In a simulator or live vessel you will need both open water and a fixed reference point (moored vessel or dock). At first, you will need open water to provide a cushion for making and recovering from mistakes. It is easy to lose control of the vessel when you first learn to walk. Do not be discouraged if you find yourself spinning in circles or feeling as though your head is tied in knots. The balance point between the thrust of the two drive units that produces lateral motion is quite narrow and elusive. Outside that sweet spot, the vessel can get out of hand rapidly. This is part of the learning process. Just make sure you leave plenty of room for mistakes.

Once you have a feel for walking in open water, you will refine that skill by adding space restrictions and steering requirements.

# Learning Scenarios

1. Walking in a straight line, open water
2. Walking straight with space restriction
3. Walking around a buoy
4. Walking diagonally

Walking in a Straight Line.

Open Water
In open water—well clear of obstructions—practice walking to port and to starboard.

What It Looks Like in Your Mind

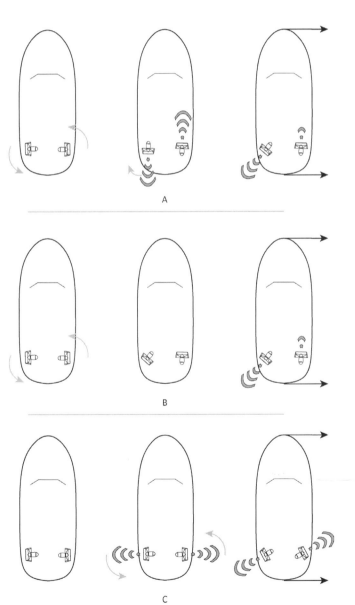

Fig. 11-5
Starting a walk

Starting the walk is one of the more difficult steps in the learning process. You may have a very clear picture in your mind of the drive unit configuration, but that picture may become outdated as soon as the drive units are clutched in. Once engaged, you must start making quick and appropriate adjustments. It is a bit like catching a wave as a surfer. While you are resting on the board, waiting for a wave, you can analyze the size and set of the waves and project an image of how you will ride the wave. But once you are on your feet and rocketing down the wave face, your body immediately engages in shifting your weight, maintaining your balance, and steering the board. At this point, if you allow your thought process to get in the way of your feet, you will wipe out. There is no time to think about it. Walking a Z-drive can be much the same. If you think too much once you are underway, your mind may impede the timely reaction of your hands and you will spin out.

When learning to walk, start simply. First, make sure the vessel is dead in the water. Second, decide whether to walk to port or starboard and which walking configuration you will use. This may sound obvious, but it is not unusual for a new operator to intend to walk in one direction and end up going in the other. The vessel will always walk toward the same side as the drive unit that is thrusting aft. This is the case even if the drive unit is only slightly aft of 90° to the centerline of the vessel (fig. 11-3C). If the propeller wash of the starboard drive unit is forward of the beam and its thrust is aft, the vessel will walk to starboard. The final step is to concentrate on adjusting the RPM and azimuth of one hand once the drive units are engaged. As much as possible, leave the other static. Remember, this is just a starting point. Eventually you will be able to transition in and out of walking without having to take the time to stop, set up, and experiment.

There are many methods that instructors use to initiate a walk. Three common ones are listed.

The first method is to keep the drive units clutched out and rotate them so one is thrusting straight back and the other is thrusting straight ahead (fig. 11-5A). Clutch both drive units in simultaneously, match their RPM at about one-third power, and begin to make azimuth and RPM adjustments to the drive unit thrusting ahead.

The second is to keep the drive units clutched out and rotate them so they are set up to have one unit thrusting straight back and the other thrusting at a 45° angle ahead (fig. 11-5B). Clutch both drive units in simultaneously, match their RPM at about one-third power, and begin to make azimuth and RPM adjustments immediately.

The third is to start from the feathered position (fig. 11-5C). Match the engine RPM at one-third power and then rotate both drive units so that one is thrusting slightly forward and the other slightly aft.

Regardless of the starting method, once the drive units are clutched in and in a walking configuration, you must make small adjustments immediately. At this point you are sliding down the face of the wave, and it is time to let your hands do the thinking.

On the first couple of tries it may help to focus on making adjustments to only one drive unit. This simplifies the learning process. Some find it easier to leave the drive unit thrusting astern static, while some find it easier to leave the one thrusting ahead static. Either way, concentrate on manipulating one hand only. Practice this until you find yourself instinctively reaching for the static control handle. That is your signal that you are ready to bring the other drive unit into play.

### What It Feels Like in Your Hands

Once you have found the balance-of-thrust point that produces lateral motion, you will sense the sweet spot. You will be in the narrow zone in which you, the controls, and the machinery are working together seamlessly and perfectly. In that state, it should take very little hand movement to stay in the zone and keep the vessel on its lateral track.

### Walking in a Straight Line with Space

### Restrictions

Using a moored vessel or dock as reference point, practice walking to port and starboard while maintaining a constant distance off the reference and a perpendicular aspect to it (fig. 11-6). As you become more skilled, close the distance between the vessel and reference object until you can walk the vessel, keeping it within 1 or 2 feet of the reference object. Give equal time to maneuvering bow toward and stern toward the reference object.

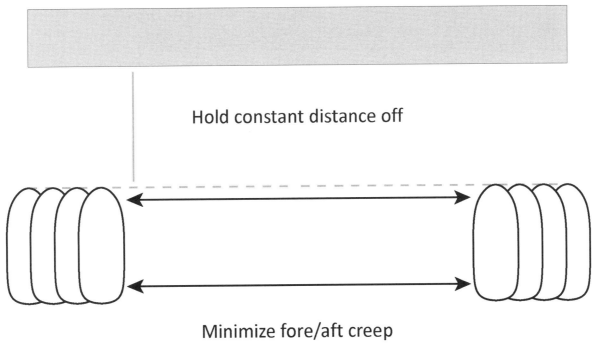

Hold constant distance off

Minimize fore/aft creep

Fig. 11-6
Walking and managing fore/aft creep

### What It Looks Like in Your Mind

The objective of this exercise is to walk and refine your skill at managing the vessel's fore and aft position relative to an object. In the previous exercise, you may have noticed the vessel's tendency to creep forward or aft when walking. This is not a problem in open water, but it is a factor in most practical walking applications. There is often a physical barrier that restricts the space either in front of or behind the vessel. In these situations there is little tolerance for fore or aft creep.

### What It Feels Like in Your Hands

The difficulty in this exercise is constantly solving the relationship between steering and propulsion. One factor creating the vessel's lateral motion is that the two drive units work against each other to negate the forward and aft thrust component of each. To adjust the distance off the reference object, you must be able to tip that balance one way or the other as necessary, but changing the fore and aft balance will also affect steering. You will have to compensate for steering effects at the same time that you adjust your fore and aft position. Your hands are solving a multivariable equation that is constantly evolving.

To complete this exercise successfully, you must first attain the sweet spot. You must feel that you are the vessel's driver, not its passenger. Once in that state, your hands become microprocessors that juggle the steering and propulsion factors required to keep the vessel on its lateral track.

The hands make two common errors when solving these multivariable equations. The first is an unintended escalation of thrust. In open water, the operator's center of attention is commonly directed toward the speed of lateral motion. He may ask himself, "How fast can I move sideways?," with a secondary regard for his fore and aft creep. Next to a dock or ship, his primary focus shifts to managing the vessel's fore-and-aft relationship to the reference object. In this case the internal conversation may be "let's not worry about how fast we move sideways; just don't hit the ship." If the operator is in this state and not quite in the sweet spot, there may be a sequence of escalating thrust, followed by the vessel becoming harder and harder to control.

As an example, when the vessel moves away from the ship, the natural tendency is to close the distance by applying more power to the ahead engine. A new Z-drive operator has a tendency to overcompensate and apply too-much power. To counteract this error, the operator brings up the RPM of the reversing drive unit. If this too is overdone, the operator counters with more ahead thrust, etc., etc. This produces a stairstep sequence of ever-increasing RPM that makes the vessel move and react faster and faster. If the speed of the vessel's response passes the threshold of the operator's skill, he may lose control of the vessel.

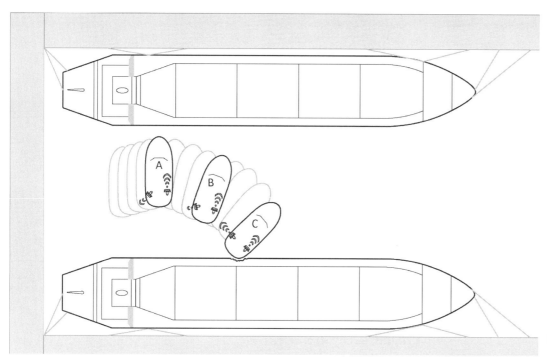

Fig. 11-7
Walking and losing track of the
steering and propulsion link

The second common error is to lose track of the relationship between steering and propulsion. To make the vessel move on parallel rails, both the bow and stern must move sideways at the same speed, while at the same time the two drive units negate the fore and aft effect of each. When the new operator recognizes a change in the vessel's aspect—movement toward or away from the reference object or a difference between the bow's and stern's lateral speed—he tends to adjust for the most obvious changed aspect but may neglect to compensate for the other. Fig. 11-7 illustrates a common scenario.

In this example, the operator has increased the RPM of the starboard (backing) drive unit to keep the vessel from closing on the ship (fig. 11-7A). However, the increase in RPM also causes the bow to move laterally more rapidly. In an attempt to compensate, the operator's instinct is to increase the angle of the ahead drive unit to give more sideways push to the stern (fig. 11-7B). Without a change in RPM, the increased azimuth angle has also altered the fore and aft thrust balance between the drive units—the port drive unit's ahead component has been diminished and the vessel begins to come astern too rapidly. In the operator's mind, the port unit is still the "ahead" drive unit, so he applies more power to compensate for the vessel's excessive sternway. But without an appropriate azimuth adjustment, he drives the vessel's starboard quarter into the ship instead of coming ahead (fig. 11-7C). This is just one example of how losing the feel for the sweet spot in combination with increasing and

misdirected thrust can lead to a cascade of errors. Under these types of circumstances it can take only seconds to go from hands on the controls to hands filling out an accident report.

In this example, one corrective option would be to increase the RPM of the port engine as the azimuth is increased. This is but one of many possible azimuth or RPM changes that would work. The key is to remember that any adjustment must account for the effect both of steering and propulsion.

This concept must become part of the muscle memory in your hands, as well as a conceptual memory in your mind. The mind may pick up this concept quickly, but the hands require multiple repetitions. It may feel counterintuitive when you first attempt this exercise and are forced to have fine control both of lateral and fore and aft motion. But with practice and many repetitions, the sweet-spot feeling will spread throughout this maneuver. Your senses will perceive the subtle change in the vessel's motion and aspect while your hands instinctively manipulate the controls with a light touch.

### Walking around a Buoy

Using a buoy as a reference point, practice circumnavigating the object by walking around it, paying particular attention to maintaining a constant distance off and a consistent heading toward the object (fig. 11-8). Give equal time to maneuvering bow toward and stern toward the reference object.

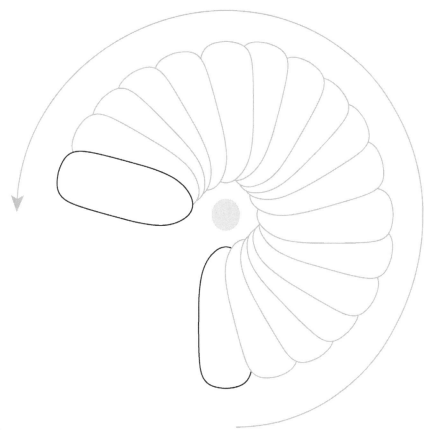

Fig. 11-8
Walking around a buoy

### What It Looks Like in Your Mind

The previous practice exercises focused on keeping the vessel on a steady, straight track—bow and stern on straight, parallel rails—while walking. In this exercise the rails are still parallel, but they curve around corners. You will notice in fig. 11-8 that there are no drive unit azimuths illustrated. That is because there are many different configurations that will work in these circumstances. At this point in your learning, you should be developing an individual style that is reflected in the way you set up and manipulate the controls. That being said, two elements are common to these successful configurations.

The first is that the two drive units are always working against each other; one is always in a position to counter the effect of the other. Second, they create a balance of thrust that can be tipped to immediately alter three maneuvering aspects: fore and aft advance, yaw, and lateral direction.

### What It Feels Like in Your Hands

Throughout this book we have used several terms to describe the different feels associated with driving a Z-drive—sweet spot, driving the vessel, the dead zone, the bite, one with the vessel, and nervous stern. It may seem odd to use such human terms to describe the proper way to use machinery, but driving a Z-drive requires a human to connect with the machinery, not just mechanically but on an intuitive level as well. Successful execution of this practice exercise requires light-vessel handling skills at a high level. At this level it is appropriate to introduce a new term to describe the feel of being connected intuitively to and in command of the vessel: "make that tug or towboat talk."

When we talk, we do not think about the letters or sounds that make up the words, and we do not see a stream of sentences in our mind; rather, we speak instantly. Talking draws both on mind and muscle memory. Our mind pulls the proper words from the vocabulary files in our heads, and our facial muscles remember how to form the sounds of words.

Successfully walking the vessel around a buoy requires you to make that tug or towboat talk. You know the Z-drive's basic maneuvering vocabulary: turning, managing speed, stopping, hovering, and walking. Your hands have a good deal of muscle memory ingrained in them. You should be ready to make the vessel talk. The key is to take command of the conversation between the tug or towboat and the buoy.

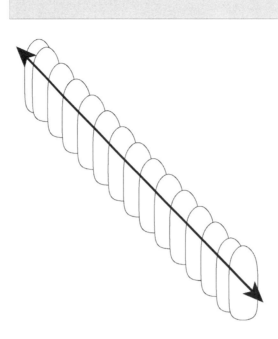

Fig. 11-9
Walking diagonally

### Walking Diagonally

Using a dock or vessel as a reference point, practice walking laterally while at the same time advancing ahead or astern. Pay particular attention to maintaining a perpendicular heading toward the object (fig. 11-9).

### What It Looks Like in Your Mind

The ability to intentionally walk diagonally has many applications in shipwork and barge work. As in previous walking exercises, the key is to first find the sweet spot—the balance of thrust that allows you to control fore/aft, lateral, and rotational motion simultaneously. Once you have that, subtly manipulate the balance so that either the headway or sternway components overpower the other to advance the vessel in the desired direction. But just as in all Z-drive maneuvers, steering and propulsion are always linked. You will have to adjust the steering forces so the vessel maintains its perpendicular aspect to the reference object when you manipulate the fore-and-aft balance.

## Three [3] Common Mistakes

Many operators will make one or all of the three common mistakes while learning to walk a Z-drive:

- Turning the drive unit thrusting ahead the wrong way when trying to make the stern catch the bow
- Changing azimuth but not compensating for the effect on headway and sternway
- Overcorrecting with either hand

The source of these mistakes usually lies in old habits learned driving conventional tugs or towboats. One phenomenon of walking is that the variables of azimuth, RPM, and lateral, fore, aft, and rotational motion assault the operator immediately. In most cases there is no time to think, only time to respond instinctively. Operators with years of previous experience on conventionally propelled vessels will default to the instincts that served them so well in the past. These instincts are embedded in hand motions, many of which are opposite to those required to maintain a walk in a Z-drive. This is the predominant source of the following common errors.

### Turning the Ahead Drive Unit the Wrong Way

To walk, both the bow and stern have to move laterally at the same speed. Typically either the bow or stern will begin to outpace the other and require the operator to make a slight control adjustment to compensate. In fig. 11-10, the vessel's bow is moving laterally to starboard faster than the stern. A conventional tug or towboat solution will use more left-rudder angle to steer the stern to starboard to catch up with the bow (fig. 11-10A). On a conventional tug or towboat the hand motion is to the left to move the steering stick or jog lever. In other words, to make the stern go to starboard the hand and rudder go left.

If this same instinctual hand motion is applied to the controls of a Z-drive, it tends to rotate the azimuth of the port drive unit counterclockwise or thrust less to starboard—precisely the wrong motion. The result is the operator makes the correction and only makes the situation worse (fig. 11-10B).

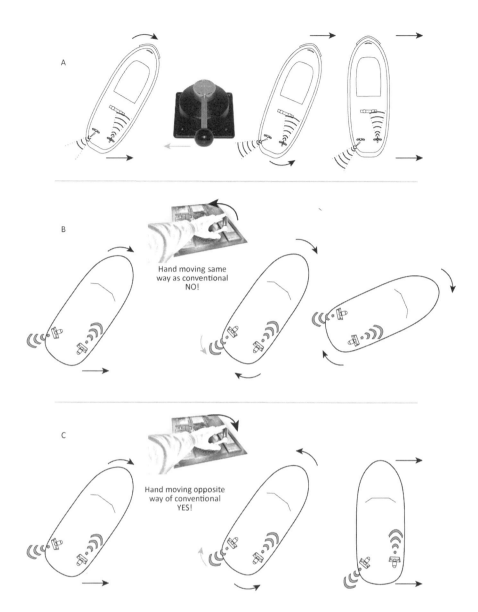

Fig. 11-10
Effect of turning the drive unit the wrong way
A: Conventional propulsion correction
B: ASD propulsion turning port unit the wrong way
C: ASD propulsion turning the port unit the correct way

The correct hand motion is to rotate slightly clockwise and increase the azimuth angle to push the stern more rapidly to starboard (fig. 11-10C). However, changing the azimuth alone is not the complete solution, and if only azimuth is changed, it leads to the next common mistake.

### Changing Azimuth but Not Compensating for the Fore and Aft Effect

In the previous example, we recognized that the stern needed to catch up to the bow and move laterally to starboard faster. The azimuth correction applied the necessary corrective steering force, but azimuth alone is not the solution. Steering and propulsion are always linked. When the operator changed the azimuth in fig. 11-10C, he also changed the fore-and-aft equation of the balance of thrust. By giving the port drive unit more angle, he also took away some of the forward thrust countering the aft thrust of the starboard drive unit. If no additional adjustment is made, the vessel will gain sternway, as well as lateral movement. Either the port drive unit's RPM must be raised or the starboard drive unit's must be lowered to restore the balance-of-thrust equation that will move the vessel laterally without rotating or moving forward or aft.

Walking is an excellent example of the application of the "1 = 2" and "2 = 1" principles. Anytime you make one control adjustment to alter an aspect of the walk—lateral speed, heading, fore and aft movement, etc.—you will always get two effects. If you want to have one effect, you must make two control adjustments. In this case—applying more steering force to the stern but keeping the fore-and-aft balance the same—requires two control adjustments: one to increase the steering force, and the other to compensate for the loss of ahead force.

## Overcorrecting

One aspect of learning to drive a Z-drive is getting used to the idea that small hand motions create greater control and large hand motions create less. It seems counterintuitive, especially to an experienced conventional tug or towboat operator. In the conventional-propulsion world, if you want the vessel to move faster, respond quicker, or increase the rate of turn, it typically requires "more"—more RPM, more rudder, and the larger hand motions associated with these actions.

In Z-drives, you can typically do more with smaller hand motions, and in fact, large hand motions many times will either do nothing or place the vessel wildly out of control. This is clearly apparent when a new Z-drive operator is practicing walking and resorts to large hand motions to control the vessel.

There is a tremendous amount of steering thrust in the stern of a Z-drive. Walking requires that the steering thrust of the two drive units works against each other so that the vessel's heading does not change while moving laterally. If the azimuth of one drive unit changes in large increments, the steering thrust becomes grossly imbalanced and the vessel immediately starts to rotate. It is similar to a player holding a basketball in two hands, standing and moving the ball laterally back and forth across his body. The ball moves laterally, but the control rests in the amount and direction of push in each hand. The pressure of one hand and the counterpressure of the other have to be directed toward each other. If one hand suddenly shifted the angle to push, the ball spins out of the player's hands and he loses control.

When walking a Z-drive, the operator must maintain the same nuanced feeling of balance in the hands, keep the steering forces of the drive units in fine balance, and avoid sudden large azimuth changes. In other words, it does not take much change in angle of push (basketball) or thrust (Z-drive) to have the ball or vessel spin out of control.

It should be emphasized that these errors and corrections can be made with subtle hand motions on the controls. It does not take but a hand twitch in either direction either to regain control of the walk or spin the vessel out of control. These types of errors can be extremely frustrating to the new operator because it can happen so quickly and cause the vessel to accelerate in the wrong direction in the blink of an eye. Many a new Z-drive operator has found himself "locked up," frozen in place with a blank look in the eyes, a furrowed brow, and confused hands while the vessel does 360° turns. If this happens to you, it is time to go to the happy place, regroup, and attempt the maneuver again. But the next time, fight the instinct in the hand that made the error, turn it the correct way, and begin laying down the new "brain wiring" required to walk.

## Practice Drill

The objective of this drill is to practice walking the vessel in a straight line and around corners. You will require a reference object (vessel or dock). In a simulator or live vessel, set the drill up by designating a starting point and two hold points on each side of the corner. There are many variations of this drill, depending on available equipment and the type and number of skill set(s) to practice. Fig. 11-11A uses a barge to practice lateral movement and walking around corners. Fig. 11-11B adds the complexity of touching up after walking around a corner. Fig. 11-11C adds the challenge of walking around a corner with a slack headline.

1. From the start point, begin walking down the reference object.
2. Walk the vessel around the corner, keeping the same distance off the object.
3. Round the corner and stop at the designated hold point.
4. Go back and forth between the two hold points, walking around the corner.
5. Add the challenges of 11-11B and 11-11C when ready—touching up on either side of the corner and walking around a corner with a slackline.

The practice objectives are to

• maintain a consistent distance off the reference object,
• maintain a perpendicular aspect to the reference object while walking,
• touch down accurately at the designated landing points (± 1 foot), and
• have no virtual collisions (in a simulator) or instructor intervention (live tug).

This practice drill, as well as several previous practice drills in this book, has required transitions—changing the tug's or towboat's primary motion from one direction to another. The next chapter looks at this topic in more detail and discusses techniques to keep control of the vessel before, during, and after a transition.

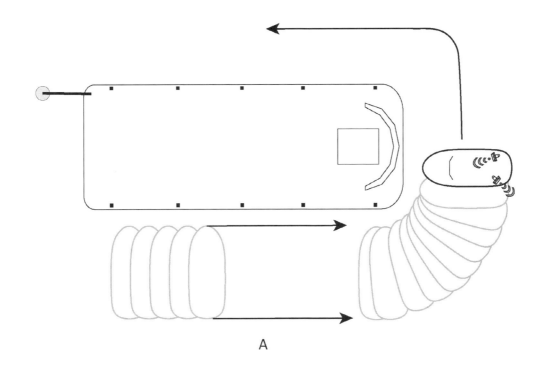

A

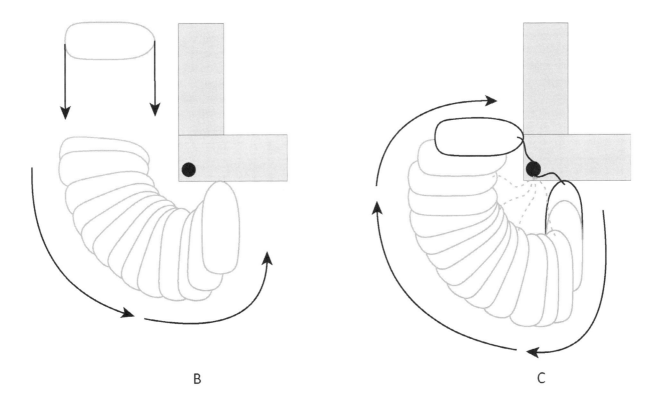

B                                                    C

Fig. 11-11
Walking drill

# *Chapter Twelve*
## Transitions

## Overview

Transitions are those points in a maneuvering sequence when the vessel's motion changes from one primary direction to another. The Z-drive tug or towboat has three basic types of motion: linear, lateral, and rotational. The Z-drive operator uses the three movements individually or in combination to achieve his maneuvering objective. Some transitions are simply a reversal of direction within one of these individual motion aspects. For example, reversing from headway to sternway is a transition within linear motion. However, most maneuvers are more complex and require transitioning through combinations of motion (fig. 12-1).

Your training to this point has focused on the basic Z-drive handling skills as separate components: turning, managing speed, stopping, hovering, and walking. During your practice of these skills as separate entities, there were undoubtedly times when you experienced transitions, but they were never identified as a specific skill set. Transitions link the sequence of Z-drive skills required for a specific maneuver. If that link is weak or broken, the tug or towboat will not shift smoothly from one direction to another, and the operator's Z-drive handling will appear rough around the edges. This chapter offers a structured approach to mastering transitions.

## Why This Is Important

Competence at transitioning is as important as mastering any of the other Z-drive tug- or towboat-handling skills. Transitions are an everyday occurrence in the life of a Z-drive vessel. Light tug or towboat handling, barge work, and shipwork all have multiple points within their array of standard and extraordinary maneuvers in which transitions will occur. From simply leaving the dock light boat, to working a line on a ship, to facing up to a barge, the Z-drive may change its primary direction of motion multiple times.

Becoming competent in transitions is important, because this skill is also critical to maintaining control of the vessel. As common as they are, transitions are also ripe with opportunities for a Z-drive to drive the operator, rather than the other way around. They are a predominant source of a new Z-drive operator's frustration and loss of control. This is because the vessel, the drive unit configuration, and the operator's hand orientation are shifting simultaneously. In addition, the Z-drive may feel less responsive and predictable. This may create confusion in the mind and uncertainty in the hands of a new operator. His connection with the tug or towboat may become weak. A mistake made in these conditions may not be easy to detect. Its cause may be hidden amid all the activity of vessel, hands, and body in motion. A lag in error recognition, particularly during the critical juncture of a transition, increases both the difficulty of controlling a Z-drive and the operator's exasperation.

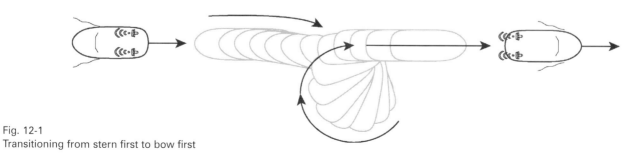

Fig. 12-1
Transitioning from stern first to bow first

# What It Looks Like in Your Mind

The purpose of this chapter is to help you work through transitions by breaking them down into three steps:

1. Entry
2. Exit
3. Shift

Each of these steps is associated with a drive unit configuration and a feeling in the hands. The mental process of managing a transition consists of picturing the drive unit configurations that will be required ahead of time. At first glance, it may seem the steps are out of order. Wouldn't it make more sense to think in terms of entering, shifting, and exiting? It is true—that is the sequence the vessel and your hands follow. However, your mind should follow a different order. You must have a clear picture of your start point and end point before you can figure out how to get there. As a Z-drive operator, you must know how your drive units are going to be configured going in and coming out of the transition before you can decide how to shift them in the most efficient and effective manner. One source of confusion for a new operator is entering a transition without an exit plan. As a new operator, if you do not have a preplanned exit configuration going into the transition, you will find it difficult to create one while the tug or towboat is spinning around or sheering off in the wrong direction.

Your mind should anticipate when and where these three steps will occur in the maneuvering sequence, and should have a clear picture of the drive unit configuration required at each step. In other words, before you go into a transition you should preplan how you will enter, exit, and shift. Having this picture in your mind helps keep you oriented throughout the maneuver and creates mental "rest stops" along the journey through a transition.

## Entry

This is the point just prior to commencing the transition. You should have a clear picture in your mind of the drive unit configuration that is creating the vessel's initial direction of motion. This image is the foundation that anchors your mental orientation throughout the transition. If it is blurry going in, it will not get any clearer as you go through the next two steps.

## Exit

This juncture marks the beginning of the vessel's new primary direction. The drive unit configuration required for the exit is the one you will rely on to propel the vessel in the new desired motion. Confidence is a key factor in your choice of configuration. Many transitions require you to "drive" out of them; that is, you may have to power out of the transition to initiate and create momentum in the new direction. You need confidence that the configuration you have chosen for an exit will work. Applying more power to a Z-drive when you are uncertain of the outcome is like driving down a mountain road, taking your hands off the steering wheel, and punching the accelerator. Not only are you no longer driving the vehicle or vessel, but you are inspiring it to accelerate off in unpredictable directions.

## Shift

This is the most critical step in a transition. Your choice of how to rotate the drive units to the exit configuration should assist—not fight—the vessel's change in direction. The choice may seem simple: the drive units turn either clockwise or counterclockwise. However, there are two factors to take into account. The first is to remember that the stern drives the tug. The rotation of the drive units should move the stern in the direction required to complete the transition. You must anticipate how the tug—and particularly the stern—will react to the rotating drive units. The second is the distance of the drive unit's arc of rotation. There is usually a short or long way around from the entry position to the exit position. The shortest path is best most of the time. There are circumstances in which the long way around works better.

Fig. 12-2 illustrates a simple maneuver: transitioning from bow first to stern first, slow ahead to fast astern, by rotating the stern to starboard. In fig. 12-2A, the operator has chosen to rotate both units the shortest distance, the port unit moving clockwise through 135° and the starboard moving counterclockwise through 135°. Both end up thrusting straight astern. However, the starboard drive unit "fights" the desired rotational motion until it is thrusting straight astern. To make the stern rotate to starboard, the port unit must overpower the starboard's tendency to retard or stop the rotation. In the hands of a new operator, this type of transition typically results in a "rough" transition—lots of thrashing about, with propeller wash and froth surrounding the hull, and the vessel rotating in fits and starts and at times coming to a complete halt.

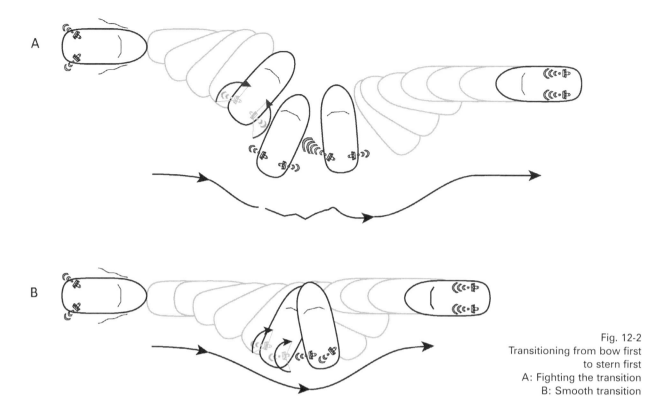

Fig. 12-2
Transitioning from bow first
to stern first
A: Fighting the transition
B: Smooth transition

In fig. 12-2B, the operator is attempting the same maneuver by rotating the port unit the same but rotating the starboard unit clockwise, the "long way" around: 225°. The starboard unit assists rather than fights the turn to starboard the entire time it is rotating. Rotating the starboard drive unit through the "outside semicircle" seemingly violates the Z-drive axiom of never having one drive unit's propeller wash directed toward the other. In this case, the starboard drive unit's wash will not negatively affect the port's wash, since the two units' thrust is staggered and in the same general direction. This type of transition results in a smooth, rapid transition with minimal use of horsepower.

This example illustrates the effectiveness of thinking your way through a transition before attempting one. In this case, rotating the starboard drive unit the long way around is the most efficient, even though it has a greater distance to travel and will be in transition for a longer period of time.

Fig. 12-3 illustrates the three steps of transition in shifting from stern first to bow first. In this example, the operator chooses to rotate the drive units clockwise and in unison to swing the stern to port to line the tug up with the new bow-first heading.

Fig. 12-4 illustrates the change in pivot point as a vessel completes a stern-first to bow-first transition. There is a point during the shift at which the stern is no longer pulling the bow, but instead pushing it toward the new heading. This marks the point at which the vessel's pivot point shifts from the after part of the vessel to the forward part. All these events—entry, exit, shift, and pivot point migration—are mental benchmarks to help you keep connected to the vessel and retain a clear picture of the changing thrust and its effect throughout the transition.

### What It Feels Like in Your Hands

In addition to a picture in your mind, there are feelings in your hands that are associated with the three steps of a transition. These sensory signals also benchmark your progression through the transition. When you are first learning transitions, you will most likely feel confident entering, doubtful during the shift, and hopeful as you exit. As you gain more experience you will feel confident throughout all three steps.

### Entry

You should have a high degree of confidence in your hands as you enter a transition. The tug or towboat should feel nimble and responsive to small control changes, and you should be kinesthetically and mentally connected to the vessel—your hands instinctively responding to the vessel's actions and your mind out ahead, anticipating the next drive unit shift, the vessel's movement, and the feeling in the hands associated with both.

Fig. 12-3
Three steps in a
transition

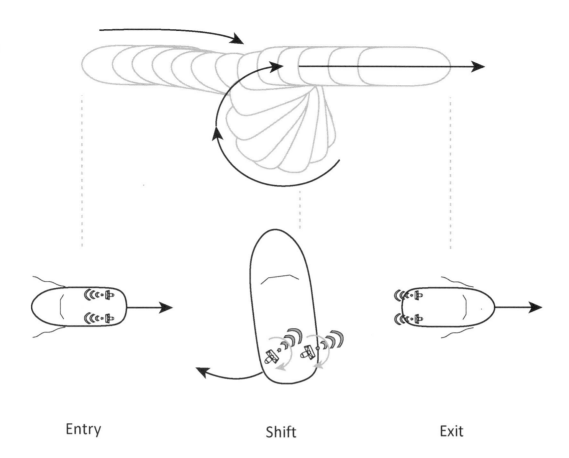

Entry                    Shift                    Exit

Fig. 12-4
Pivot point changes
during a transition

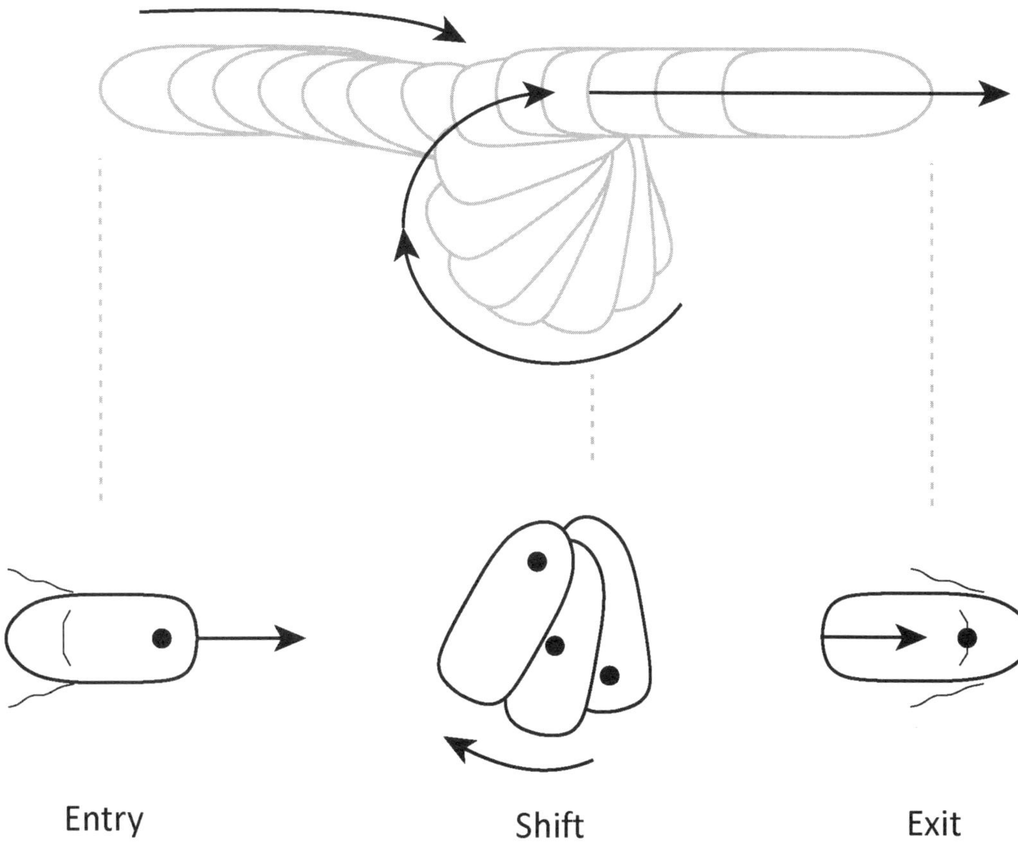

Entry                    Shift                    Exit

### Shift

This is the point at which a new Z-drive operator is most vulnerable to losing control of the tug. As the vessel's drive units and hull turn, the water flow around each becomes more turbulent. This may create some degree of propeller cavitation, causing the controls to feel mushy and the vessel's response to be less predictable. If the maneuver is new to the operator, he may start to question whether he has turned the drive units correctly. Because the tug or towboat may be less responsive, the operator is not getting the instant feedback through his hands that affirms he has turned the handles the correct way. The seeds of self-doubt will have been planted. At this point, he may begin to twist the control handles back and forth in an attempt to reconnect with the vessel. Under these circumstances a hand movement without a known outcome is just as likely to lose as to regain control of a Z-drive.

This is why it is so important to have a transition plan. The plan is the bridge between the entry and exit. It carries you past the self-doubt and ambiguity that sometimes occurs during the shift, and it will give you the confidence to keep the drive units turning from the entry to the exit configuration.

As you gain more experience, your perception of the shift step will evolve. You will see it as a vantage point rather than a valley of doubt. The disturbed water associated with a transition may create propeller cavitation, but it also offers an opportunity to rotate the drive unit while thrusting and effectively to be in neutral.

This can be handy, since there are transitions in which the shortest arc of change for a drive unit may be the best choice in the overall context of the maneuver but be in a direction that would retard rather than enhance the vessel's transition motion. In these instances an experienced operator creates enough momentum to carry the tug through the transition while the drive units are repositioned to the exit configuration. The disturbed water somewhat neutralizes the effect of the drive units' thrust, enabling them to be rotated with little contrary effect on the vessel's smooth course of transition.

We used the example in fig. 12-2A to illustrate the pitfall of rotating a drive unit through the shortest path in which it fights the required vessel motion during a transition. The same situation can also illustrate how an operator can neutralize the effect of a drive unit thrusting in a contrary direction by taking advantage of cavitation and water turbulence.

In fig. 12-5, the operator is transitioning from slow ahead to fast astern by turning bow to port, stern to starboard. The port unit rotates clockwise and increases power, and the starboard unit rotates counterclockwise and simultaneously decreases

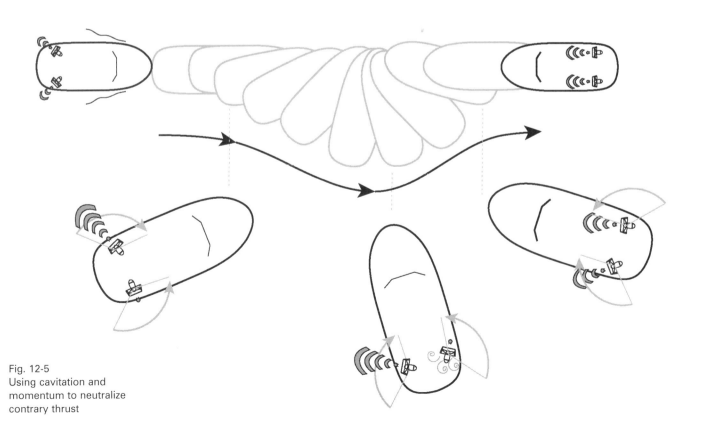

Fig. 12-5
Using cavitation and momentum to neutralize contrary thrust

power. The port unit becomes the propelling force throughout the transition. The thrust imbalance between the two drive units powers the stern to starboard; at the same time it creates light cavitation and negative water flow in the starboard drive unit. The disturbed water effectively allows the starboard drive unit to rotate to the exit position through the short arc and neutralize its contrary effect during the transition.

### Exit

As the vessel approaches its exit point from the shift step, the drive units will be coming around to the exit configuration. This point is also an important juncture. It is not uncommon to have to power the vessel out toward the desired direction. The new operator may be too tentative if his mind is still clouded in doubt, and if he does not apply sufficient power coming out of the shift. Rather than powering his way out and driving the Z-drive, he lines up the drive units and hopes that the vessel will settle down and steady up in the desired direction. In contrast, the experienced operator recognizes and anticipates this critical juncture and applies the necessary power in a timely fashion to drive the vessel out of the shift.

The new operator may feel anxious and unsure about applying power in the midst of a cloud of ambiguity—the vessel turning, the controls feeling mushy. After all, we just alluded to applying power to a Z-drive in uncertainty as the equivalent of punching the accelerator and driving off a cliff in a car. The operator who has thought through the transition and is clear on the exit configuration will not crash and burn when he applies power. Rather, his faith in his thought process will be rewarded— once power is applied, the feeling of tentativeness and ambiguity in the hands fades and a sense of positive control returns.

The sensations associated with the three steps can be clearly felt when transitioning from stern first to bow first (fig. 12-6). The operator has a great deal of confidence in the entry configuration as he steers in a straight line stern first (fig. 12-6A). As he enters the transition, he starts to swing the drive units and the stern in a clockwise direction. The vessel responds immediately and begins to turn (fig. 12-6B). As the drive units continue to rotate, the operator senses the "bite" into the water as the vessel rapidly slows while continuing to rotate. This is a critical moment. The vessel has sufficient momentum to keep rotating about its pivot point, there is turbulent water all

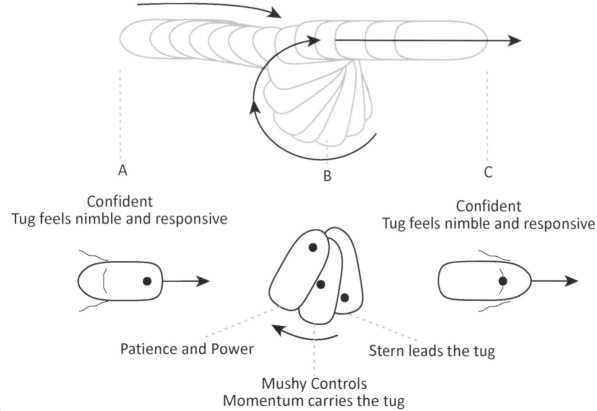

Fig. 12-6
Transitions—how it feels

around the hull created by wheel wash and wake, the drive units are cavitating a bit in the disturbed water, and the pivot point is rapidly shifting from the stern to the bow. The controls feel mushy and the vessel is less responsive. The operator no longer feels the vessel's stern pulling the bow; rather, he feels he is just at the point where he will have to thrust the stern toward the bow to push the vessel in the desired direction. It is near this point that the experienced operator has the patience to wait for the drive units to come around into the exit configuration, and the confidence to apply power once they and the vessel are lined up to exit. As he judiciously applies power, the tug or towboat comes back alive under his hands, and he regains firm control of the vessel (fig. 12-6C).

Use the three-step process both to think and feel your way through the practice exercises that follow.

## Learning Scenarios

The objectives of the learning scenarios are to become proficient at transitioning between

1. bow-first and stern-first movement,
2. linear and lateral movement,
3. linear and rotational movement, and
4. lateral and rotational movement.

In a simulator or live tug, you will need to create a training scenario that has a reference object (dock or vessel) of about 500 feet in length. The space can be defined by a vessel, or a dock with bollards, cones, or signs to mark the boundaries.

## Learning Scenarios: Transitions

1. End-to-end transitions
2. Linear-lateral transitions
3. Linear-rotational transitions
4. Lateral-rotational transitions

The illustrations that accompany the practical exercises give a visual representation of the practice pattern. The diagrammed drive unit configurations are not the only possibilities; you may find other configurations that work better for you. This practice is an opportunity to find not only what works for the tug or towboat, but also what works for you. As discussed earlier in this chapter, confidence is a key factor in successfully completing a transition. Seek solutions to these practice exercises that fit in your comfort zone.

## (1) End-to-End Transitions

The objective of this exercise is to practice end-to-end transitions within space restrictions. Start at one end of the practice zone and transition from bow first to stern first and vice versa, completing the entry, shift, and exit steps within the 500-foot distance (fig. 12-7). Try to limit the amount of ground you cover during the transition, and keep a consistent distance off the reference object throughout the maneuver. Start at a slow speed and work your way up to full speed. As you become more proficient, you will be able to perform the transition smoothly and confidently while remaining within a few feet of the reference object.

You should note the different feel between a bow-to-stern and a stern-to-bow transition. The difference has to do with the pathway of the vessel's stern and the effect of the pivot point. In a bow-first to stern-first transition, the stern rotates first around a pivot point toward the vessel's bow (fig. 12-7A). Once the tug begins to rotate, the pivot point begins to move aft and the stern begins to pull the bow toward the original course line.

This happens seamlessly, and it feels as if the vessel's stern is always being driven in the general direction of the desired track line. This makes for an easy shift step. Once the tug or towboat begins to rotate, it is a simple matter of keeping the drive units thrusting toward the desired direction and letting the bow rotate around the new pivot point near the stern (fig. 12-8). This transition can be done with minimal loss of speed along the track line.

As discussed earlier in this chapter, a stern-first to bow-first transition requires the stern to move opposite of the original track line to get the pivot point forward and the stern in a position to push, rather than pull, the bow down the track line (fig. 12-7B). This does not feel as seamless as the bow-to-stern transition and typically results in the vessel losing some or all of its speed of advance while it is rotating.

~500'

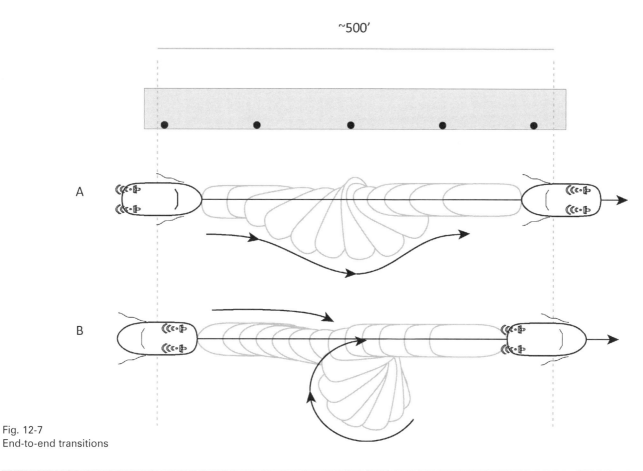

Fig. 12-7
End-to-end transitions

Fig. 12-8
Bow-first to stern-first transition
Thrust and control handles
continue to point toward the
desired exit direction.

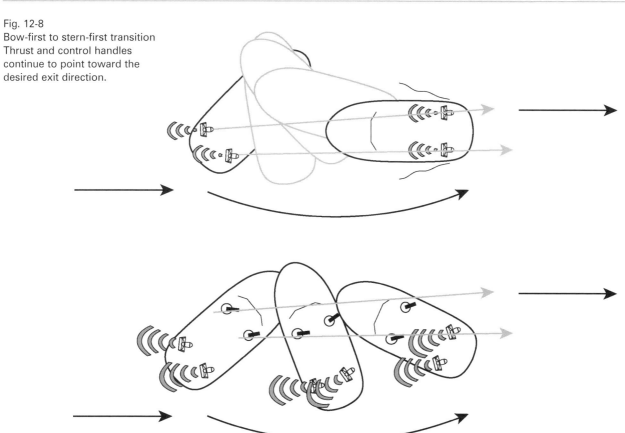

# (2) Linear-Lateral
# Transitions

The objective of this exercise is to practice linear-to-lateral transitions (and vice versa) within a limited space. The vessel's wake should outline a rectangle so that there is a transition at each corner (fig. 12-9). Proceed around the box clockwise, then repeat the practice counterclockwise. Try to limit the amount of ground you cover during the transition, and keep the vessel as close as possible to the track line throughout the maneuver. Start at a slow speed and work your way up to full speed as you become more proficient.

Fig. 12-9
Linear-lateral transitions

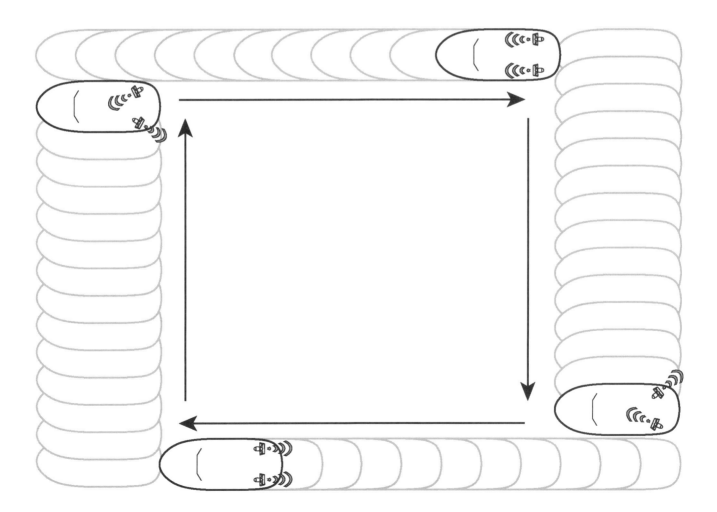

## (3) Linear-Rotational
## Transitions

The objective of this exercise is to practice linear-to-rotational transitions (and vice versa) within a limited space. The vessel's wake should outline a rectangle so that there is a transition at each corner of the box (fig. 12-10). Proceed around the box clockwise. At each corner the vessel rotates 90° counterclockwise to attain the exit heading. Repeat the practice going both directions around the box. Try to limit the amount of ground you cover during the transition, and keep the vessel as close as possible to the track line throughout the maneuver. Start at a slow speed and work your way up to full speed as you become more proficient.

Fig. 12-10
Linear-rotational transitions

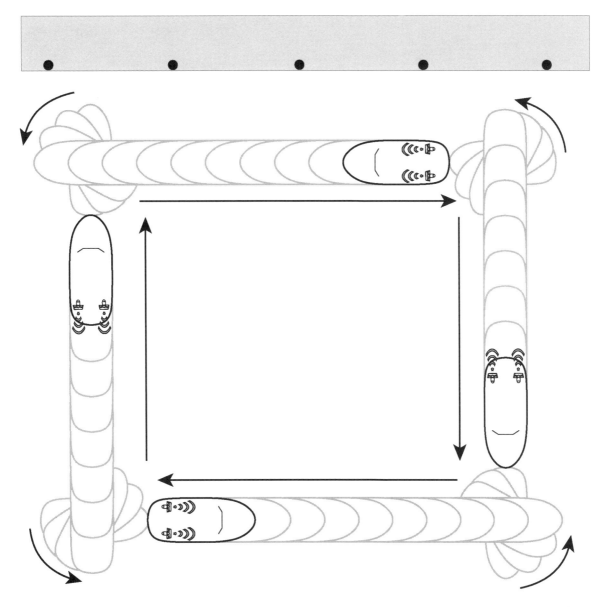

# (4) Lateral-Rotational Transitions

The objective of this exercise is to practice lateral-to-rotational transitions (and vice versa) within a limited space. The vessel's wake should outline a rectangle so that there is a transition at each corner of the box (fig. 12-11). Proceed around the box clockwise. At each corner the vessel rotates 90° counterclockwise to attain the lateral exit heading. Repeat the practice going in both directions around the box. Try to limit the amount of ground you cover during the transition, and keep the vessel as close as possible to the track line throughout the maneuver. Start at a slow speed and work your way up to full speed as you become more proficient.

Fig. 12-11
Lateral-rotational transitions

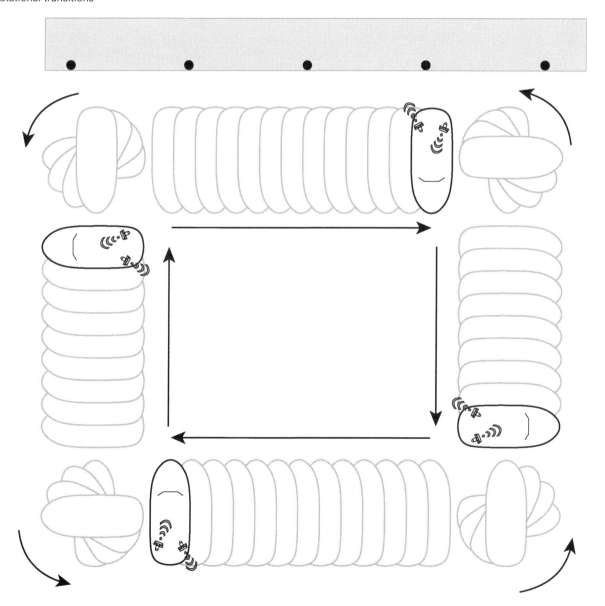

# Practice Drill

The objective of this drill is to practice basic transitions in combination. Although similar to the previous practice exercises, it requires more precision and finer control. In a simulator or live vessel you will need to create a training scenario that has a reference object (dock or vessel) approximately 500 feet in length. The space can be defined by a vessel, or a dock with bollards, cones, or signs to mark the boundaries.

Fig. 12-12 positions:

(Position 1) Walk diagonally to starboard and ahead.

(Position 2) Transition from a diagonal walk to running stern first.

(Position 3) Transition from running stern first to a lateral walk to port.

(Position 4) Transition from a lateral walk to running bow first.

(Position 5) Transition from running bow first to a diagonal walk to starboard and astern.

(Position 6) Transition from a diagonal walk to hovering.

The practice objectives are

• maneuvering the vessel accurately along the pattern,
• keeping within the boundaries defined by the reference object,
• maintaining the perpendicular aspect to the reference object at all times,
• maintaining smoothness in transition from one motion to another, and
• having no virtual collisions (in a simulator) or instructor interventions (live tug).

Steering, stopping, managing speed, walking, and transitions are the basic tools in the Z-drive operator's tool chest of maneuvering skills. When those individual tools feel familiar in your hands, you will be ready to move onto the next training level: using them in combination to practice maneuvers associated with the everyday work of tugs and towboats.

Fig. 12-12
Transition practice drill

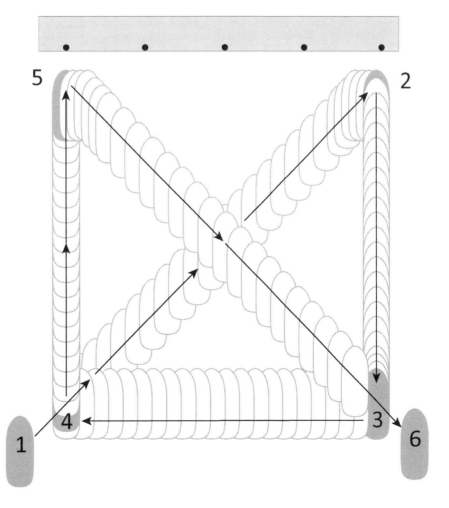

# Chapter Thirteen
## Light-Boat-Docking Maneuvers

## Overview

Once you become proficient in the basic Z-drive skill sets—steering, stopping, speed management, walking, and transitions—you are ready to apply these skills in close-quarter scenarios. Light-boat docking, barge work, and shipwork are three common work environments that call upon simple and complex combinations of these basic skills. This chapter introduces you to the basic principles and techniques of light-boat docking and guides you through practice under controlled circumstances.

Many of the previous learning exercises were done in open water, or in artificially created situations that had built-in cushions of time and space to allow for mistakes. I hope that there was an element of fun in your practice while you learned the basic skill sets. Now it is time for a more serious focus. The stakes are much higher in this chapter's practice maneuvers—a mistake maneuvering close aboard docks or other vessels can be costly. These practice maneuvers require an experienced trainer to be close at hand, ready to intervene if necessary to prevent damage to vessels or personnel. This is true even in a simulator.

A simulator is an excellent learning tool and offers a safe environment for making mistakes. It is good to be able to make mistakes and learn. At this point in your learning sequence, your experience in a simulator should be as real as possible. Replicating an onboard docking experience should include not only the vessel and dock, but the person who may be called on to intervene as well. The simulator provides a platform to physically practice maneuvers and refine the relationship between trainer and trainee. The trainer should set the rules of engagement, just as he would in a live vessel.

Follow the steps emphasized previously in the chapter 8 section "The Role of the Trainer." Set ground rules and a clear boundary line between a learning experience and protecting personnel and property. Ensure that the trainer is in a position to physically intervene quickly if necessary. If on a live vessel, it is also important to communicate to other personnel that this is a training session and that a trainee is at the controls.

## Your Mind and Hands Must Work Together

Docking and undocking require your mind and hands to work together as described in chapter 2, with your mind two to three vessel lengths ahead of the boat, and your hands instinctively reacting to the vessel's movement in the present. In most docking maneuvers there is simply not enough time to "think" your way completely through the maneuver. Close to the dock, a Z-drive demands instant directives to keep it under control. The hands must drive the vessel. However, busy hands need guidance of forethought so they will not be caught out of position as the docking maneuver unfolds. Both mind and hands must work together.

## Words of Caution: Don't Forget the Basics

A Z-drive vessel is highly responsive and maneuverable. Its quickness and omnidirectional performance are well beyond the capabilities of a conventionally propelled vessel. Nevertheless, it is best to utilize five pieces of conventional-boat wisdom when practicing close-quarters maneuvers in a Z-drive:

1. Plan ahead.
2. Consider the "what-ifs."
3. Make a good approach.
4. Stay in your comfort zone.
5. Always leave an "out."

## Plan Ahead: Identify Transition Points

Part of keeping your mind ahead of the vessel is anticipating transition points during a maneuvering sequence. Most docking maneuvers have one or more points when the vessel's primary direction of motion changes. For example, a vessel that undocks by swinging its stern away from the dock and backs away in a straight line has a point at which the stern's lateral motion transitions into sternway. This transition point requires a significant change in the drive unit's configuration. Your mind should anticipate this change so that your hands and the vessel make a smooth transition from one direction of motion to another. Identifying these transition points ahead of time, and the associated drive unit configuration, helps keep your mind ahead of the vessel.

It is a good idea to identify these points prior to attempting a maneuver in a simulator or live situation.

Prior to first attempting a new maneuver, some operators find it helpful to draw on paper the drive unit configurations they anticipate using at transition points. Fig. 13-1 is an example of a drive unit configuration associated with departing a berth and backing away. At transition point A (fig. 13-1A), the operator is preparing to change from all stop to swinging the stern away from the dock. The drive units are clutched out, opposed at 90°, and ready to thrust or counter the movement of the stern away from the dock. Transition point B (fig. 13-1B) marks the point at which the lateral motion of the stern shifts to sternway of the vessel. At transition point C (fig. 13-1C), the operator changes to a configuration that facilitates steering with sternway. Of course, these are not the only possible configurations; others may work as well or better. The key is to have a plan in mind before embarking on a new maneuver.

### The "What-Ifs"

During the planning process and as the maneuvering sequence unfolds, ask yourself the "what-ifs." In the undocking scenario of fig. 13-1, ask these questions: What if the vessel creeps ahead or astern while you swing the stern out? What if the stern begins to close on the vessel moored behind you while you are backing away? What if a small vessel in the main channel suddenly appears behind you? Do you have a drive unit in position to accommodate these circumstances? Part of planning ahead is developing contingency plans that cover unexpected "what-ifs."

### Make a Good Approach

As a Z-drive operator, you have your hands on an array of powerful maneuvering tools, but having the self-discipline to set up a good approach minimizes the tools you may need to pull out of the box. The rest will lie ready for the time when you really need them. A good approach may sound easy and obvious but in practice can be complex and unclear. As an example, it is easy to visualize the end result of a docking maneuver: the vessel is stopped and in position at the berth. But there are many options in getting there. You must decide on speed and angle of approach and must judge the vessel's momentum through the water and what it will take to bring it to a stop. These are the building blocks of a good approach. A little investment in mental homework before starting into the dock pays multiple dividends by the time you get there.

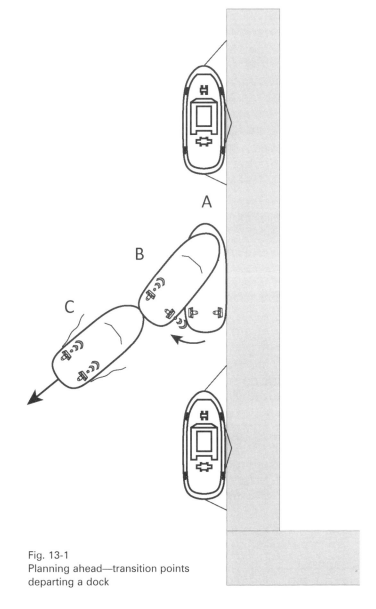

Fig. 13-1
Planning ahead—transition points departing a dock

### Stay in Your Comfort Zone

Choose a maneuvering technique that is within your comfort zone. A good approach is paramount, but you must also know how to make the vessel follow the approach. You must know how to manipulate the Z-drive controls to make the vessel turn, slow down, reverse direction, or stop as required by your transit plan. As noted, you have a number of tools in your maneuvering tool box. You should choose the tools that have a comfortable and familiar feel.

### Always Leave an Out

Always have in mind a technique that will enable you to quickly check the vessel's motion toward the dock or other obstacles, or to abort the maneuver if the approach becomes untenable. In a Z-drive, this means keeping the drive units in a balanced-thrust configuration, where one drive unit is in a position to counteract the other. This will provide the quickest response if the dominant thrust direction needs to be reversed and the primary direction of the vessel's motion changes immediately.

### Z-TPPs

This chapter marks the introduction of Z-TPPs, which stands for the following:

Z: Z-drive
T: Tug or Towboat
P: Polish
P: Points

The Z-TPPs sections in this and following chapters list some tricks of the trade that have been gathered from the collective experience of knowledgeable Z-drive operators. As you work through your learning path, you need not learn by duplicating the mistakes of others who have come before you. Rest assured, you will make plenty of mistakes uniquely your own. Z-TPPs are not the "laws of Z-drive handling"; they are nuggets of knowledge that come from the trials and errors of experienced Z-drive operators.

Before embarking on the learning exercises, note that two Z-TPPs have general application:

• Coasting has very limited effective applications.
• Clutching in and out should be minimized.

Coasting and clutching in and out may look reasonable on paper but do not work well in general practice.

# Coasting

Z-drive vessels do not coast or dead stick well. On your first docking approach, you may be tempted to take both drive units out of gear and let the vessel's momentum carry it toward the dock, but without the drive unit's thrust, the vessel lacks predictable directional stability and could sheer off one way or another. This is due to a number of factors: the Z-drive's hull shape, the drag of the drive units, and the lack of rudders. No matter the cause, the Z-drive needs to be driven right up to the dock.

# Clutching In/Out

The second technique to avoid is rapidly clutching the drive units in and out to change the balance of thrust. This does not work well for three reasons. First, each time you clutch out, you lose the connection between your hand and the vessel. Your hand on a live control is a key source of sensory feedback—constantly processing the cause and effect of the Z-drive's thrust and the resultant motion. When this connection is lost, even for a few seconds, it takes time to regain the feel once the drive unit is clutched back in. The delay in reorienting the hands can be critical.

Second, the balance of thrust is maintained by the drive units working against each other. When one source of thrust is suddenly taken away, this balance is grossly tipped one way. If this effect is not anticipated, the operator will often overcompensate with the other control, taking large and often-too-extreme corrective actions. There are maneuvers when clutching out may be appropriate, such as docking a vessel with only one functional drive unit or clutching out to let the vessel's momentum carry it gently to the dock the last few feet. An experienced operator uses this technique sparingly and appropriately.

Third, the clutch mechanism in a Z-drive is not engineered for day-in and day-out, constant in/out gear shifts. Although a Z-drive's performance has been compared to a Formula 1 race car, a Z-drive operator should not be working the drive unit clutch as though he were a Grand Prix driver. A Z-drive clutch is not built for that type of use. It is designed to spend most of its working life engaged, transferring the power of the engine to the thrust of the propeller over the complete range of engine loads—from idling around as a light vessel to a maximum dead push. The capability of the clutch to engage and disengage is a necessary and utilitarian function; it is not a high-performance feature.

Also, the time it takes for the clutch to engage or disengage varies from vessel to vessel and may even differ from one drive unit to the other in the same vessel. When rapidly approaching a dock at close quarters, the timing factor adds one more variable for the operator to juggle in an already complex situation.

# Learning Scenarios

The objectives of the learning exercises are to become proficient at

1. docking and undocking the vessel in restricted space,
2. docking/undocking bow first,
3. docking/undocking stern first,
4. docking/undocking straight in/out approach,
5. docking/undocking walking approach, and
6. docking/undocking in current.

In a simulator or live vessel, you need to create a dock configuration that restricts the berthing space to approximately two vessel lengths (fig. 13-2). The space can be defined by other vessels, or cones or signs on the dock to mark the boundaries.

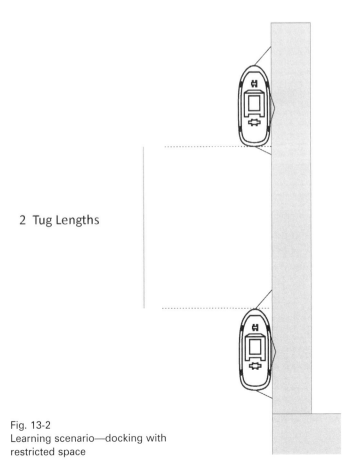

2 Tug Lengths

Fig. 13-2
Learning scenario—docking with restricted space

The illustrations that accompany the learning exercises have two purposes. One is to give a visual representation of the exercise maneuvers. The other is to diagram one set of possible drive unit configurations associated with the maneuver's transition points. The diagrammed configurations are only one of many possible successful solutions. You may find other configurations that work as well or better for you. At this point in your learning practice, you should be developing your own style of Z-drive handling, which may include drive unit configurations that are not "textbook." However, they should facilitate your ability to follow the five principles of conventional vessel wisdom:

1. Plan ahead.
2. Consider the "what-ifs."
3. Make a good approach.
4. Stay in your comfort zone.
5. Always leave an "out."

# Undocking: Stern First

Beginning from a docked position with restricted space, swing the vessel's stern out and back away from the berth in a straight line (fig. 13-1).

### Z-TPPs

- Begin with the units clutched out in the feathered position—propeller wash to be directed 90° away from the vessel's keel.
- In close quarters, have one drive unit in position to counter either the thrust of the other or the primary motion of the vessel.
- Be prepared that once clutched in and the vessel starts to move, the sequence of transitions—stern lifting, checking the bow, gaining sternway, steering clear of the other vessels—happens quickly!

# Docking: Bow First

Approach the berth bow first and dock the vessel in a restricted space (fig. 13-3).

### Z-TPPs

- As you approach the berth, slow the vessel down by bringing the drive units toward the feathered position.
- Stop and hover for a moment 10 feet from the dock.
- Make sure you are rooted in your comfort zone before moving in the last 10 feet.

- You must find the "sweet spot" before you commit to the final approach.
- If you do not feel that you have confident control 10 feet away from the dock, you will not find it when you are 10 inches away.
- Spot the bow first, put up a breast line, and swing the stern toward the dock.
- Watch the stern!
- Make sure the other drive unit is in position to check the stern's swing toward the dock.
- If you do decide to clutch out once the bow breast line is up, clutch both units out *simultaneously*.

Fig. 13-3
Docking bow first
Restricted space
No current

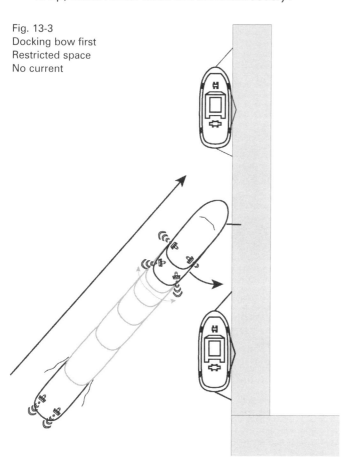

# Undocking: Bow First

Beginning from a docked position with restricted space, swing the vessel's bow out and come away from the berth, bow first in a straight line (fig. 13-4).

## Z-TPPs

- Avoid jamming the stern too forcefully into the dock.
- "Twin screw" the bow out.
- Be wary of the stern coming back into the dock as you swing the backing unit around to come ahead.

- Be ready to counter a sheer back toward the vessel/dock when you first gather headway.

Fig. 13-4
Undocking bow first
Restricted space
No current

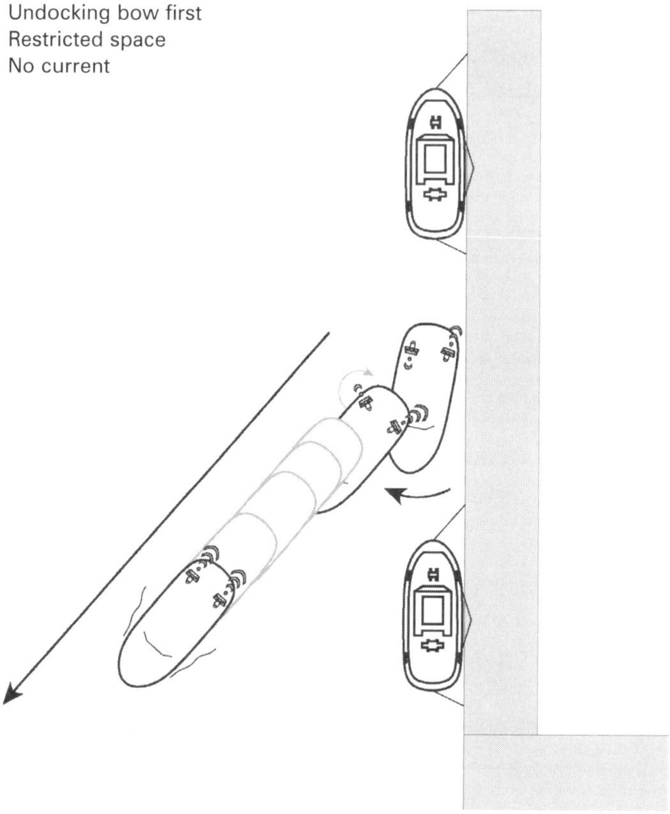

# Docking: Stern First

Approach the berth stern first and dock the vessel in a restricted space (fig. 13-5).

## Z-TPPs

- As you approach the berth, slow the vessel down by bringing the drive units toward the feathered position.
- Stop and hover for a moment 10 feet from the dock.
- Make sure you are rooted in your comfort zone before moving in the last 10 feet.
- You must find the "sweet spot" before you commit to the final approach.
- Do not tie down the stern first! Many a cleat, chock, and piling have been pulled off the dock by securing the stern of a Z-drive tug or towboat first and attempting to spring the bow in by working on the breast line.
- Walk toward the dock, or gently bring the bow in first, secure it, and finish by swinging in the stern.

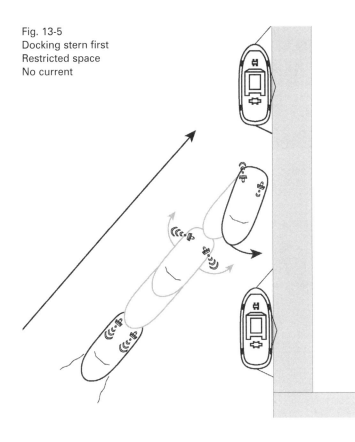

Fig. 13-5
Docking stern first
Restricted space
No current

# Undocking: Walk Out / Proceed Stern First

Beginning from a docked position with restricted space, walk away from the berth and, once clear, proceed stern first on a steady course (fig. 13-7).

### Z-TPPs

• Be wary when first clutching in alongside the dock—the drive units may not be perfectly aligned and may require immediate adjustment to find the "sweet spot" to prevent damage to the dock.
• Propeller wash toward the dock may push the stern laterally faster than the bow.
• Expect a dead zone when transitioning from lateral motion to headway or sternway.
• Be ready to counter a sheer back toward the vessel/dock when you first gather headway or sternway.
• Remember that space equals time in Z-drive maneuvering. Make sure you have ample clearance on the moored vessel before committing to transition from lateral motion to headway.

# Undocking: Walking Out / Proceed Bow First

Beginning from a docked position with restricted space, walk away from the berth and, once clear, proceed bow first on a steady course (fig. 13-6).

Fig. 13-6
Undocking walking out
Proceeding bow first
Restricted space
No current

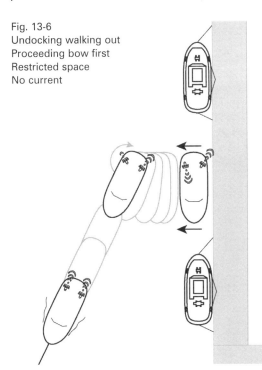

Fig. 13-7
Undocking walking out
Proceeding stern first
Restricted space
No current

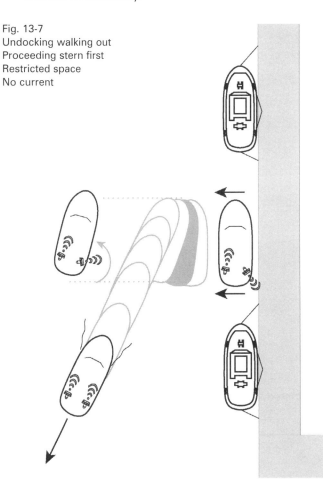

# Docking: Stern First / Walk In

Approach the berth stern first, stop approximately two to three vessel lengths off the dock, and walk the vessel into its berth in a restricted space (fig. 13-8).

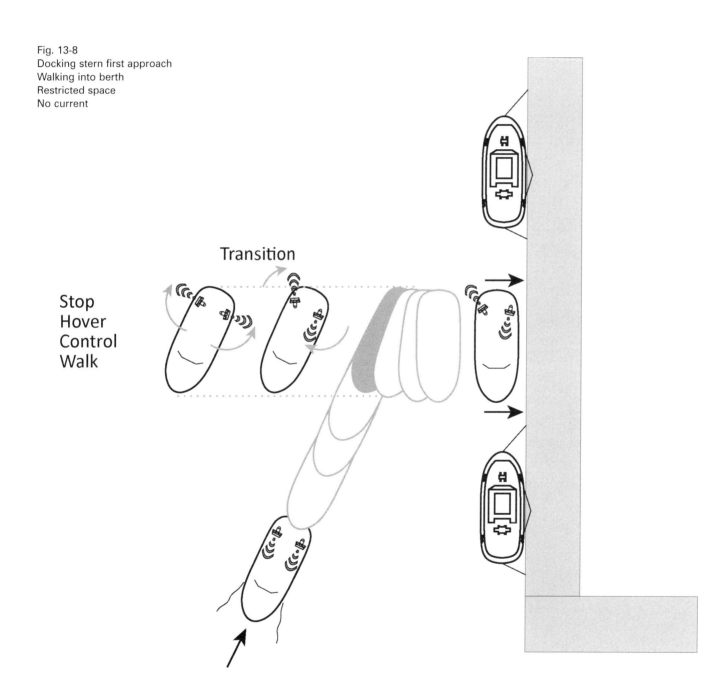

Fig. 13-8
Docking stern first approach
Walking into berth
Restricted space
No current

Transition

Stop
Hover
Control
Walk

# Docking: Bow First / Walk In

Approach the berth bow first, stop approximately two to three vessel lengths off the dock, and walk the vessel into its berth in a restricted space (fig. 13-9).

## Z-TPPs

- Stop and hover before walking toward the dock.
- Make sure you have found the "sweet spot" and have control of the vessel before beginning the walk.
- Expect a dead zone when transitioning from headway or sternway to walking.
- Give yourself space and time to get on top of managing lateral, fore/aft, and yaw motion prior to entering restricted space.
- Be wary of creating too-much lateral momentum, resulting in a hard landing.
- A walking configuration when alongside the dock can keep the boat pressed in and minimize the contrary effect of propeller wash hitting the dock structure.
- If you do decide to clutch out to "soak" in the last few feet, clutch both units out *simultaneously*.

Fig. 13-9
Docking bow first approach
Walking into berth
Restricted space
No current

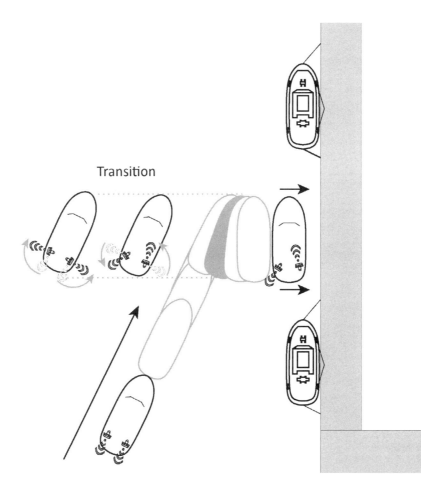

Transition

Stop
Hover
Control
Walk

# Approach Berth, Turn 180°, Bring into Berth

Approach the berth bow first, turn 180° while remaining approximately two to three vessel lengths off the dock, and walk the vessel into its berth in a restricted space (fig. 13-10).

### Z-TPPs

• Use the 180° turn to take off the vessel's headway.

• Expect a dead zone when transitioning from rotating to walking.
• Give yourself space and time to get on top of managing lateral, fore/aft, and yaw motion prior to entering restricted space.
• Manage lateral speed to avoid a hard landing.
• A walking configuration when alongside the dock can keep the boat pressed in and minimize the contrary effect of propeller wash hitting the dock structure.
• If you do decide to clutch out to "soak" in the last few feet, clutch both units out *simultaneously*.

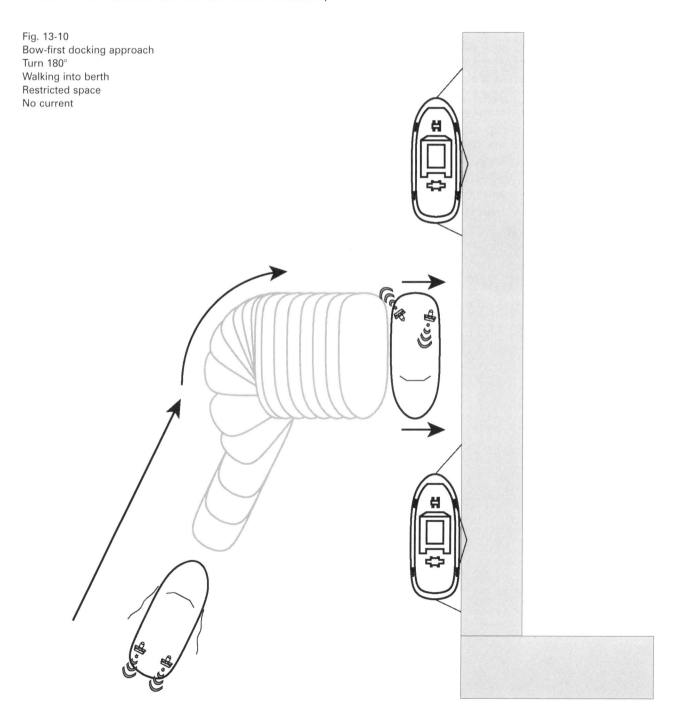

Fig. 13-10
Bow-first docking approach
Turn 180°
Walking into berth
Restricted space
No current

The scenario in fig. 13-10 is an excellent example of how thinking ahead can assist you in attaining your maneuvering objective. The 180° turn is a maneuvering requirement of this scenario, but it also offers the opportunity to transition smoothly from a drive unit configuration appropriate for headway to one appropriate for walking. There are multiple thrust configurations that will produce the 180° turn, but one in particular will set you up nicely for the walk toward the dock (fig. 13-11).

Just before your bow is abeam of the berth, begin to rotate the outboard (in this example port) drive unit counterclockwise (fig. 13-11A). This begins to spin the vessel clockwise. The starboard drive unit continues to thrust ahead at reduced RPM and assists in steering and managing the vessel's headway while the port drive unit continues to rotate counterclockwise (fig. 13-11B). If you have timed this correctly, you will end up abeam of the berth in a walking configuration once the vessel has completed its 180° turn (fig. 13-11C).

### Z-TPPs

- Timing, boat speed, and momentum are key factors in performing this maneuver with finesse and accuracy.
- One key is to regulate the headway and rate of turn of the vessel by the increments and pace that you turn the port Z-drive control handle.
- Once you commit to the 180° turn, the maneuvering and control adjustments that follow come at a rapid and continuous pace—too quickly to "think" your way through the maneuver. You have to be able to adjust intuitively.

# Docking in Current

All the previous docking exercises can also be practiced in current, but there are several Z-TPPs to keep in mind.

The basic rules of boat handling in current still apply:

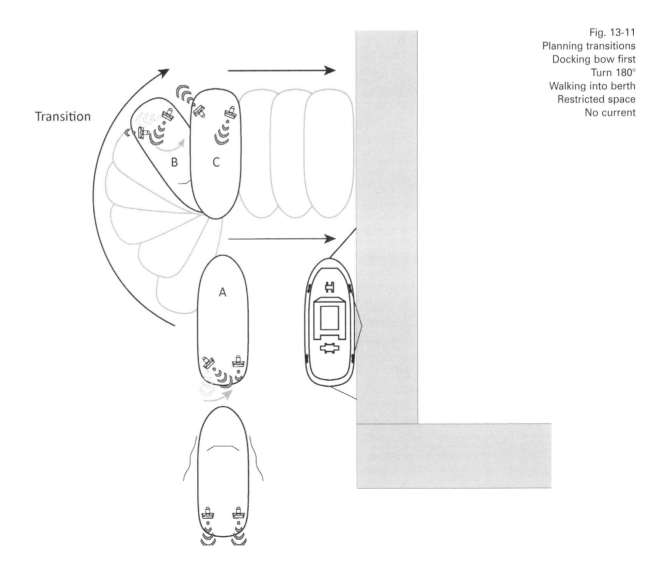

Transition

Fig. 13-11
Planning transitions
Docking bow first
Turn 180°
Walking into berth
Restricted space
No current

- When landing parallel to the current, land the up-current end (bow or stern) first.
- Use the current to counter the momentum and direction of the boat's motion.
- Use the current to assist, rather than fight the maneuvering objective.

Drive unit configurations will be different—sometimes subtly, sometimes dramatically—than ones that are effective in still water (fig. 13-12):

- A simple docking maneuver in still water becomes primarily managing speed and steering in current (fig. 13-12A).
- A "walking configuration" to get the boat to move laterally in current may be unnecessary and potentially disastrous (fig. 13-12B).
- Operating stern to the current (stern up) offers a paradox of easier control of the boat but is ruthlessly unforgiving of a loss of attention or oversteering.

Fig. 13-9 illustrates a bow-first approach to a berth in still water. The steps are headway, stopping and hovering, rotating to be parallel to the dock, and walking into the berth. Fig. 13-12A illustrates a Z-drive making the same approach, but with a two-knot head current. In this case, there are the same transition points and the boat appears to follow the same path to the dock, but the drive unit configurations are different. In current, this is a two-part maneuver of managing speed and steering (fig. 13-12A). The operator must keep enough headway through the water to remain fixed over the ground and use steering techniques to tip the bow in and let the current move the vessel laterally.

Using the walking configuration that worked well in still water to move laterally may be disastrous in current. Fig. 13-12B shows an unfortunate operator who chose this methodology. His initial approach is the same as in fig. 13-12A, but at the transition point he starts rotating the starboard drive unit to the backing position. As soon as he begins this rotation, the bow dives to starboard, the boat loses headway, and he starts sliding rapidly toward the downstream vessel. At this point he has no way out; both drive units are out of position to arrest the slide. His only hope is that the starboard drive unit gets aft of 90° in time for him to start backing away faster than the bow is swinging in. If he is lucky he will miss by inches. More often than not there will be a dented boat and ego to repair.

# Practice Drill

The objective of this drill is to practice docking and undocking in restricted space. This is similar to the previous learning exercises but requires more precision and finer control. In a simulator or live vessel, you will need to create a dock configuration that restricts the berthing space to approximately 10 to 15 feet of clearance both on bow and stern (fig. 13-13). The space can be defined by other vessels, or cones or signs on the dock to mark the boundaries.

1. Start alongside the dock, drive units clutched out, and the vessel made fast to the pier (fig. 13-13A).
2. Cast off the lines and take the vessel off the dock, using your preferred technique.
3. Once clear of the berth, rotate 180° in place.
4. Come back into the berth for a "touch and go"—bringing the vessel alongside the berth and holding it there, without lines, for thirty seconds (fig. 13-13B).
5. After thirty seconds, come away from the berth, using your preferred technique.
6. Once clear of the berth, rotate 180° in place (fig. 13-13C).
7. Come back into the berth and make fast to the dock with two lines (fig. 13-13D).

The practice objectives are

- conducting the whole maneuver within the boundaries defined by the restricted berth (dotted lines in fig. 13-13),
- on the "touch and go," keeping the vessel's side pressed flat against the dock,
- minimizing the degree of line use required to get the vessel into the berth (less is better), and
- having no virtual collisions (in a simulator) or instructor interventions (live vessel).

Once you have completed the drill multiple times successfully and without instructor intervention, you are ready to move on to the practical applications of Z-drive maneuvering in barge work and shipwork.

Fig. 13-12
Docking in current, head to current

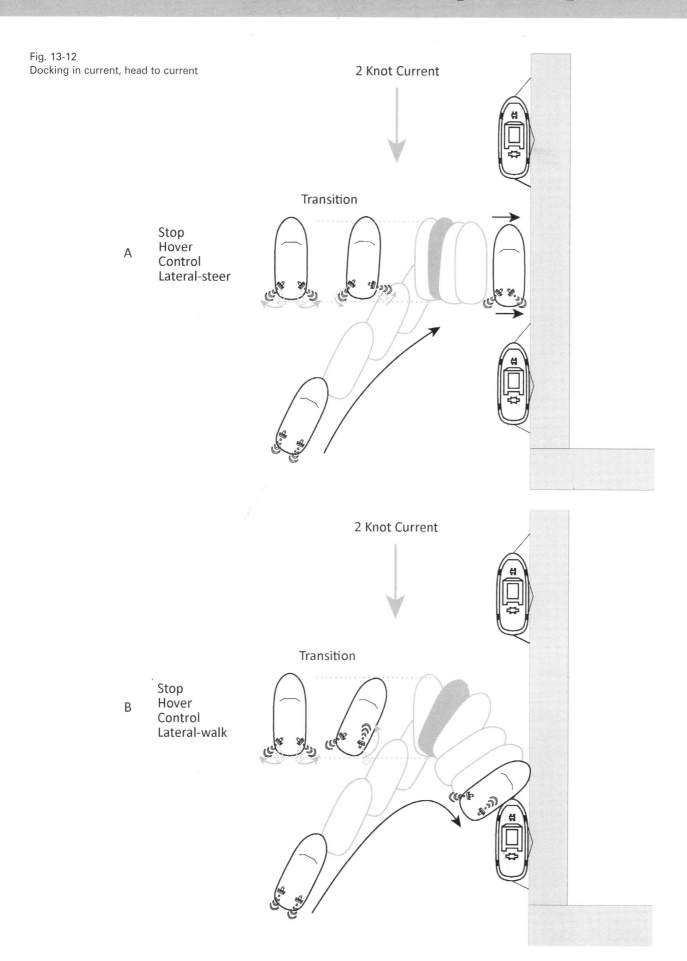

2 Knot Current

Transition

A    Stop
Hover
Control
Lateral-steer

2 Knot Current

Transition

B    Stop
Hover
Control
Lateral-walk

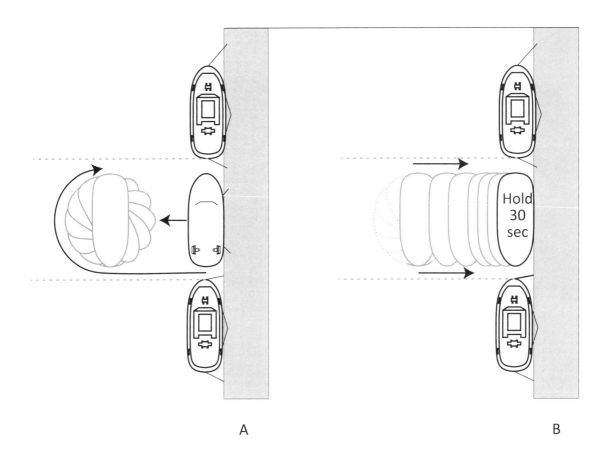

A

B

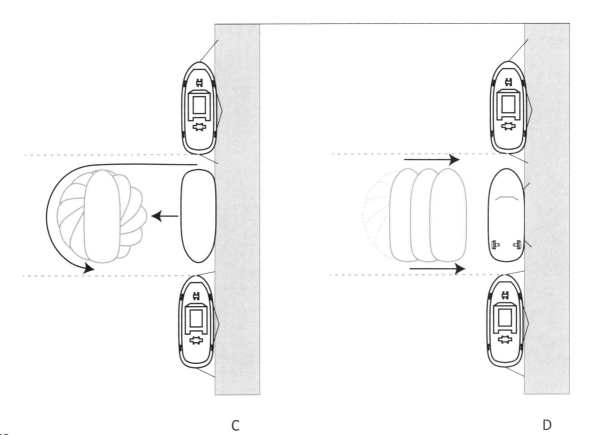

C

D

Fig. 13-13
Practice drill: docking/undocking

# Notes

# Chapter Fourteen
## Preparing for Barge Work

## Overview

At this point in your training you should be able to competently perform basic light-tug maneuvers: steer, stop, walk, transition, dock, and undock. The controls should have a familiar feel in your hands. Your mind should be able to maintain a clear picture of the drive unit configurations associated with the tug's or towboat's motions. The next application of your skills is to actively engage in barge work or shipwork.

This chapter will focus on skills specific to basic barge work: facing up, making up alongside, and towing astern, alongside and pushing. However, there is an intermediate step prior to putting these skills to use in a working environment:

1. Getting the light tug or towboat into position
2. Shifting the tug or towboat precisely relative to a moored or drifting barge

Practicing with moored barges is a good way to introduce and hone these skills prior to applying them in practical application.

## Role of the Trainer

All the practical exercises require the presence of a skilled and experienced trainer in the wheelhouse. Follow the steps outlined in the chapter 8 section "The Role of the Trainer." Set ground rules, create learning boundaries, and ensure that the trainer is in a position to physically intervene quickly if necessary. In addition, it is important to communicate to other personnel that this is a training session and that a trainee is at the controls. Deck personnel handling lines need to know who is at the controls. When they are working lines, their safety depends on the skill of the operator.

## Learning Exercises

The exercises that follow are applicable both to towboats and tugboats and can be conducted in a simulator or onboard. Some of the descriptive terminology used is towboat or tugboat centric, but the maneuvers translate into skill sets that are essential for both types of vessels. For example, "facing up" is a common towboat term that describes maneuvering a light towboat into push mode, but the skill of maneuvering head to current or stern to current and landing the bow at a specific point has applications both in the towboat and tugboat world. The illustrations that follow will portray one type of vessel or the other, but that does not mean the exercise is limited to a specific type of towing vessel.

## Facing Up Head to Current

Facing up to a barge is an everyday occurrence with a towboat. The learning exercise illustrated in fig. 14-1 should be practiced in still water or head to current. Make sure you spot the tow knees exactly where they need to be to face up—do not rely on a capstan line to center up. Once you can successfully complete the exercise consistently on the outside tier (fig. 14-1A), move closer to the inside tier, where there is restricted space (fig. 14-1B).

## Z-TPPs

- Most operators find a variation on the "feathered" configuration to be effective on the approach.
- Bring the towboat to a stop 2–3 feet from the barge—you may need this time to find the sweet spot that gives you the control required to land the tow knees precisely.
- Creep in the last foot—the rate of closure with the barge should be no faster than "a leaf drifting on a pond."
- Resist the temptation to immediately swing both units to thrust straight ahead once you have touched up. You do not need that much azimuth to keep the towboat pressed into the barge, and you will lose some of your steering sensitivity if you do.

# Alternate Knee Touching

Facing up requires precise positioning of the tow knees. There are many circumstances in which it is helpful to have one tow knee touch up before the other. This exercise is designed to help you develop the finesse to lightly touch down one knee and then the other.

1. Pick a timberhead or kevel on the barge as a designated touchdown point.
2. Touch up one knee and then shift to touch up the other knee.
3. Try to stay only a foot or two off the barge as you alternate back and forth.

## Z-TPPs

The keys to precise maneuvering and positioning of the tow knees are to:

- find and work in the sweet spot,
- keep the hands calm and moving in small increments,
- use low RPM, and
- keep the maneuvering speed slow.

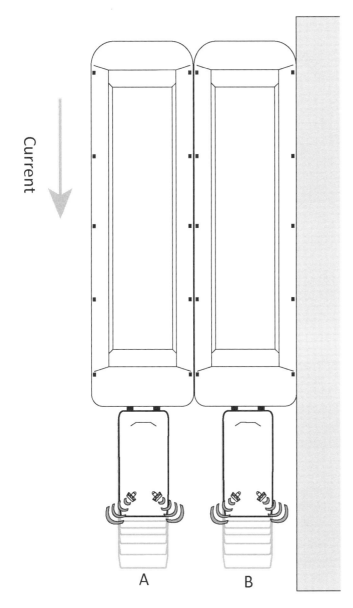

Fig. 14-1
Facing up

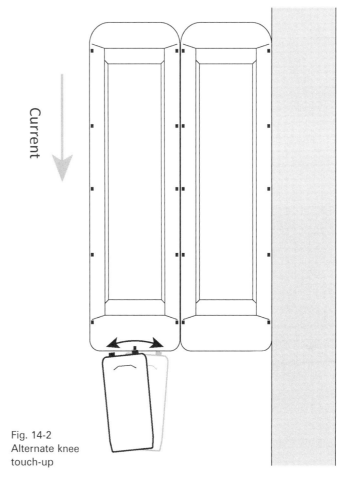

Fig. 14-2
Alternate knee
touch-up

# Coming Downstream, Rounding Up Head to Current, and Facing Up

This exercise is designed to string together several skill sets: managing speed, steering, rotating with precision, and facing up.

1. Start at the head end of the tow or, if in current, start at the upstream end of the tow.
2. Come down and swing around the stern corner and face up.
3. Keep within a consistent distance of the downstream corner as you turn to face up.
4. Close the distance on the corner as you become more proficient.
5. Work toward rounding the corner only a few feet off.
6. Once around the corner, touch up in the precise position to face up.

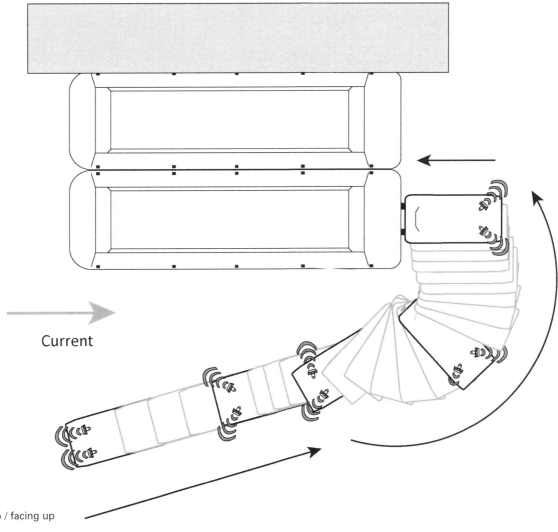

Current

Fig. 14-3
Rounding up / facing up

# Walking around a Barge and Facing Up

This exercise is best practiced along moored barges at least two tiers wide; the extra tier creates extra room to master checking the slide before overshooting the barge and possibly contacting the dock.

1. Start perpendicular to the side shell of the barge.
2. Walk down the side of the barge, maintaining the same distance off.
3. Maintain the boat's perpendicular aspect to the barge.
4. Walk around the end corner.
5. Touch up in the precise position to face up.

If there is current, start at the up-current end and work your way to the down-current end. The difficulty in this exercise lies in the rapid sequence of transitions rounding the corner of the barge:

- Walking laterally to walking around a corner
- Walking around a corner to checking the slide
- Checking the slide to gaining headway to face up
- Managing headway to steer and stop at a designated point

These transitions require rapid, intuitive adjustments with little room for error. As you gain proficiency, close up the distance to the barge so that you are within 1 to 2 feet of the barge during the whole exercise.

## Z-TPPs

- Plan ahead for the transitions.
- Expect to use judicious bursts of thrust at appropriate times.
- Checking the slide requires forethought and timing of thrust configurations and control handle movements.

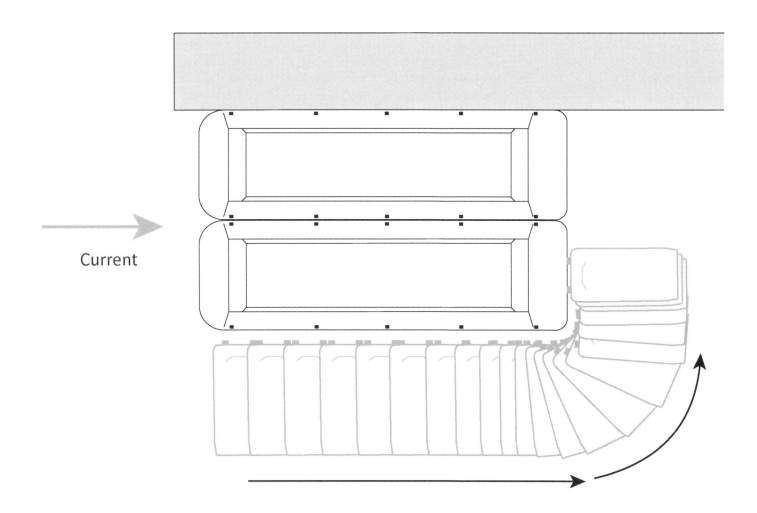

Current

Fig. 14-4
Walking around a barge

# Shifting Laterally, Dragging One Knee

This exercise is best practiced along moored barges at least two tiers wide and even on the downstream end.

1. Start this in a faced-up position on the inside barge.
2. Initiate a walk toward the outside barge.
3. Once walking laterally, work your way back toward the barge.
4. Drag one push knee as you slide down the barge.
5. Keep the boat at a slight angle to the barge so that one tow knee drags and the other is about 1 foot off.
6. Experiment with different amounts of pressure on the knee to regulate the lateral speed.
7. Stop in a faced-up position when the outboard knee is even with the outboard corner of the outside barge.
8. Do not overshoot the outboard corner.
9. Add intermediate stops along the way at kevels, timberheads, or other specific landing points as you gain proficiency.

The final objective is to develop the finesse and touch to be able to shift the tow knee laterally just a few feet, touch up, and then square up in a faced-up position.

There are circumstances when it is advantageous to be able to lightly drag one push knee when sliding laterally. Experienced towboaters will use this technique to help check a lateral slide when facing up, or to keep close to the barge while a deckhand is shifting a boat line into a new position. It requires finesse and a light touch to be able to regulate the amount of friction between the push knee and the barge, check the slide at a precise point, and touch up gently on the barge.

### Z-TPPs

- Small control adjustments and small hand movements are essential.
- Be aware that as the tow knee friction increases, the stern will tend to outpace the bow.
- Experiment during the shift to determine what will be required to check the slide *before* you get to the designated landing point.
- Checking the slide can be as challenging as initiating the walk.

# Downstreaming

Downstreaming is one of the most hazardous maneuvers in towboating. Done improperly, it is a maneuver that with the wrong boat, in the wrong hands, or under the wrong conditions can result in serious injury, death, or damage to the vessel. Some operators avoid this maneuver all together, but for others, it may come with the job (e.g., fleet boats).

The design of Z-drive towboats, with omnidirectional thrust at the stern, offers a powerful tool in managing the risk of downstreaming. Having precise steering control while thrusting astern is a key element to downstreaming safely. However, this very trait can cause the untrained Z-drive operator to lose control of this maneuver in a heartbeat. When the current is striking the stern at an angle and setting it down to one side, the operator of a Z-drive can easily counter it with the *appropriate amount* and *angle* of thrust. The key word is *appropriate*. A mistake in this situation is like hitting the accelerator instead of the brake when backing a car into a garage. If the wrong control is moved, or the wrong azimuth or power applied, the Z-drive towboat can immediately set down on the barge in an unrecoverable position.

The key to learning to downstream in a Z-drive is to work up to it in steps. The *trainee* must have confidence and competence at each step before moving to the next. The *trainer* must have the experience to conduct an accurate risk assessment of the training conditions and the trainee's level of competence. He must also have absolute authority to step in at any time and abort the exercise or training session.

These exercises should not be conducted if it is a violation of any company or vessel owner policies or procedures. Additionally, a qualified trainer must be present in the wheelhouse, close at hand, and ready to abort the exercise in an instant. Downstreaming exercises should be practiced only if the trainer has determined that the current velocity and maneuvering circumstances are at an appropriate magnitude for the operator's skill level.

Fig. 14-5
Shifting laterally, dragging one knee

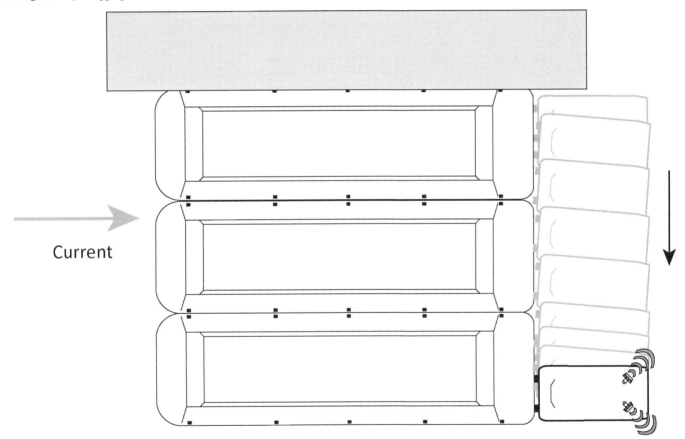

Current

# Downstreaming Step 1: Controlling the Stern

This exercise is practiced alongside moored barges.

1. Go to a spot about two to three boat lengths off a moored barge.
2. Turn the towboat "tail up" with the stern to the current.
3. Practice hovering stern to the current, neither moving upstream nor downstream, nor closing on the barge.
4. Once the vessel is stabilized, slide toward the barge, closing the distance.
5. Stop and hover when within one boat length of the barge side shell.
6. Slide toward the barge and slightly downstream to touch up with the tow knee even with a kevel or timberhead on the barge side shell.

This exercise appears simple on paper but can be quite challenging on the first attempt. The first challenge may be figuring out how to hover with the stern up current. Many an operator on his first attempt at turning and holding tail-up has completed a few 360° before finding the configuration that stabilizes the stern in current. That is why the first attempt is several boat lengths off the barge. The second challenge is checking the slide toward the barge; that is why there is an intermediate stop and hover position before the final position. The last challenge is landing next to the barge in the precise position, but not letting the towboat's bow or stern make hard contact.

## Z-TPPs

• There is no one-size-fits-all Z-drive configuration for downstreaming.
• The Z-drive configuration can vary widely, depending on the amount of current.
• Some prefer a feathered aft position and adjust RPM to steer.
• Some prefer a constant RPM and adjust azimuth.
• The position of the stern dictates the position of the bow.
• Be disciplined about not approaching the barge unless you are in the comfort zone.
• You must find the sweet spot before closing on the barge.
• If you can't control the towboat in open water, you will not be able to control it when you are inches from the barge.
• Be aware of the propeller wash effect as you approach within a few feet of the barge.
• Have your abort configuration in mind before committing to the final approach to the barge.

Fig. 14-6
Downstreaming exercise
Controlling the stern

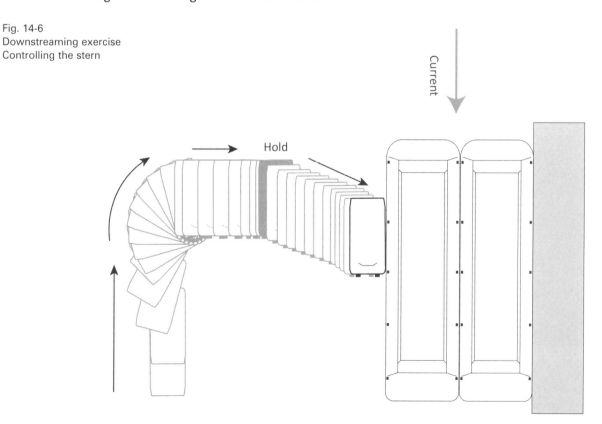

# Downstreaming Step 2:
# Touching Up One Tow Knee

1. Go to a spot about two to three boat lengths up current and off a moored barge.
2. Turn the towboat "tail up" with the stern to the current.
3. Practice hovering, stern to the current, neither moving upstream nor downstream, nor closing on the barge.
4. Once the vessel is stabilized, slide toward the barge, closing the distance.
5. Stop and hover when the inboard tow knee is about 10 feet off the barge.
6. Hold this position for one minute.
7. If successful holding for one minute, slide toward the barge and slightly downstream.
8. When the inboard tow knee is 2–3 feet off the barge, hover and hold position.
9. Hold position for one minute.
10. Move in and "touch and go" the inboard tow knee on the outboard, upstream corner of the barge.
11. After several "touch and goes," come in and "stick" and hold the push knee on the outboard, upstream corner of the barge.

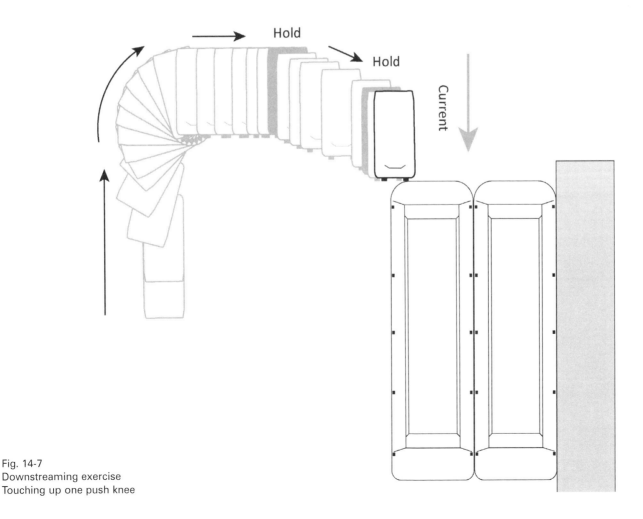

Fig. 14-7
Downstreaming exercise
Touching up one push knee

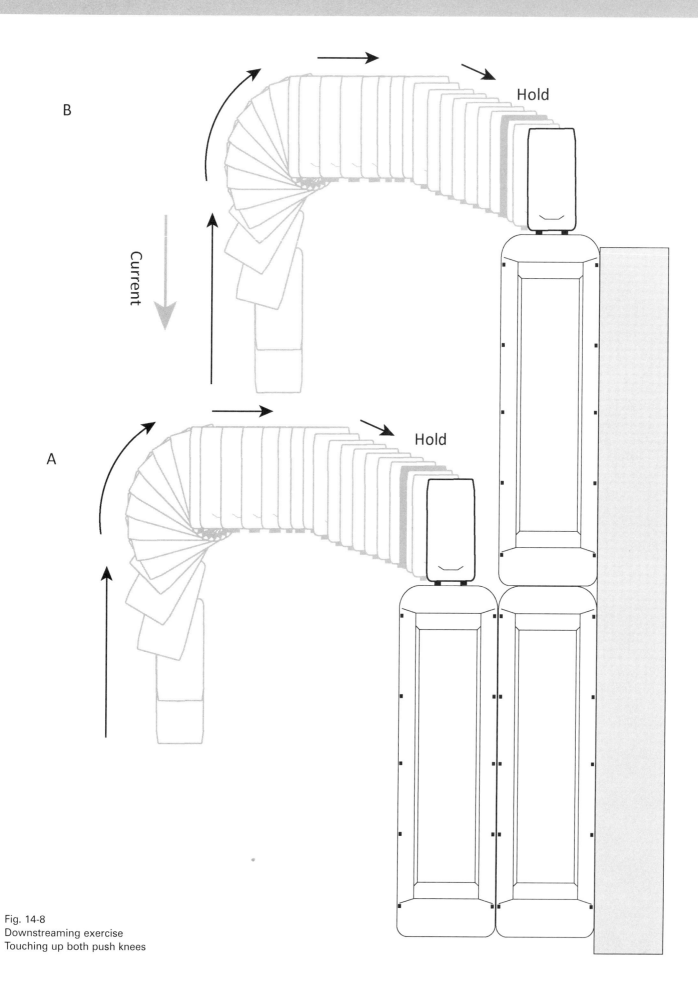

B

Current

Hold

A

Hold

Fig. 14-8
Downstreaming exercise
Touching up both push knees

# Downstreaming Step 3: Touching Up Both Tow Knees

This exercise should be taken in steps, and only after you can complete the previous two downstreaming exercises consistently and successfully. Use the scenario illustrated in fig. 14-8A first. The inside barge tier creates a safety barrier in the event the trainee can't check a slide toward the shore. Fig. 14-8B is the final step and should be attempted only if both the trainee and trainer have confidence in the trainee, and the trainer has witnessed multiple successful completions of the previous downstreaming exercises.

Different operators have different approaches to downstreaming. Some prefer to go well upstream, top around, line up with the barge, and settle straight down on the barge. Others prefer to go upstream of the barge, top around just outside the side shell, slide over into position, and settle down on the barge. Use your preferred approach in the following exercises.

Regardless of your choice, you will have to master the Z-drive skills of hovering and controlling lateral, rotation, and advance of the boat while stern to the current to complete the maneuver safely and successfully.

1. Go to your preferred downstreaming approach point.
2. Turn the towboat "tail up" with the stern to the current.
3. Practice hovering stern to the current and neither moving upstream nor downstream, nor closing on the barge.
4. Once the vessel is stabilized, close toward the barge.
5. Stop and hover when the tow knees are about 10 feet off the barge.
6. Hold this position until stabilized and in the sweet spot.
7. Slide toward the barge and downstream.
8. When the tow knees are 2–3 feet off the barge, slow the rate of closure to a "creep."
9. Move in and touch up in a position to face up.
10. Stick and hold the tow knees in the position to face up.

### Z-TPPs

- Make sure you are in the sweet spot before moving in toward the barge.
- Small hand movements are the key to working around the sweet spot.
- Keep the maneuvering speed slow.
- Keep the maneuvering speed to a creep the last few feet.
- Be wary when making contact with the barge; you will have to make immediate control adjustments to hold the stern in a stable position.
- Resist the temptation to "stick" the tow knees by rolling the controls around to thrust straight ahead.
- Have your abort configuration in mind before committing to the final approach to the barge.

# Boat-Handling Maneuvers Relative to a Moving Barge

Once you are comfortable completing the previous exercises, it is time to add an additional layer of complexity: relative motion of a drifting barge. Maneuvering around fixed objects is one thing, but catching a drifting barge is quite another. There is usually a lot going on in a short time frame that challenges a new operator. Drifting barges rarely stay stationary: they tend to drift in the current or wind, one end of the barge may drift faster than the other, and they may spin. In addition, there is usually a time restriction—the maneuver has to be completed before the drifting barge encounters other floating or shoreside obstructions.

This requires a Z-drive operator who can instantly create and constantly revise an evolving strategy of where to best position the boat to catch the barge, and have the Z-drive skills to maneuver the boat with precision. Catching a drifting barge requires strategy, timing, rapid transitions, and finesse.

# Swap Ends of a Floating Barge

This exercise requires a moderate-size barge and an open area to practice. The barge should be one that the tug or towboat can easily handle once made up, but also large enough to dampen the effects of wind or current. The practice area should have ample room for the operator to maneuver around the barge and be able to drift unobstructed.

This exercise can be done with a towboat faced up on one end, breaking out and facing up on the opposite end (fig. 14-9A), or a tugboat made up alongside one end, breaking tow and making up alongside on the diagonally opposite end (fig. 14-9B).

1. Position the tow upwind or up current to ensure enough space/time to practice the maneuver.
2. Take in lines and shift away from the barge.
3. Observe the barge motion and plan the transit and approach to the opposite end.
4. Face up or make up on the opposite end and regain control of the barge.

## Z-TPPs

- When breaking tow, use a method that minimizes the tug's or towboat's effect on the barge's drift and rotation.
- Once lines are off and the tug or towboat has backed away from the barge, take a moment to observe the set and drift of the barge.
- Create a transit and approach plan that uses the barge set and drift to assist catching the other end, rather than chasing it.
- Start the approach to the opposite end several boat lengths off—this gives you time to settle the boat down, find the sweet spot, and move in toward the barge with confidence and control.
- Keep the approach speed slow.
- Avoid large, rapid hand movements when closing in on the barge.

Fig. 14-9
Swapping ends of a tow

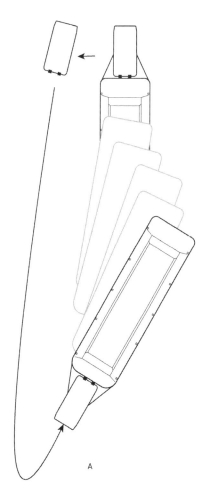

A

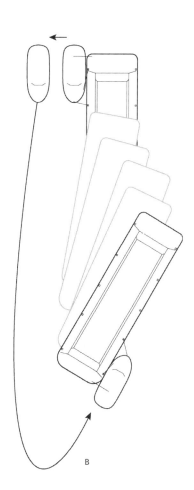

B

# Swap Ends of a Barge: Variations

Once you have swapped ends a few times, you can add some additional components to the exercise. There are many circumstances while switching ends in which you may need to nudge the barge to check up an undesired swing or set. One way of remaining in position to nudge is to walk from one end to the other, remaining close to the side shell (fig. 14-10). Use the same barge and space parameters as the previous exercise.

1. Position the tow upwind or up current to ensure enough space/time to practice the maneuver.
2. Take in lines and begin walking around one corner of the barge.
3. Once perpendicular to the side shell, continue walking down the length of the barge.
4. For practice, or if required to steer the barge, stop the walk and come in and gently bump the barge at one or two locations.
5. Walk around the corner of the barge.
6. Face up or make up on the opposite end and regain control of the barge.

## Z-TPPs

- Once the walk is initiated, use minimal RPM to continue.
- Too-much RPM and the associated propeller wash may set the barge away from your vessel.
- Try to stay off the side shell by 1 to 2 feet.

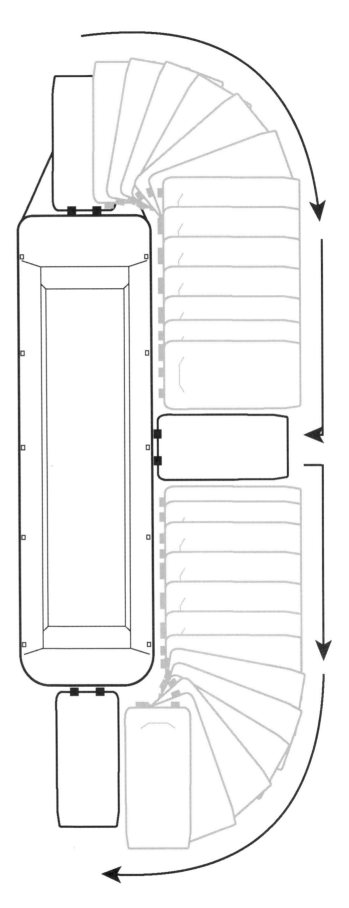

Fig. 14-10
Swapping ends—walking to the opposite end

# Transition from Towing Astern to Towing Alongside

The terminology describing the maneuver to transitioning from towing close astern to towing alongside varies from region to region: "flopping," "taking the barge alongside," and "hipping up" are some of the common terms. Regardless of the terminology, it is a basic, everyday maneuver for coastal tugs with the same challenging parameters as swapping ends of a tow. It requires strategy, timing, rapid transitions, and finesse. This exercise is best practiced with a pace vessel pushing a barge.

1. Have the pace tug/barge unit advancing ahead at 1 to 3 knots on a steady heading.
2. Maneuver the training tug in front of the barge, matching the barge's speed and heading.
3. Hold the training tug in a position approximately one boat length in front of the barge, continuing to pace it.
4. Steer until the stern of the training tug is outside the side shell of the pace tug/barge.
5. Turn so the training tug is stern up, paralleling the barge side shell and matching the barge's speed.
6. Work over to the barge, landing and holding in a position to make up alongside.
7. Pass lines and make up to the barge.

### Z-TPPs

- Have patience in holding position in front of the barge.
- Find the sweet spot before committing to the "flop" (fig. 14-11A).
- If you can't find the sweet spot while holding a stable position relative to the barge running in front of it, you will not find it while transitioning and turning stern up.
- Make sure the stern of the tug is outside the barge side shell before transitioning (fig. 14-11B).

- Be wary of using too-much thrust or large hand movements. It is easy to overrotate the tug before it is clear of the oncoming barge.
- It may be appropriate to clutch out to let the barge pass by (fig. 14-11C).
- Watch the stern! The wrong application of azimuth and thrust can easily send the stern rocketing toward the barge or underneath the rake.
- Watch the stern! This pitfall is even more pronounced if the tug is connected to heavy-chain bridles and surge gear.
- Always, always, *always* have a drive unit positioned to check the stern from closing on the barge.
- Land on the flat of the barge—avoid overlapping the rake until you have made your initial landing alongside the barge (fig. 14-11D).
- Many operators find it useful to use a walking configuration to shift the tug once alongside the barge (fig. 14-11E). This walking configuration is a walk toward the barge, keeping the tug pressed in position. Varying power and azimuth from this position enables the operator to shift the tug fore and aft, to keep the stern from going under the rake and to hold the tug in position while lines are deployed.

# Summary

New Z-drive operators comment that one of the most challenging aspects of barge work in a Z-drive is just getting the boat in position and attached to the barge. The previous training scenarios were created to give you an opportunity to hone your basic boat-handling skills in barge work applications. Real-world application of these skills will undoubtedly hold more challenges: space restrictions, time restrictions, current, and wind. Repetition is the key to competence. Use every opportunity to drill on the skill sets described in this chapter. You will learn something new on every repetition, and over time, you will gain confidence, experience, and expertise.

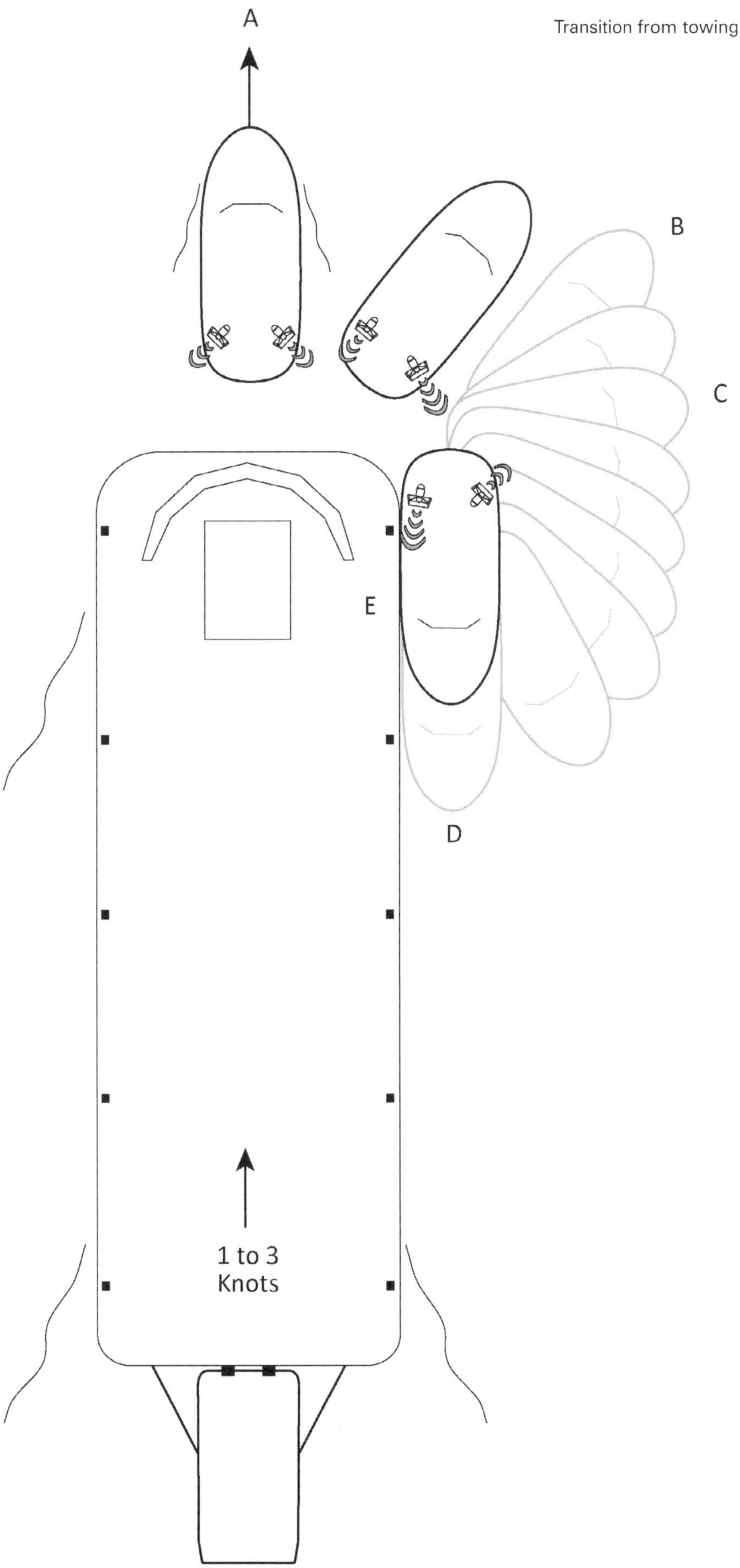

A

Fig. 14-11
Transition from towing astern to towing alongside

B

C

E

D

1 to 3
Knots

# *Chapter Fifteen*
## Barge Work

## Overview

Azimuthing Stern Drive tugs and towboats engage in all aspects of barge work: fleeting tugs, line-haul towboats, coastal tugboats, articulated tugs and barges, etc. A Z-drive tug or towboat is particularly well suited for handling barges. Their omnidirectional thrust and the capability to steer while backing sets them apart from conventionally propelled tugs or towboats. They can replicate conventional tug or towboat barge maneuvers more efficiently and with a greater safety margin, and they can engage in maneuvers that are beyond the capability of a conventionally propelled vessel.

However, it takes time, experience, practice, and an efficient learning process to maximize the capability of handling barges with a Z-drive. It is not a simple matter of transferring light-boat-handling skills and techniques to handling barges. Many Z-drive thrust configurations that are appropriate and effective for handling a light boat are inefficient with barges. Describing the details and nuances of handling barges with a Z-drive is beyond the scope of this book, but it is appropriate in the context of basic Z-drive training to introduce the fundamental principles of handling barges with Z-drive propulsion.

Many new Z-drive operators are immediately assigned to barge work once they have learned basic light-boat handling. These operators should also have knowledge of basic Z-drive barge-handling principles when they step aboard to work and continue their on-the-job training. This chapter introduces some basic guidelines to handling barges with a Z-drive. The guidelines and illustrations that follow are equally applicable to Z-drives that are pushing ahead or hipped up. There are five [5] guiding principles to keep in mind:

1. Mass—the new balance-of-thrust variable.
2. Steering and speed—maximize the link between the two.
3. Keep it simple—look for the simplest thrust solution.
4. Transitions—pre-position a drive unit.
5. Connections—stay attached to the barge.

## Mass: The New Variable

The mass of the barge adds a new variable to the balance-of-thrust equation. You can use the barge resistance to changes in motion (inertia) or its kinetic energy once in motion (momentum) to find effective and efficient balance-of-thrust configurations. You do not have to know Newton's law or the theory behind these terms. In tug- or towboater's language, you simply have more weight that you can use to your advantage by appropriately working against it or with it.

One of the principles of light-boat Z-drive handling is to use thrust configurations in which one drive unit can counter the other and the boat's primary direction of motion. That is because tugs and towboats have so much power relative to their weight. Thrust is required to stop the boat's motion. In most light-boat-maneuvering circumstances, you can't count on the weight of the boat to slow things down predictably or sufficiently. Barge handling is different. Barge mass is an additional variable in the balance-of-thrust equation that allows more flexibility in drive unit configurations.

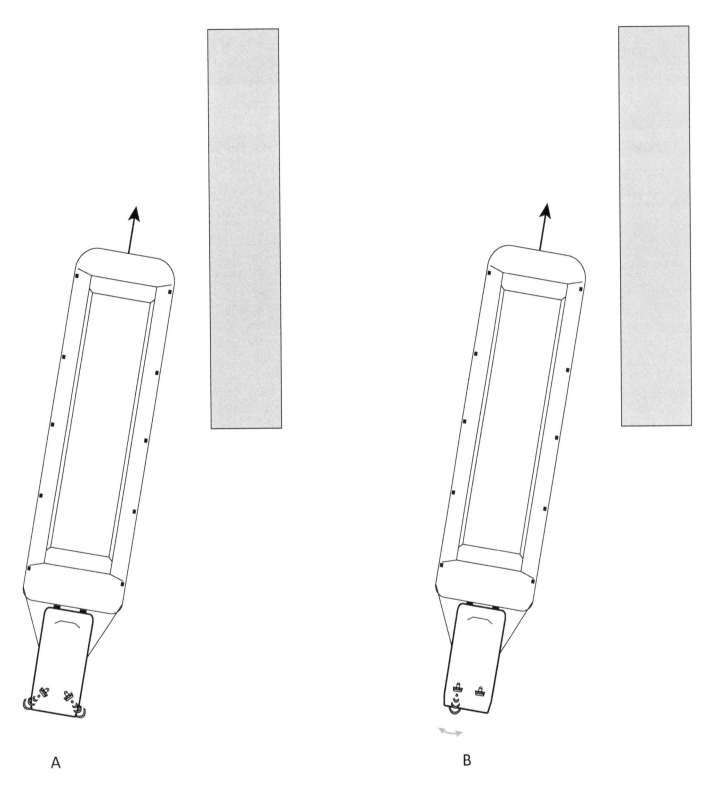

A

B

Fig. 15-1
Barge handling
Using barge mass to advantage

As an example, take the simple case of tow approaching a berth (fig. 15-1). On the approach, the objective is to maintain an appropriate speed and steer. The typical Z-drive light-boat configuration for this type of maneuver is a variation of the feathered position, in which one drive unit is opposed to the other (fig. 15-1A). However, using this with a barge results in a wasteful use of power. In other words, this configuration is using power for dual purposes: to create balance of thrust as if there was only a light boat, and to overcome the barge's inertia (resistance to motion). There is no light boat, and it is wasteful and unnecessary to use a drive unit configuration to control a light boat when there is none. The drive unit configuration should be appropriate for a self-propelled barge and should maximize the differences between the mass of a light boat and the mass of the barge. This difference gives the tug and tow characteristics that are absent on a light Z-drive tug:

- The tug and tow unit have directional stability—a light boat does not.
- The tug and tow unit does not immediately react to changes in thrust or azimuth—a light boat does.
- The mass of the barge offers a large counterbalance to the boat's thrust—the mass of the light boat is much less.

Fig. 15-1B illustrates a drive unit configuration that is simpler and more efficient: using just one drive unit to steer and manage speed. The resulting force created by one drive unit's azimuth and RPM can be the same as the combination created by two drive units. This configuration eliminates the wasted fuel of having two drive units working against each other, and substitutes barge mass for the thrust of one drive unit in the balance-of-thrust equation. In addition, it creates the option of pre-positioning the drive unit not in use. This configuration creates a balance-of-thrust equation between the barge's resistance to headway and turning, and the one drive unit thrusting ahead and steering.

# Steering and Speed: Maximize the Link between the Two

Steering and speed are always linked, whether handling a Z-drive light boat or made up to a barge. This is what creates the Z-drive 1 = 2 and 2 = 1 equations. A single change in one drive unit's azimuth or power will have two effects. The key in barge handling is to make the two effects assist in the maneuver, rather than have one assist and one fight.

Fig. 15-2 illustrates a barge making an approach to a berth that requires turning to starboard and slowing down simultaneously. A light-tug technique would be to feather both drive units in toward each other to slow down and at the same time increase the power on the starboard unit to affect the starboard turn (fig. 15-2A). However, a good portion of the starboard unit's thrust is required to overcome the port unit's undesired effect of countering the starboard turn. This is appropriate when handling the light tug or towboat, but with a barge, this is effectively fighting yourself.

A better choice would be to take advantage of the 1 = 2 equation and leave the port unit thrusting ahead and swing the starboard unit close to a 90° angle (fig. 15-2B). This one change on the starboard unit has two desired effects. It slows the tug/barge unit down because it is diminishing the starboard's headway component, adding the braking effect of the transverse-arrest position and thrusting the stern to port (bow to starboard) with no counter from the port unit. Maximizing the effect of a drive unit azimuth or power change is the key to handling barges efficiently.

It is important to have an awareness of the link between steering and speed, not just to be efficient in barge handling but also to be safe. The example in fig. 15-3 illustrates a Z-drive towing up short in which the operator created a dangerous situation by forgetting the link between steering and speed. In fig. 15-3A, the operator is on a straight heading, setting up for a turn to starboard. In fig. 15-3B, the operator has changed the azimuth on the starboard unit to turn the tug to starboard but did not compensate for the loss of speed. The 1 = 2 equation resulted in two effects—one desired, one not. The desired was turning to starboard, while the undesired was losing speed relative to the barge and being overrun.

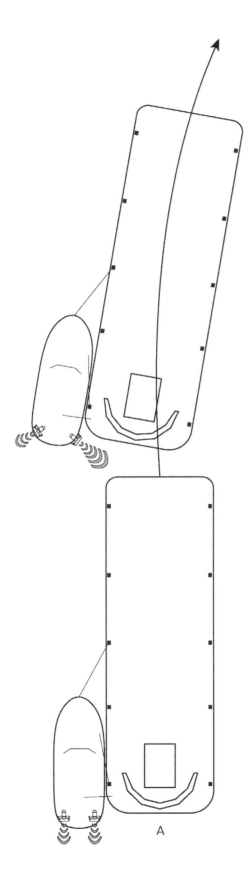
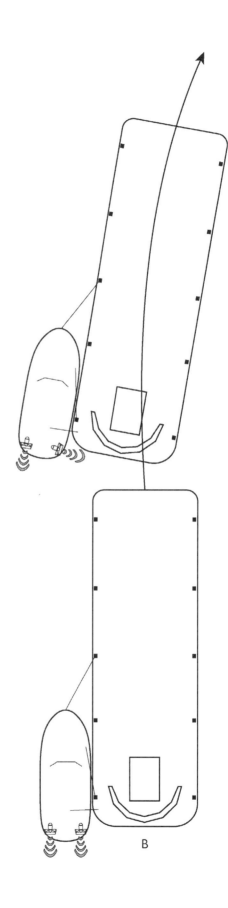

Fig. 15-2
Barge handling
Leveraging the link between steering and speed

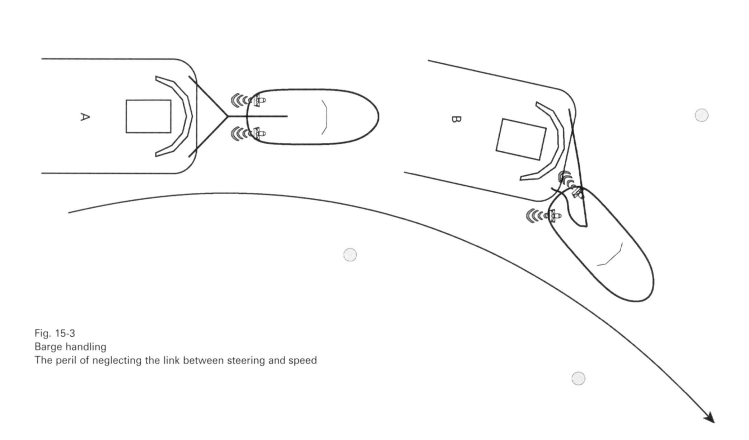

Fig. 15-3
Barge handling
The peril of neglecting the link between steering and speed

# Keep It Simple: Look for the Simplest Thrust Solution

Z-drives have an infinite number of azimuth and power combinations at the operator's disposal. It is easy for a new operator to be overwhelmed by trying to accommodate the variables of azimuth and power in two drive units, by the barge's heading and momentum, and by wind, sea, current, and obstructions and simultaneously maneuver with precision and efficiency. An experienced operator will recognize the factors that are either irrelevant to the task at hand or can be eliminated, and he will create a simple thrust solution. Most of the time the simplest thrust solution is the most efficient and most effective in handling barges.

Fig. 15-4 diagrams a simple maneuver: topping around in current but not falling downstream. The maneuver requires rotating the tow and simultaneously holding the stern up in the current. A new Z-drive operator may default to using a conventional-propulsion configuration: "twin screwing" with one drive unit backing and the other ahead and steering (fig. 15-4A). This configuration utilizes a Z-drive as an enhanced conventional towboat and does not maximize the unique capabilities of a Z-drive. A conventionally propelled towboat accomplishes this by dividing the functions between two propellers and having them work against each other to create the necessary torque to turn the tow but not set downstream.

An experienced Z-drive operator will complete this same maneuver by using one primary drive unit with minimal power and rotating it throughout the maneuver to hold the stern in place while the head of the tow carries around in the current (fig. 15-4B). The secondary drive unit (in this case the starboard) continues to rotate as well and is always in a position to augment the port unit if necessary. There is no need to have one drive unit oppose the other, as in fig. 15-4A. The simple solution is the most effective and efficient in this case.

Fig. 15-4
Complex versus simple thrust solutions

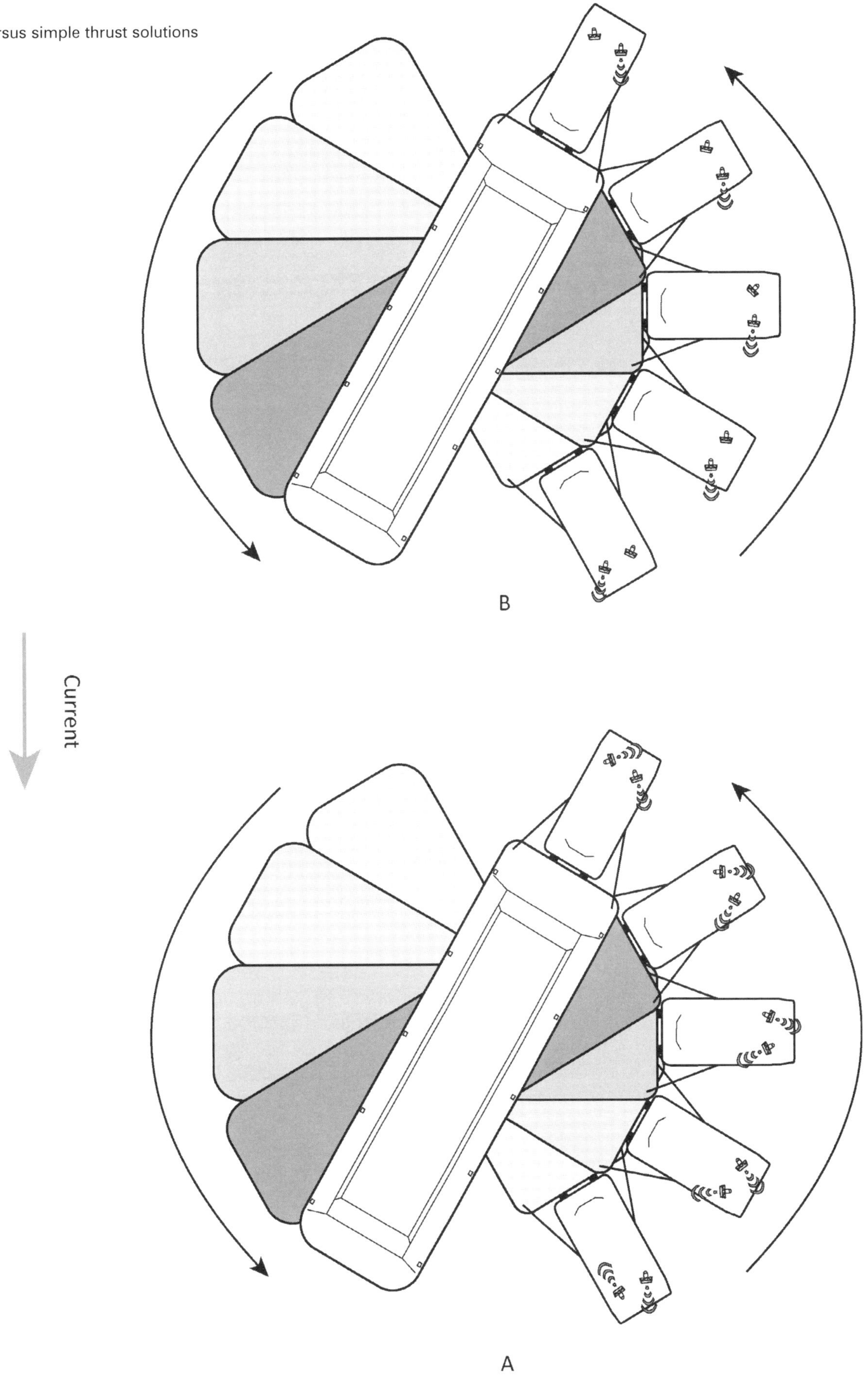

B

Current

A

# Transitions: Pre-position a Drive Unit

One of the maxims for handling a Z-drive light boat is to avoid clutching in and out. This is for engineering reasons and to maintain a balance of thrust between the two drive units to control the boat. Barge *mass* adds an additional balance-of-thrust factor that enables the operator to allow judicious clutching out and pre-positioning a drive unit with minimal effect on the heading and speed of the tow. Barge *momentum* gives the operator time to clutch out and rotate a drive unit in anticipation of the next critical thrust position.

This is a beneficial attribute, since most Z-drives do not have a means of immediately changing the rotation of the propeller. In other words, there is no immediate "reversing" a single drive unit. It can take anywhere from eleven to eighteen seconds to rotate a drive unit 180°. With a light boat, we compensate for this by working closely around drive unit configurations in which one drive unit is thrusting opposite of the other (e.g., feathered or walking configurations). This works well with a light boat due to the high power-to-weight ratio of light boats—it takes small changes in the balance to gain or check headway, sternway, rotation, or lateral movement. A barge reacts slower and takes more power to affect its motion due to its mass. It may require both drive units thrusting in the same direction just to get it moving or turning. There are circumstances when opposing thrust is appropriate in barge handling, but there are also times when using this light-boat configuration and technique just makes the boat and tow fight each other. Keeping both drive units thrusting in opposition in barge handling can be like driving a semitruck with one foot on the accelerator and one on the brake all the time. It can be done, but a lot of power and fuel is used just to overcome the effect of the self-induced opposing force.

The ability to clutch out and pre-position a drive unit is both handy and critical in barge handling. Many barge-handling circumstances call for one unit to be ready to quickly check the swing, headway, or sternway.

Fig. 15-5 illustrates a tug with a barge alongside coming into a slip to butt up against a bulkhead. Both drive units are required to thrust ahead initially to get the barge moving. Once the barge gains momentum, both drive units are brought down to low power to manage speed and steer. As the tug/barge unit approaches the slip, the operator needs to take off headway and steer simultaneously. This presents an opportunity to clutch out and rotate one drive unit to a backing position (fig. 15-5A). Clutching out reduces forward thrust and allows the drive unit to rotate with minimal effect on the barge heading. The pre-positioned drive unit is now standing by, ready to clutch in and instantly check the barge's headway as it closes on the end of the slip (fig. 15-5B).

# Connections: Stay Attached to the Barge

Staying connected to the barge sounds obvious. All the power and capability of a Z-drive is dependent on the connecting gear that transfers its thrust to the barge. However, it is easy to underestimate the power and leverage that a Z-drive may generate when made fast to a tow, and to overestimate the strength of bitts, kevels, chocks, and wires. Overzealous Z-drive operators have torn off bitts, kevels, and chocks from barges; parted mooring lines and wires; and broken up multibarge tows. A Z-drive thrusting 90° at full power on both engines generates a tremendous amount of strain on lines, wires, and attachments due to the combination of thrust and leverage created by the vessel's length. The design of a Z-drive tug or towboat can accommodate these loads, but many barges, especially older ones, cannot. If you must use full power—and there are times you must—bring the power up gradually. This reduces shock loads and lets the connecting gear take the strain slowly.

# Summary

Barge handling with a Z-drive offers the operator a wide choice of effective and efficient maneuvering options. The key is not just to replicate conventional-boat maneuvers, or Z-drive light-tug techniques, but to maximize the Z-drive's capability. Discovering this capability, harnessing it, and applying it in appropriate situations is an ongoing process. A good place to start the learning process is by replicating conventional-boat barge maneuvers and then stretching the envelope as you gain experience and confidence and a greater understanding of your Z-drive's capability. You will undoubtedly discover basic maneuvers you can safely complete in more restrictive space, time, and environmental conditions. You will also discover maneuvers that are Z-drive unique—maneuvers that you would not dream of attempting in a conventionally propelled towing vessel, but that you can do safely and consistently with a Z-drive.

You may find that you can hold up the head end of a tow in crosswinds that have conventional tows holding up on a bank. Or hold a tow stern to a heavy current while waiting for traffic to clear a bend, and not sweat that you will be carried down prematurely. Or back a barge stacked high with containers into a forty-knot wind that previously had you waiting at the dock. A Z-drive towing vessel connected to a barge is a powerful maneuvering tool; under skilled hands it can expand the repertoire of safe and efficient barge handling.

Fig. 15-5
Pre-positioning a drive unit

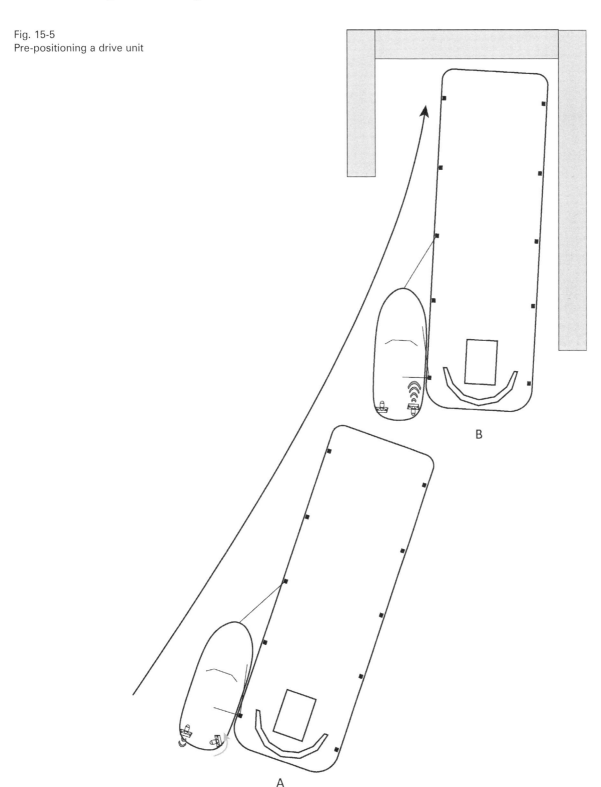

# Chapter Sixteen
## Preparing for Shipwork

## Overview

At this point in your training, you should be able to competently perform basic light-tug maneuvers: steer, stop, walk, dock, and undock. The controls should have a familiar feel in your hands. Your mind should be able to maintain a clear picture of the drive unit configurations associated with the tug's motions. The next application of your skills is to actively engage in shipwork. However, there is an intermediate step prior to beginning your on-the-job shipwork training, involving two essential shipwork skills:

1. Getting the tug into position
2. Paying out and hauling in a working line

Practicing with another tug as a reference vessel is a good way to introduce and hone these skills prior to working around live ships. As in your previous learning exercises, you will learn by making mistakes. Practicing in this training environment carries lower risk. Bouncing off the fendering of another tug is a much-better alternative than denting a ship. Although practicing with another tug is not a substitute for on-the-job learning, it will better prepare you to begin that process.

## Role of the Trainer

All the learning exercises require the presence of a skilled and experienced trainer in the wheelhouse. Follow the steps outlined in the chapter 8 section "The Role of the Trainer." Set ground rules, create learning boundaries, and ensure that the trainer is in a position to physically intervene quickly if necessary. In addition, it is important to communicate to other personnel that this is a training session, and that a trainee is at the controls. Deck personnel handling lines need to know who is at the controls. When they are working lines, their safety depends on the skill of the operator.

## Shipwork Learning Exercises

The objectives of the learning exercises are to become proficient at

1. getting the tug in position to work,
2. putting up and paying out a working line,
3. running with a slackline, and
4. hauling in and letting go of a working line.

In a simulator or live tug you will need open water and a pace (reference) vessel in motion. The exact speed of the pace vessel and the tug should be determined by a competent trainer, taking into account vessel types, design, and capability, as well as the skill level of the trainee. A well-fendered tug is an ideal live pace vessel; a small ship with low freeboard and minimal sheer or tumble is a good reference vessel in a simulator. The speeds listed in the practice exercises are general recommendations. When working through the practice scenarios, remember the five principles of conventional tug wisdom:

1. Plan ahead.
2. Consider the "what-ifs."
3. Make a good approach.
4. Stay in your comfort zone.
5. Always leave an "out."

## Getting into Position

The first step in handling an ASD tug in shipwork is getting the tug into position to work a line or push. There are three (3) basic ship assist positions:

1. Tail tug: tug bow tethered to the ship's stern
2. Tug alongside: tug either bow first or stern first to the ship's forward shoulder or aft quarter
3. Lead tug: tug tethered to the ship bow to bow

The next series of learning exercises provide opportunities to practice getting into these positions in a controlled environment.

## Tug's Bow to Pace Vessel's Stern

In a live tug or simulator, start out well aft of the pace vessel that is underway. Come up to the center of the vessel's stern and push lightly, holding position for one minute, then fall back astern. Start this practice with the pace vessel proceeding ahead on a straight course at a slow speed (3–4 knots; fig. 16-1A). Once you are comfortable at that level, practice getting into position while the pace vessel is in the middle of a slow turn (fig. 16-1B). Continue your practice by varying the pace vessel's speed and rate of turn. If the pace vessel is another ASD tug, it can create different degrees of wake turbulence by directing each of its propellers' washes slightly toward each other (fig. 16-1C).

Fig. 16-1
Tail tug getting into position

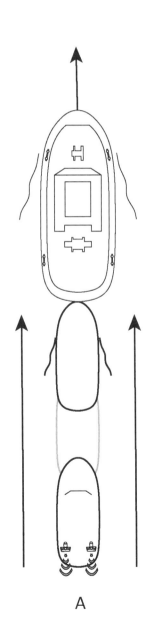

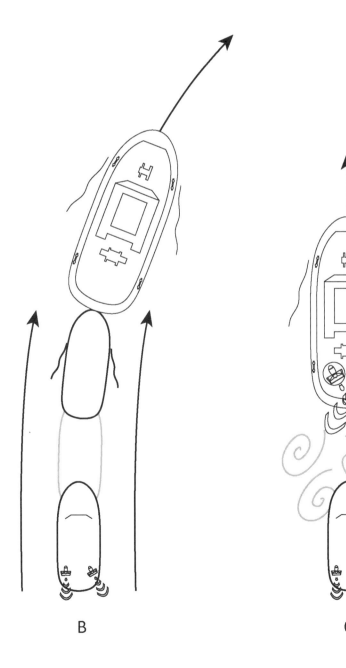

A                                          B                                          C

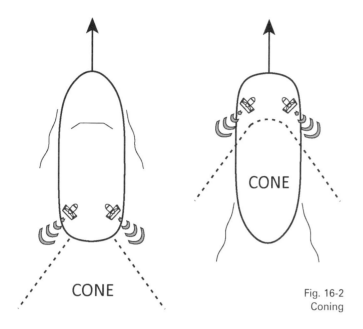

Fig. 16-2
Coning

### Coning

Coning is a term used to describe a drive unit configuration in which both units are angled in at approximately equal angles. It is a common configuration used when getting into position relative to a moving vessel. The name is derived from the shape outlined by the tug's propeller wash produced by this configuration (fig. 16-2). It is a useful configuration, since it allows the ASD operator to have precise and simultaneous control of the tug's speed and heading—the two factors most important in getting into position relative to a moving vessel.

There are two derivatives of the coning method that may be utilized to get into position as a tail tug: the first is to control the tug principally by azimuth; the second is to control it by power.

The azimuth method begins with the drive units angled in and both engine RPMs matched and set at a level that has your tug closing the distance on the pace vessel at a comfortable rate (fig. 16-3A). Speed and steering are controlled by varying the azimuth angle as your tug approaches the stern of the pace vessel. The power method begins in a similar fashion, but speed and steering are controlled by varying RPM (fig. 16-3B).

The purpose of having a primary focus on azimuth or RPM is to minimize the number of control variables the operator must juggle while maneuvering the tug. In real shipwork, you not only will be jockeying the tug into position but may also be operating the winch and talking on the radio. In addition, you will be maneuvering close aboard to the ship and its wake. Your tug may be jostled about, requiring your quick reaction and the tug's nimble response.

Many experienced ASD operators prefer the azimuth method to position the tug as a tail tug. In general, the tug responds more quickly to changes in azimuth than it does to changes in power. This difference in response time can be critical when the tug is being buffeted about by a ship's propeller wash.

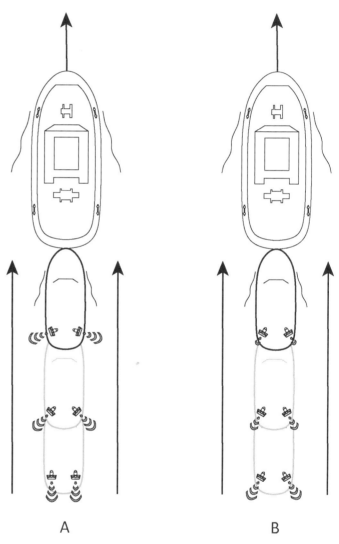

A                    B

Fig. 16-3
Coning
A: Control by azimuth
B: Control by power

Practice making different approaches to the pace vessel's stern. Become familiar with the effects associated with coming up from dead astern, directly in the center of the pace vessel's wake, and coming up off to the side, pacing the stern and moving laterally over into position (fig. 16-4).

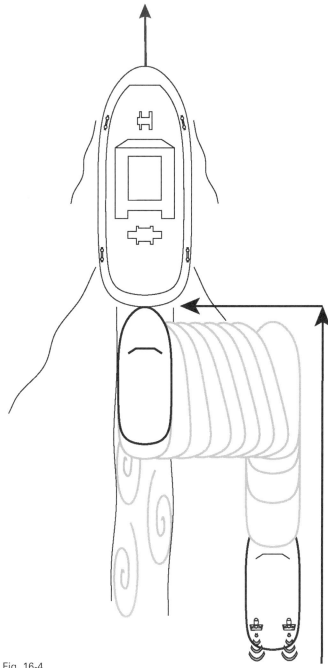

Fig. 16-4
Tail tug getting into position
Lateral approach

# Tug Alongside

In a live tug or simulator, start out aft of a pace vessel that is underway at slow speed (3–4 knots). Come up alongside the vessel and make controlled, light contact, as if to drop off a pilot or pass a working line. Hold this position for one minute and then break away. Give equal time to maneuvering both bow first (fig. 16-5A) and stern first (fig. 16-5B).

Start this practice with the pace vessel proceeding ahead, on a straight course at a slow speed. Once you are comfortable at this level, practice getting into position while the pace vessel is executing a slow turn and varying the pace vessel's speed and rate of turn.

## Z-TPPs

Whether approaching bow first or stern first, break this maneuver down into steps:

1. Come up alongside, remaining a few tug widths off the pace vessel.
2. Pace the vessel.
3. Begin to move laterally toward the vessel.
4. Close to within 10 feet of the vessel and square up, running parallel again.
5. Hold this position until you are sure you have control of the tug.
6. Move laterally toward the vessel, touch up lightly, and hold position.
• Watch the stern when maneuvering bow first!
• Become comfortable doing this maneuver stern first.
• A stern-first approach is easier to abort than a bow-first approach.
• When breaking away from alongside, bring the tug's leading end away first—bow when running bow first, stern when running stern first.

## Tiller Method

In a nautical context, tiller refers to a horizontal bar fitted to the head of a rudder for the purpose of turning the rudder to steer. Typically it is found on small vessels in which the vessel has only one rudder to steer by. ASD operators equate a single drive unit to a single rudder and adopted this term to refer to a method of managing speed and steering with one drive unit. It is an effective technique, particularly when coming alongside stern first. In the case of coming alongside the pace vessel, one drive unit is the tiller unit, while the other drive unit stands by to push the stern toward or away from the pace vessel if necessary (fig. 16-5B). The advantage of this method is its simplicity—speed and steering lie under one hand. It works well going stern first because all the critical action is taking place at the stern: steering, propulsion, pivot point, and contact point are located in close physical proximity to the drive unit being utilized as a tiller. The tug's stern quickly responds to any changes in amount and direction of thrust, and the operator has pinpoint control of the stern and the tug.

### Coning Method

The coning method can be used to come alongside either bow first or stern first, adjusting azimuth, power, or both to control the tug. It is the preferred method when running bow first (fig. 16-5A).

The tiller method is not as effective when an ASD tug is bow first coming alongside another moving vessel. The reason is simple. When you are running stern first, the stern is your point of initial contact. To move your point of contact closer to the pace vessel, it takes a small hand movement and small change in thrust to move the stern a few feet.

Remember, the stern steers the tug. Bow first requires a larger movement of the stern to move the bow a few feet and subsequently larger hand movements, and a larger change in thrust. If using only one drive unit, a large change of thrust is required to get the bow to move toward the pace vessel. Once the tug begins to close the distance to the pace vessel, the operator may find the drive unit too far out of position to recover in time. There may not be enough time or space for the stern to swing toward the pace vessel and check the bow, and as a result the tug makes hard contact with the pace vessel.

Fig. 16-5
Coming alongside
A: Bow first
B: Stern first

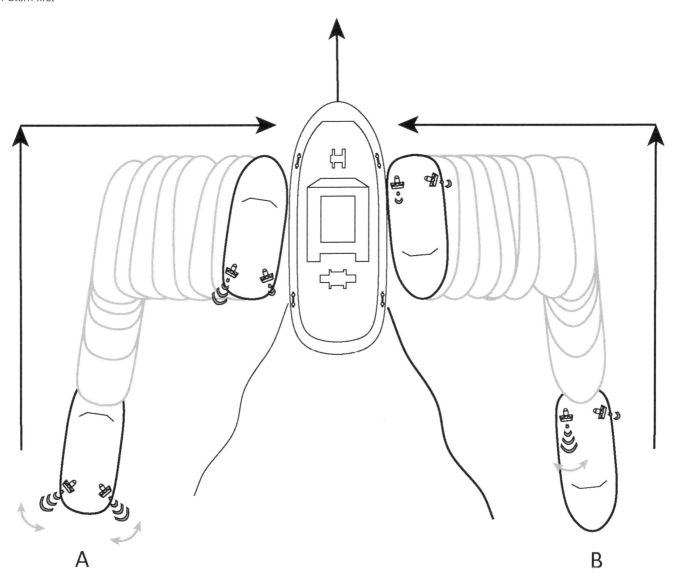

A

B

When coming alongside a moving vessel bow first, the danger is in "losing the bow." That is, letting the bow fall off so far that room is lacking to swing the stern around to "catch the bow" (fig. 16-6A). This requires that you have pinpoint control of the stern and can instantly adjust the stern in either direction. Coning with two drive units—each able to quickly counter the other—can instantly move the stern in the direction required as you close on the pace vessel (fig. 16-6B). However, the tiller method does not provide the same quickness running bow first. The tiller drive unit must rotate quite a few degrees and takes too long to catch the bow when running close aboard another vessel.

### Holding Position

Once alongside, keep the tug pressed into the pace vessel by using the outboard engine to work ahead a little stronger when bow first (fig. 16-7A), or thrust toward the pace vessel when stern first (fig. 16-7B).

### Breaking Away

Breaking away is accomplished by getting the leading end of the tug to break away from the pace vessel first. When running bow first, it is the bow; when running stern first, this is the stern.

In the bow-first mode, breaking the bow away can be challenging. One method is to turn the outboard unit 90°, thrusting toward the pace vessel at an idle. This will create drag on the outboard side of the tug, causing the stern to tip in and the bow to break away from being alongside. Once the bow is tipped out, power is applied to the inboard unit to clear the tug's stern and drive away from the pace vessel (fig. 16-8A). In the stern-first mode, breaking away is easier. Simply turn the drive units so they are thrusting away from the pace vessel to break the stern away, apply power, and steer clear (fig. 16-8B).

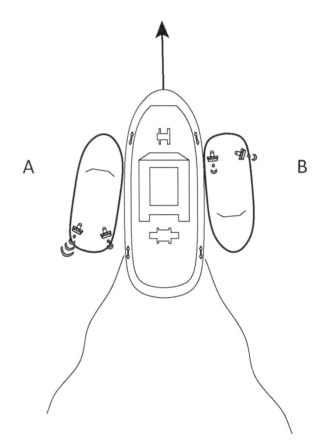

A                                        B

Fig. 16-7
Holding position

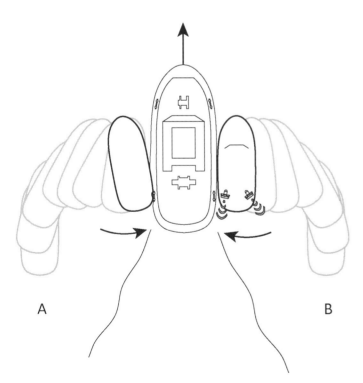

A                                        B

Fig. 16-6
Watch the stern
A: "Lost the bow, hit the stern"
B: Control the stern, control the bow

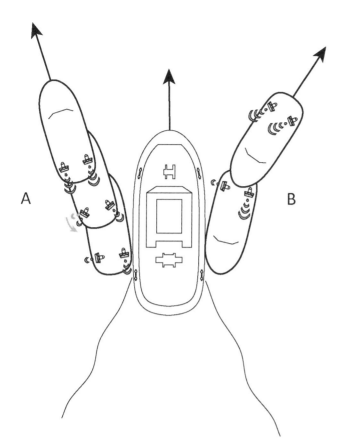

Fig. 16-8
Breaking away from alongside

## Bow to Bow

Going bow to bow with a moving vessel requires intense concentration and a deft touch on the controls. This exercise gives you the opportunity to practice this maneuver until you trust your hands to drive the tug in this position.

In a live tug or simulator, start out forward of a pace vessel that is underway at slow speed (3–4 knots). Approach the pace vessel bow to bow (fig. 16-9):

1. Make light contact on the pace vessel's port bow and hold position for one minute (fig. 16-9A).
2. Shift to a stem-to-stem position and hold for one minute (fig. 16-9B).
3. Shift to the pace vessel's starboard bow and hold for one minute (fig. 16-9C).

Repeat this exercise multiple times. Start this practice with the pace vessel proceeding ahead, on a straight course at a slow speed. Once you are comfortable at this level, practice getting into position while the pace vessel is executing a slow turn and by varying the pace vessel's speed and rate of turn.

### Note
There is a critical difference between this learning exercise and working a live ship. You would not routinely be touching the stem of a live ship under these circumstances. There are two reasons for this. One is that ships have large flairs and overhangs at the bow and may have a bulbous bow as well. Any contact could result in damage to the tug or ship. Second, the tug loses maneuverability if the bow touches up when the tug is running stern first, bow to bow with a ship. Bow-to-bow contact can cause the tug's stern to sheer or its bow to be pushed away, causing the tug to get spun around and caught under the ship's flare.

The learning exercise includes making bow-to-bow contact for two reasons. The first is to give you a feel for the loss of tug maneuverability caused by bow contact. The second is to challenge your tug-handling skills. It requires quick reactions to hold position once the tug's bow makes contact.

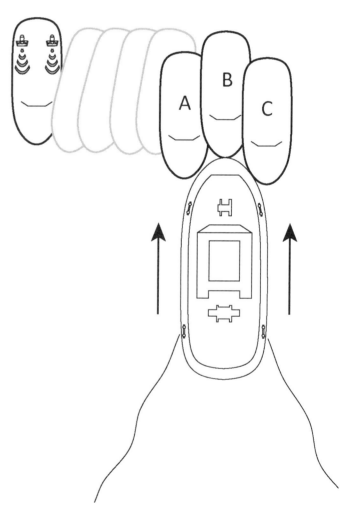

Fig. 16-9
Bow to bow

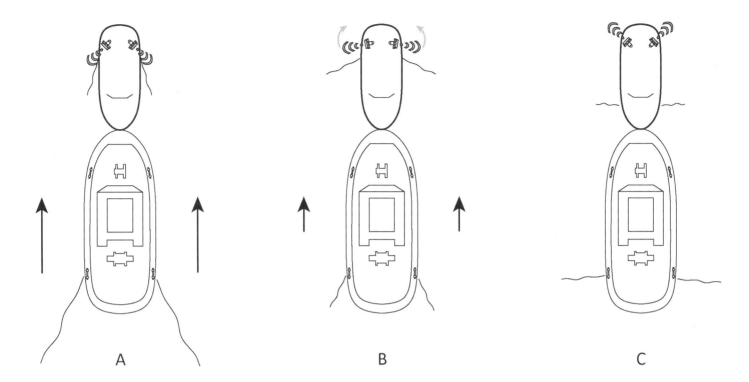

Fig. 16-10
Bow to bow, bringing the pace vessel to a stop

You can make this practice exercise even more challenging by going stem to stem and gradually pushing harder and harder against the pace vessel until you bring it to a stop (fig. 16-10). First, make light bow-to-bow contact (fig. 16-10A); second, slow the pace vessel by pushing against the pace vessel stem, still holding position (fig. 16-10B); and third, increase the push until you have brought the pace vessel to a stop by matching its forward thrust (fig. 16-10C). Throughout the exercise, the pace vessel should maintain a constant heading and amount of forward thrust.

### Z-TPPs

Going bow to bow with a moving vessel is challenging. No single tried-and-true method works every time on all ASD tugs. The key is to find a technique that both matches your skill level and accommodates the tug's handling characteristics. The shape of the stern, beam of the tug, length of the keel, and location and size of the skeg all affect how the tug handles moving stern first. Specific ASD designs may lend themselves better to one over another technique.

The methods for going bow to bow fall into three categories—canting, coning, and tiller.

### Canting Method

Canting is similar to coning, except that the drive units' propeller wash is slanted in toward the tug's keel (fig. 16-11A). This technique is favored by many ASD operators because it tends to "calm" the tug's bow. One of the difficulties of going bow to bow is that you do not have direct, positive control of the tug's bow. It follows the stern but may wander back and forth. You are simultaneously positioning both ends of the tug but have direct control over only one end—the stern. The canting method stabilizes the bow so that it follows the stern in a more predictable fashion. Once the operator finds the correct, canted azimuth to keep the tug and its bow tracking straight, he steers the stern (and thus spots the bow) by adjusting the power of each drive unit.

### Coning Method

The coning method can also be used when going bow to bow (fig. 16-11B). When utilizing this configuration, many ASD operators prefer to steer and manage speed by varying power and keeping the azimuth constant as much as possible. There are two principal advantages to this method. The first is that it helps dampen the motion of the tug's stern. The second is that it simplifies the task of maneuvering by minimizing the azimuth variable. One of the common pitfalls of going bow to bow is that the new ASD operator has a tendency to oversteer the stern. Because the tug reacts slower to changes in power than it does to changes in azimuth, using power as the primary maneuvering tool helps dampen the tug's motion. However, one of the disadvantages of the coning method is that the bow may be more skittish than in the canting or tiller methods.

### Tiller Method

The tiller method is also favored by many experienced ASD operators when the pace vessel is moving at a relatively slow speed (fig. 16-11C). It combines the advantages of the canting method with the simplicity of the tiller method. Usually the drive unit closest to the pace vessel is designated as the tiller drive unit. Because this unit is offset from the tug's centerline when it thrusts straight astern, it will tend to turn the tug's stern away and the bow toward the pace vessel. To counter this effect, the operator will naturally slant the drive unit in, bringing into play the bow stabilization associated with the canting method. The non-tiller drive unit is usually standing by at a 90° position to thrust the stern one way or the other. The choice is personal. Some prefer to position the non-tiller drive unit to thrust the tug's stern toward the pace vessel to help push the tug's stern into position. Others prefer to have it positioned to thrust away should aborting the maneuver become necessary.

Note in fig. 16-11C that it looks like the drive unit configuration should continue to move the tug's stern to starboard. This is not necessarily the case. This is a good example of the tipping point between a drive unit's drag and its thrust. The starboard drive unit is canted in and the port drive unit is idling, thrusting straight to starboard. While the port drive unit is idling and thrusting to starboard, it is also creating significant drag in the water. In this case the drag effect tends to turn the tug's stern to port. The thrust effect is to starboard. Whether the effect of the port drive unit is to starboard or port depends on which effect overrides the other. The tug's speed through the water and the braking effect of the propeller wash determine the amount of drag; the power setting determines the amount of thrust force to starboard. It is a multivariable equation best solved by the hands on the basis of how the tug feels and the operator's maneuvering objective.

This practice scenario offers an opportunity for you to become familiar with all three techniques. Take advantage of it to get a sense of which method works best for you and the tug.

Fig. 16-11
Bow to bow
Canting, coning, and
tiller methods

A    B    C

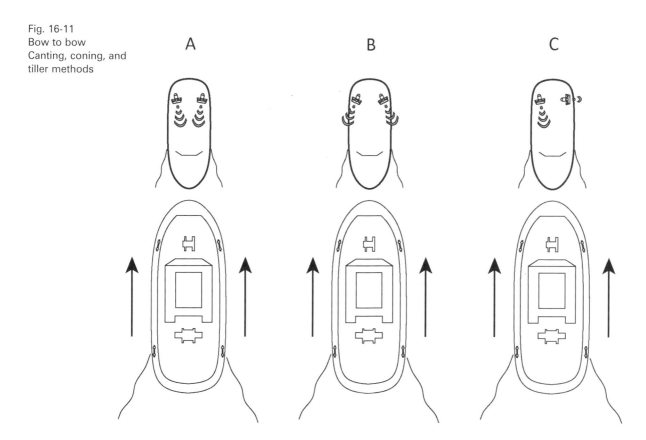

# Paying Out and Hauling In

The most basic skill of working a line is to be able to pay it out smoothly and haul it back without putting in too-much slack or jerking on it during the process. Applying pull to a line is not an all-or-nothing affair. It is not like an on/off switch; rather, it is like a rheostat. A competent ASD operator must be skilled at applying varying amounts of pull to a line while simultaneously maneuvering the tug. This requires a skilled and light touch both with drive unit and winch controls. The following exercises practice this skill both in static and dynamic environments.

This exercise is best done in a live tug, since it provides you with an opportunity to become familiar with the idiosyncrasies of the winch system aboard your tug. Start out with a headline attached to a dock bollard (fig. 16-12A).

1. Back out slowly, paying out approximately 100–150 feet of line.
2. Stop the tug.
3. Set the winch brake.
4. Slowly take a light strain to stretch the line.
5. Hold this strain and tug position for one minute.
6. Ease off, release the winch brake, and begin hauling in.
7. As you haul in, keep the same amount of slack in the line as you drive back to the bollard or bitt.

Break this skill down into three learning steps:

1. Have the trainee operate the vessel and the trainer run the winch.
2. Have the trainee run the winch and the trainer operate the tug.
3. Have the trainee operate both simultaneously.

Repeat this exercise multiple times. Once you are comfortable in this static environment, practice utilizing a pace vessel proceeding ahead on a straight course and at a slow speed (3–4 knots; fig. 16-12B). Make the tug's headline fast to the stern of the pace vessel. If practical, lead the line through the pace vessel's centerline aft chock or make the line fast to the pace vessel's tow bitt. Continue your practice by varying the pace vessel's speed and rate of turn.

## Z-TPPs

- Try to make either the winch or the tug speed constant and adjust the other to match.
- When first taking a strain on the headline, ease into it slowly. Most ASD headlines are high modulus polyethylene (HMPE) lines with no or little stretch.

- Be wary of putting too-much slack in the headline and having it hang up on the tug's fenders. Some tugs have protrusions in their fendering that could snag the line if it has too-much slack and drifts down onto the bow of your tug. This is a good way to ruin a very expensive line.
- Winch speed is usually the limiting factor on tug speed when hauling in. You want to make sure you do not overrun the line as you are hauling in.

## Lead Tug: Tethered Bow to Bow

Positioning a tug bow to bow with a ship is used primarily to assist in steering the ship's bow and to tow the ship forward at minimal speed. A difficult aspect of this maneuver is holding the tug in position while the line is passed to or cast off. Working the winch and the Z-drive controls simultaneously can be a challenging task, all the while remaining in position. The purpose of the exercises that follow is to acquire these skills in a controlled environment.

In a live tug or simulator, start out forward of a pace vessel that is underway at very slow speed (2–3 knots). Practice the following maneuvering sequence while the pace vessel is still moving ahead:

1. Go bow to bow and pass the tug's headline. Do not contact the pace vessel's bow.
2. Pay out 100 feet of headline and run in line / slackline for one minute (fig. 16-13A). Be careful to keep the slack headline from going underneath the pace vessel.
3. Stretch your line and begin to tow the pace vessel on a steady course (fig. 16-13B).
4. Have the pace vessel stop its propulsion and use your tug to turn the pace vessel both to port and starboard (fig. 16-13C).
5. After executing several port and starboard turns, tow the pace vessel on a steady course.
6. Have the pace vessel engage its propulsion and increase to a moderate speed (5–6 knots), holding a steady course.

Once you are comfortable assisting the pace vessel at moderate speeds and on a straight course, vary its speed and direction. Try turning the pace vessel to port while it has right rudder; remain in line / slackline with the pace vessel while it executes port or starboard turns. Experiment with these variables so that you begin to acquire a feel for the limits both of the tug and your ability to operate from this position. Finish the practice by hauling in the tug's headline, holding position by the pace vessel's bow, and casting off the headline.

### Z-TPPs

- Keep your line loads low. This is a practice exercise! You can easily overpower the pace vessel.
- Remember, the stern drives the tug.

- Positioning the tug effectively means positioning the stern first.
- Be cautious about large headline angles to the pace vessel at moderate to high speeds.

Fig. 16-12
Paying out and hauling in

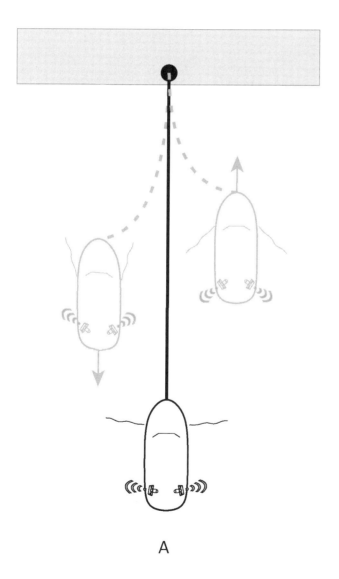

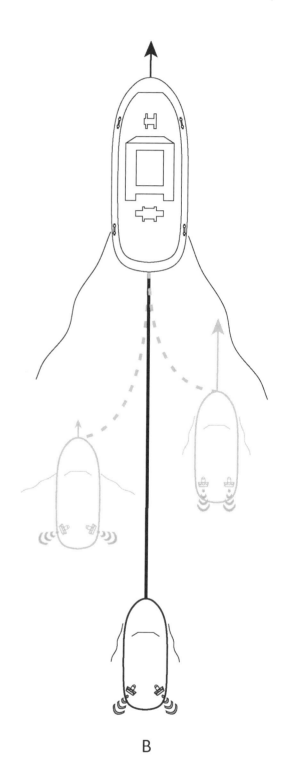

A

B

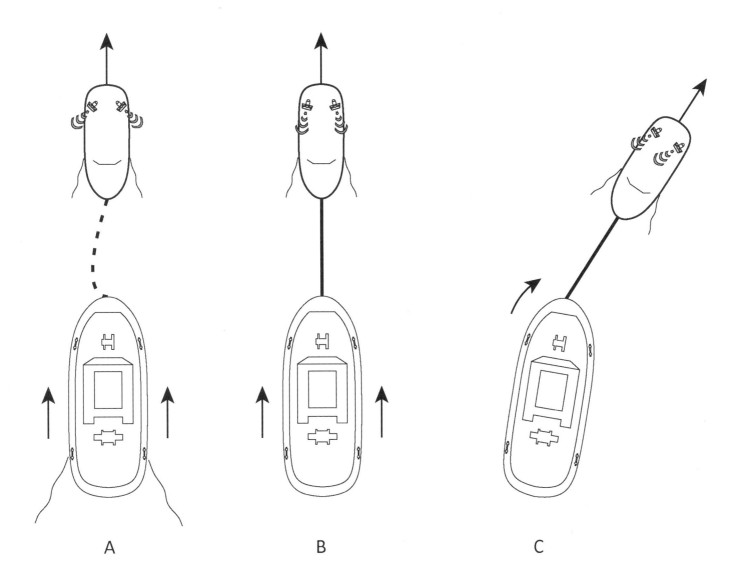

A                           B                           C

Fig. 16-13
Working a headline bow to bow underway

# Practice Drills

### Practice Drill No. 1

The objective of this drill is to practice positioning the tug in the three basic assist positions. In a simulator or live tug you will need a pace vessel proceeding ahead, on a steady course at moderate speed (5–6 knots).

1. Start aft of the pace vessel, come up from astern, and position the tug bow to stern (fig. 16-14A). Hold position for one minute.

2. Shift to the pace vessel's port side and come in alongside, bow first (fig. 16-14B). Hold position for one minute.
3. Break away, turn 180°, and position the tug bow to bow with the pace vessel. Touch lightly on the pace vessel's port bow, stem, and starboard bow. Hold position off the starboard bow for one minute (fig. 16-14C).
4. Break away and, stern first, come alongside the pace vessel's starboard side (fig. 16-14D). Hold for one minute.
5. Break away, turn 180°, and finish with the tug's bow to the pace vessel's stern (fig. 16-14A).

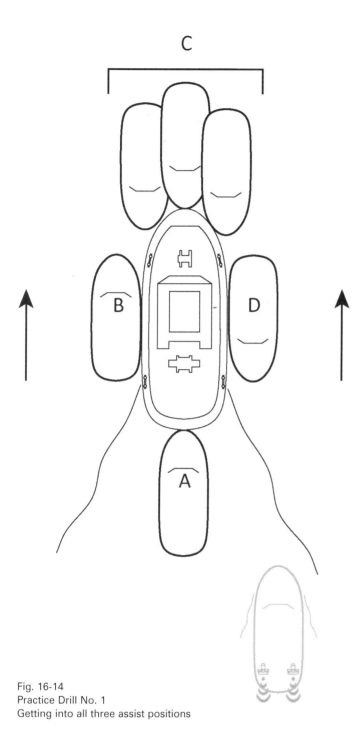

Fig. 16-14
Practice Drill No. 1
Getting into all three assist positions

## Practice Drill No. 2

The objective of this drill is to quickly reposition the tug. You will need a finger pier or a vessel moored in a manner that allows access to both sides of the pier or vessel.

1. Position the tug, pushing on the finger pier at 90° (fig. 16-15A).
2. Back away and quickly shift the tug to the opposite side of the finger pier or moored vessel.

3. Position the tug, pushing on the finger pier at 90° and directly opposite the starting push point (fig. 16-15B).

Once you have successfully completed the practice drills multiple times and your trainer feels you are ready, you should move your ASD tug learning into the on-the-job environment. Although you may have practiced either in a simulator or with smaller vessels, there is no substitute for the experience of working a large ship. The next chapter serves as a guide for safely acquiring that experience.

### Z-TPP

Be mindful of negative water flow around a clutched-out drive unit. Negative water flow is when water flows from the discharge side of the propeller nozzle to the suction side, rather than in the normal direction. This may cause the propeller to freewheel opposite its normal direction of rotation. When the drive unit is clutched in, it must first stop the rotation of the propeller going the wrong way, reverse its rotation, and bring it up to the desired RPM with the correct rotation. Too-much negative water flow may cause the drive unit clutch to slip or the engine to stall, or permanently damage the clutch and drive train—any of which will render the drive unit inoperable at a critical maneuvering point. Pre-positioning a drive unit should be done only at slow maneuvering speeds.

Fig. 16-15
Practice Drill No. 2
Repositioning the tug

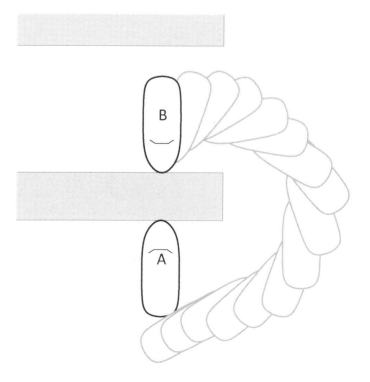

# Notes

# *Chapter Seventeen*
## Shipwork

## Overview

Before engaging in shipwork—one of the principal applications of ASD tug technology—you should be well versed in basic ASD light-tug-handling skills. "Well versed" means more than speaking about it intelligently; it means being able to run the ASD tug through its paces: turning, stopping, hovering, walking, and docking while feeling one with the tug, and having confidence that your hands are instinctively making the right movements. In other words, you can drive the tug through the basic light-tug maneuvers without thinking. Your mind will have plenty to think about in shipwork: what is the best approach to the ship, where to position the tug, and how to best meet the pilot's directions to push or pull. Your mind will be occupied figuring out *what* you want the tug to do. There will not be much thinking capacity left to figure out *how* to make the tug move. That knowledge must already be embedded firmly in your hands.

## On-the-Job Training

On-the-job (OTJ) training is the bridge between the light-tug-handling skills you have acquired and their application in shipwork. As in your previous practice, it will take repetition and experience to become competent and comfortable assisting ships. You have undoubtedly discovered by now that you have acquired many of your ASD skills by learning from mistakes. Unfortunately, the consequences of a mistake in the OTJ environment can be serious and costly to trainee, trainer, crew members, vessels, and companies. A good learning program incorporates opportunities to make mistakes while minimizing their effect. This book's practice scenarios create a controlled environment by specifying the vessel, space, and maneuvering parameters. The same principle can be applied in the OTJ environment. Although fewer parameters can be controlled, the principle still stands of minimizing risk by managing controllable factors.

## Managing Risk in OTJ Learning

The first step in managing risk in OTJ training is to take proactive control of controllable factors:

### Have a Qualified Trainer Present

A qualified trainer should be present in the wheelhouse. "Qualified" does not necessarily mean the captain with the most experience or the most senior position. An outstanding captain is not necessarily a competent trainer. The trainer utilized in OTJ training not only must have extensive experience and skill handling ASD tugs but should also possess knowledge of effective communication and teaching techniques, and experience using them in training situations. He must know when it is appropriate to intervene, and be ready, willing, and able to do so if necessary.

### Attitude

It is important to realize that most of the people and equipment involved in on-the-job training are not there to train or teach; they are there to do a job. The container ship coming into port, its pilot and crew, the longshoremen standing by at the terminal, and the corporations that operate these vessels and terminals are not in the business of training. They are in the business of marine transportation—moving goods and providing services over water in an efficient and profitable manner.

As a trainee, you must recognize and appreciate this dynamic and understand that their business has priority over your training. That being said, many captains and pilots are grateful for the OTJ training opportunities provided to them in the past, and they are pleased to be able to pass the gift on to others. However, the gift does not extend to taking on an unreasonable risk to their reputation or to the job at hand to accommodate a training scenario. An attitude of respect and appreciation for those who are enabling your OTJ training goes a long way to making it a productive experience.

### Know Your Tug

You should be familiar with the equipment you will be operating in the on-the-job training scenario. Coming alongside a ship is not the time to become familiar with the tug's controls and response. Before engaging in shipwork, you should be well versed in the tug's controls, winch operation, and handling idiosyncrasies. The risks in training should be associated with the shipwork maneuver, not basic knowledge of how your tug operates.

### Know Yourself

Just as the tug has operating capabilities and limits, so does the operator. You will bring a personal level of skill and experience each time you enter an OTJ-learning scenario. Be aware of your limits and capabilities. OTJ learning usually involves a trainee "pushing the envelope" of his capability. The key to a successful training experience is to expand the envelope, not break it. That can be done only if you know your personal limits and have the self-discipline to stay within them. If you have practiced only coming alongside another vessel at 3 to 4 knots in daylight conditions, you should be wary of attempting the same maneuver at night when the ship is moving at 8 knots. Learning when to say "I'm not ready to do this" is sometimes the most valuable lesson of all.

### Know the Job

Find out all you can about the ship job before arriving at the job site. A little homework before on-the-job training goes a long way toward preventing a training accident. Find out the length of the ship and its flair or tumble, chock and cleat location, berth location, and expected ship maneuvering sequence, as well as, of course, the position and working lines expected of your tug. The more information and details you gather ahead of time, the more your mind will be free to focus on driving the tug.

### Have a Training Plan

Both trainer and trainee should create a training plan. In general, the training plan should work from the simple to the more complex. Any maneuvering sequence is made of components. By breaking down the maneuver into its components, a step-by-step training plan can be made. These steps should be sequenced so that the trainee does not go to the next step until he is competent and qualified with the preceding steps.

Take as an example coming alongside a ship. The first step may simply be picking a spot off the ship and pacing it while maintaining a constant distance off. That step may need to be repeated until the trainee gains confidence and trust in his hands. The next step would be closing to within a tug width and again pacing the ship while maintaining a constant distance off. Once the trainee knows he can manage the rate of closure on the ship, he can proceed to the next step: making contact. Subsequent steps can add additional tasks, such as communicating on the radio and operating the winch.

The training plan should be built around learning steps that fit the trainee's skill and experience. In addition, the plan should incorporate the five principles of conventional tug wisdom:

1. Plan ahead.
2. Consider the "what-ifs."
3. Make a good approach.
4. Stay in your comfort zone.
5. Always leave an "out."

# Communicate

Pilots have a complex task. Bringing a laden ship into or out of berth; directing assist tugs; managing the personality and cultural dynamics on the ship's bridge; utilizing unfamiliar propulsion, navigational, and communication systems; and, of course, dealing with effects of wind, sea, and current can make for trying days on the job. In OTJ-training situations, the trainee should introduce himself to the pilot and ask permission to use the job at hand as a training environment. This is a professional courtesy and acknowledgment that the pilot is in the best position to decide whether a training session is appropriate under the specific circumstances of the ship's anticipated maneuvers.

In addition, the trainee should let the pilot know who the trainer will be. Pilots may get uneasy with an unfamiliar voice on the radio. All parties should be assured that the training session is under the supervision of a familiar and competent operator, and that he is standing behind the unfamiliar voice on the radio.

# Tug Handling in Shipwork

Handling an ASD in shipwork requires a high level of skill extending beyond being a competent boat handler. The design of a modern ASD tug centrally locates communication, navigation, winch, and drive control functions within easy reach of the operator. An operator may be called on to simultaneously speak on the radio, maneuver the tug, and pay out or haul in line. In short, a lot may be going on when working a tug in shipwork. At this level, tug handling is but one of many critical skills a competent ASD tug operator must possess. In addition to handling the tug, he must be able to quickly prioritize and address multiple tasks in a dynamic and high-risk environment. In this context the ASD operator must accommodate

- the relative motion of the ship,
- the hydrodynamic interaction between ship and tug, and
- the direction and amount of force to be applied to the ship.

Decision making at this level requires a solid understanding of the factors influencing the interaction between ship and tug. This interaction creates three significant differences between shipwork and light-tug docking maneuvers: relative motion, disturbed water, and the allocation of horsepower for dual purposes.

## Relative Motion

The first difference, relative motion, is due to the fact that much shipwork takes place both with tug and ship in motion. In this environment, ASD tug handling becomes an exercise in relative motion and relies heavily on visual cues. From the tug handler's perspective, the appearance of ship motion and speed becomes an added reference to judge the tug's direction and speed. This appearance can be deceptive, requiring the operator to learn a new set of visual cues and drive unit configurations to

associate with maneuvering one vessel in reference to another in motion.

## Disturbed Water

The second difference between shipwork and light-tug docking is that the tug is working mainly in and around disturbed water. The ship's propeller wash and the hull's suction and pressure zones create hydrodynamic forces that influence both the tug's speed and direction.

## Allocation of Horsepower

The third difference is that in shipwork, the operator must allocate the tug's horsepower for two primary purposes: one is to hold the tug in position relative to the ship, and the other is to apply a pulling or pushing force on the ship. Each ASD tug has a finite amount of thrust capability. In shipwork, the ASD operator must learn the thrust configurations that appropriately portion out the tug's available horsepower to meet the maneuvering requirements both of the tug and the ship.

The three differences reinforce the one-to-many principle of ASD drive unit configurations. In many shipwork maneuvers, the drive unit configurations that work well maneuvering as a light tug may fail miserably working a ship. It is not that the principles of ASD handling have changed; rather, it is a matter of applying those principles in more-complex and more-variable circumstances. It is similar to the difference in basketball between shooting a free throw and dribbling down the court and making a jump shot. At the free-throw line, the player has the time to apply fundamental shooting principles in a static situation—dominant hand behind the ball resting on the fingertips, the other hand cradling the ball, feet shoulder-width apart, eyes focused on the rim, knees bent, and the shooting hand following through toward the basket. These principles do not change when making a jump shot during a game, but the principles must be applied within the relative motion of the other nine players' movements, the bodies and hands that are attempting to disrupt the shot, and the physical effort expended to get into position to shoot the ball.

An example in the realm of shipwork is the difference between lateral motion (walking) toward

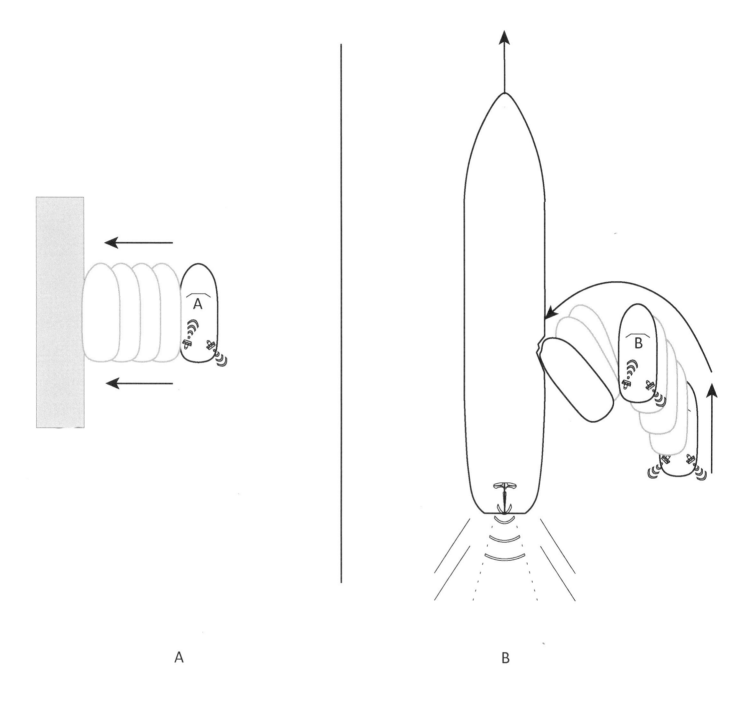

A

B

Fig. 17-1
Lateral motion
Still water versus relative motion

a dock and moving laterally to come alongside a ship underway (fig. 17-1). The drive unit configuration that is used to walk toward a dock (fig. 17-1A)—one unit angled to thrust ahead and in, the other thrusting astern—is required to manage the tug's fore and aft, heading (yaw), and lateral directions as it approaches the dock. But applying this same configuration coming alongside a moving ship can be disastrous (fig. 17-1B). Creating lateral motion relative to a moving ship shares two of the three light-tug docking requirements: managing heading and lateral motion. The third—fore and aft motion—is different. In the docking scenario, the operator must be able to move the tug both ahead and astern to position the tug relative to the dock. In the ship scenario, there is no need to position the tug by creating sternway. Instead, this position is attained by managing the tug's forward speed relative to the ship. When pacing a ship at 4 to 7 knots, the effect of reversing the drive unit closest to the ship will most likely result in an immediate loss of the tug's speed and its bow sheering uncontrollably into the ship. A single, incorrect twist of a control handle can be the source of serious damage both to tug and ship. ASD maneuvering principles have not gone out the broken wheelhouse window. It is just that the right principles must be applied in the context of the maneuvering situation. Coming alongside a moving ship is not so much about walking sideways; it is more about managing speed and steering while moving ahead. The drive unit configuration must be appropriate for the principles applied.

## Working in Disturbed Water

A tug working a ship underway must contend with the suction and pressure zones created by the water displaced as the ship's hull moves through the water. The hydrodynamic interaction between ship and tug is a function of ship speed, displacement, and hull shape. As a ship moves through the water, it creates different pressure zones and water flow velocities around its hull (fig. 17-2). In simple terms, a ship moving bow first displaces or pushes water out of its way, in essence making room for the body of the hull to pass. Water resists this displacement and builds up at the ship's bow. This results in a high-pressure zone that pushes objects—including tugs—away from the bow.

    Once the water flow has rounded the bow, it accelerates and seeks to fill in the trough left by the passing ship. This factor, combined with the low

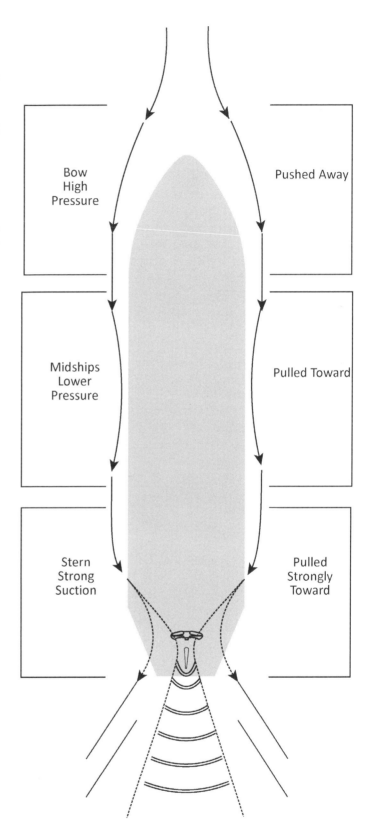

Fig. 17-2
Ship pressure zones

resistance of the ship's side, creates a low-pressure zone. The result is suction toward the hull.

As the water nears the ship's stern, it comes under the influence of the propeller. The water flow on the intake side of the propeller accelerates and accentuates the drop in pressure, increasing the suction toward the ship's hull. Just aft of the propeller, the propeller wash and ship's wake generate an additional small area of higher pressure. Generally, this area of high pressure is not as pronounced as the one encountered near the bow.

The effect of these hydrodynamic forces varies with ship speed, displacement, and hull shape. Besides disrupting the flow of water, these forces may also disrupt the ASD operator's association of specific drive unit configurations and the tug's motion. What worked in smooth water may not work in the altered water around the ship. Again, the principles of ASD handling do not change; they are simply being applied in a different hydrodynamic environment.

Creating this environment in a simulator, or with small live vessels, is difficult. It is just not the real experience unless you have a large vessel displacing tons of water. The magnitude of the ship's suction and pressure zones, propeller wash, deadweight tonnage, and momentum can be surprising. It takes on-the-job training to fully appreciate and learn how to handle the effects of tug-ship interaction.

# Allocation of Horsepower

Regardless of design, an ASD tug has a finite amount of thrust capability. Thrust capability is dictated by its engine horsepower, propeller and nozzle design, and hull shape. In shipwork, there is always a proportional relationship as to how this capability is allocated. In most shipwork situations the tug must balance three factors: its own hull resistance in the water, opposing forces when maneuvering to the desired position, and application of force to the ship by pulling or pushing. Tugs are most effective when these three factors are working in unison. An example of this is an ASD tug pulling full, positioned 45° to the bow of a stopped ship (fig. 17-3A). The tug can allocate all its thrust to the ship, since that will also meet the tug's requirements to steer and hold position. This allocation changes as soon as the ship begins to make way. Now the tug's horsepower must be allocated for dual purposes.

Portions of thrust are expended to counter the tug's increased lateral resistance and keep its position at 45°, while the remaining horsepower exerts force on the ship (fig. 17-3B). As the ship gains speed, more of the tug's horsepower is allocated to overcoming the tug's increased lateral resistance, as well as countering any suction or pressure effects created by the ship's hull. As the ship continues to accelerate, the tug's ability to pull on the ship diminishes. At higher ship speeds, even the highly maneuverable ASD tug will have to devote all its horsepower to holding position. Under these conditions, the best it can do is run with the ship with a slackline (fig. 17-3C).

The importance of the allocation of horsepower to the ASD operator is that he must continually track this allocation to ensure that there is enough horsepower available to maneuver the tug safely. In light-tug handling, he has the full horsepower to propel and steer the tug, whereas in shipwork he may have a reduced amount.

# Line Length

The length of the tug's working line is an element common to all the ship assist positions. There are four primary factors that determine the optimum length of a working line:

1. Steepness of the line angle from ship to tug
2. Effect of the tug's propeller wash on the ship
3. Distance the tug must travel to change the horizontal angle of line pull
4. Sea/swell conditions

In any specific ship job, the chosen line length will be a compromise that represents the best balance between these four factors.

### Strength in Length

A common saying in shipwork is that there is "strength in length." What this means is that longer lines preserve the working strength of a line by reducing the vertical line angle, and subsequently the line load from the ship to the tug.

The thrust produced at the tug's propellers is transferred through the winch and line to the ship. Although 60 tons of thrust will produce 60 tons of pulling force on the ship, the winch and line can

## Allocation of Tug's Horsepower

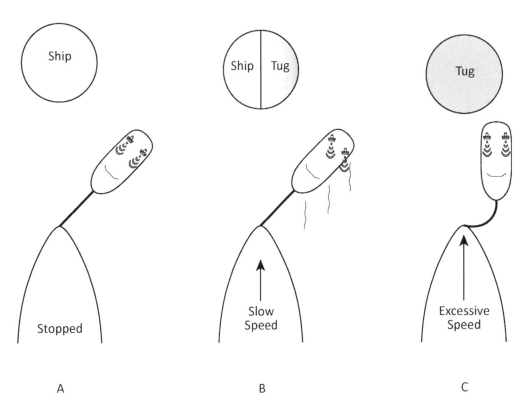

Fig. 17-3
Allocation of tug's horsepower

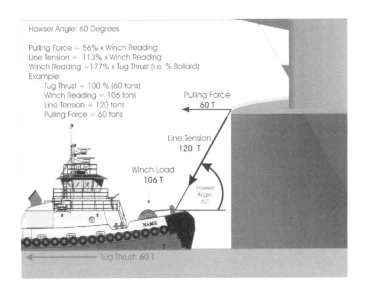

A

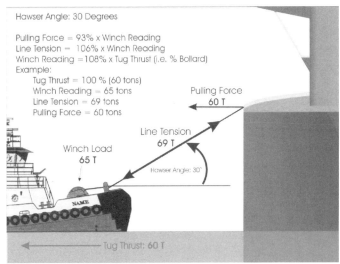

B

Fig. 17-4
Strength in length
*Courtesy of the Glosten & Associates Inc.*

have a much-higher load, depending on the vertical angle of the line. Sixty tons of thrust combined with a sharp line angle (60°) will produce a winch load of 106 tons and a line load of 120 tons (fig. 17-4A). Adding length to the line and reducing the line angle to 30° lowers the winch load to 65 tons and the line load to 69 tons (fig. 17-4B). Shorter lines and sharper angles weaken this link between tug and ship; longer lines and shallower angles strengthen it.

### Effect of Propeller Wash

Even though the ASD tug is relatively small compared to most ships, its propeller wash can have a marked effect on a ship. At shorter line lengths this effect is more pronounced, since the ship's hull is closer to the tug's wash. In fact, this effect can be so pronounced that the tug may be pulling hard one way while its wash is pushing the ship in another (fig. 17-5A). The longer the line length, the more space created for the tug's propeller wash to dissipate before hitting the ship (fig. 17-5B).

### Horizontal Line Angle

Line length also affects the amount of distance the tug must cover when repositioning to change the horizontal angle of line pull. For any given change in horizontal line angle, the shorter the line, the shorter the arc of transition when repositioning (fig. 17-6).

### Sea/Swell Condition

A common application of ASD shipwork is to provide escort towing in open roadsteads. In these circumstances, sea and swell conditions may dictate a longer line length to enhance the line's ability to absorb any additional load generated by the tug's motion in a seaway.

Determining line length requires the tug operator to weigh and prioritize the effects of vertical line angle, propeller wash, horizontal line angle, and sea/swell conditions as they apply to a specific assist job. His choice should be the compromise that is best suited for the job at hand.

## OTJ Shipwork Training

Your learning sequence in OTJ shipwork training will be determined largely by the order and type of maneuvering opportunities that arise in the course of the tug's daily work schedule. OTJ learning requires a proactive attitude. Many of the learning opportunities will come to you, and you will have to seek out others. This may mean getting up off watch or meeting a ship early to take advantage of circumstances that will allow you to practice. Some pilots may allow you to practice maneuvers other than the ones specifically required for the ship's safe arrival or departure. For example, even though a bow-to-bow position may not be required, a pilot may allow you to practice getting into that position if you have met the ship early. However, you must ask and receive the pilot's permission for this type of extra practice!

As you move through the shipwork learning process, you will rely heavily on your mentor or

Fig. 17-5
Effect of tug's propeller wash

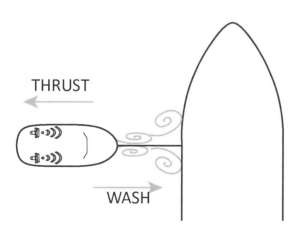

A

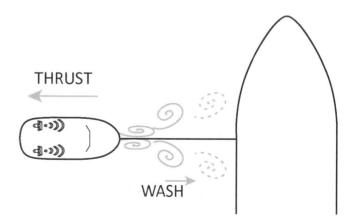

B

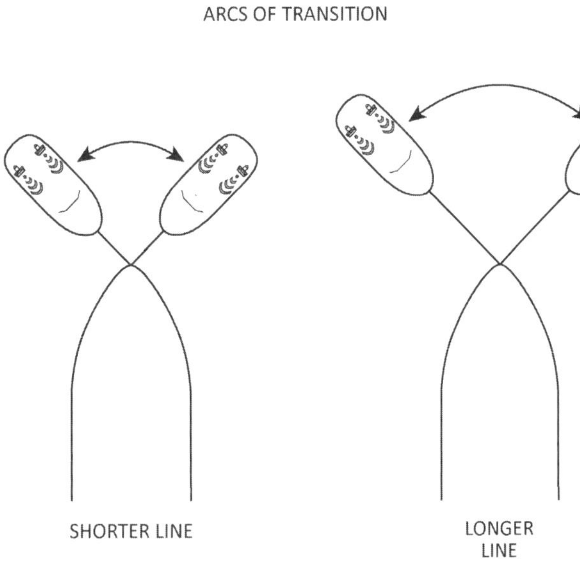

ARCS OF TRANSITION

SHORTER LINE

LONGER LINE

Fig. 17-6
Arcs of transition
Short line—short arc; longer line—longer arc

trainer to guide you. He will choose the appropriate time and place for you to learn how to apply your tug-handling skills in shipwork. And he will let you know what you did right and what you could improve on, and also make you aware of other techniques that may be applicable to your maneuvering circumstances.

The remaining sections of this chapter describe the typical shipwork scenarios you will encounter and the general tug-handling principles you should keep in mind as you apply your skills in these new situations. In addition, some Z-TPPs from experienced ASD operators are offered to help illuminate the nuances of these techniques.

# Tug Alongside

Positioning the tug alongside the ship is a good first OTJ-learning scenario. You will use many of the skills required for bow-to-bow and bow-to-stern assist positions, but you will have more room and time to maneuver.

### Getting into Position

First, pick your landing spot. This may be directly under the chock or cleat where you will place your working line, or it may be forward or aft of it. Choose a landing spot that is in close proximity to the designated working chock or cleat, but that is also

safest. It should be away from hull protrusions, overhangs, and tumble and flair. If you make a mistake, you would prefer that the tug's fenders pay the price, not the tug's superstructure. Once alongside, you can slide up or down the ship's hull to place your bow under the ship's chock to pass your line.

The location of the ship's chocks will be one of the prime factors in choosing whether you approach

Fig. 17-7
Stern-first position, alongside ship's quarter

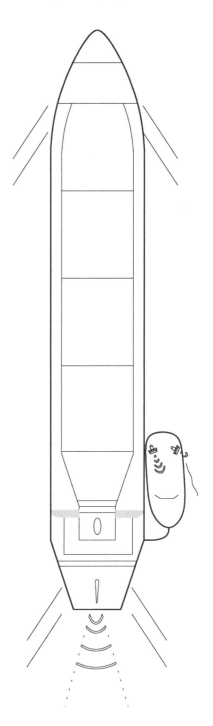

the ship bow first or stern first. For example, if you are directed to a chock on the ship's quarter near its stern, the only safe option may be approaching stern first (fig. 17-7). This allows the body of the tug to land on the flat of the ship's side shell and puts the drive units in the best position to quickly abort the maneuver if necessary.

Once you have chosen your spot, come up abeam of it and pace the ship, but stand off a good distance. This will allow you to determine the method (canting, coning, or tiller) that is best suited for you, the tug, and the ship's speed.

Before you begin to move into position, consider the "what-ifs." As an example, what if

- debris or a mechanical malfunction stops a nozzle from turning?
- a main engine stalls?
- you lose your visual reference to the ship due to snow, fog, or a ship's floodlight blinding you?
- the suction toward the ship is much stronger than expected?

Have an "out" in mind should one of the "what-ifs" becomes a "What do I do now?"

Once you are dialed in and feel your hands solidly connected to the tug, begin to move into position. Even though you have practiced this maneuver with a small pace vessel, it will be different when attempted with a ship. The effects of the suction and pressure zones you encounter along a ship's side will be much more pronounced than those associated with a small pace vessel.

## Approach

### Z-TPP

Approaching a ship to come alongside relies heavily on visual cues. Most of the time you will be looking out the side window at the ship. Look for a mark on the ship near your chosen touchdown point. It could be a chock, handrail, or rust streak—any visual mark that makes that location distinct. Focusing on one spot on the ship helps you retain your perspective and gives you the visual cues to judge your rate of closure and advance relative to the ship. If your mark on the ship is creeping up in the window frame, you

know you are closing with it. Likewise, if it is creeping forward or aft, you will know you are moving forward or aft relative to the ship. You should mainly be looking out the window, not at the azimuth or RPM indicators. Your hands should be the azimuth indicators, allowing your eyes to track the tug's closure with minimal interruption.

## Pulling on Your Line

### Z-TPP

Be mindful of your propeller wash when you are pulling on your working line (fig. 17-8A). If the ship is stopped, some operators will use a derivative of the feathered position to minimize the effect of the propeller wash by directing it farther down the ship's hull (fig. 17-8B).When the ship is in motion, some operators produce the same effect by tipping the tug's stern upstream (fig. 17-8C). The direction of the propeller wash can also affect the amount of load on the tug's engines. Some operators have found that when pulling full, the upstream engine may bog down if the crosswise position of the nozzle presents too-much angle to the flow of incoming water. Tilting the drive unit a bit more inward can relieve this condition (fig. 17-8D)

## Pushing When the Ship Has Way On

### Z-TPP

If alongside stern first and directed to push on the ship at ship speeds above 3 knots, it may be easier and safer to push with the tug's quarter, rather than roll out to 90° (fig. 17-9A). Make sure your tug has appropriate fendering aft before attempting this.

Some ASD tugs have the staple slightly aft of the bow. Be particularly cautious on these tugs if you start with a tight headline and roll out to 90° when the ship is moving ahead; it may have a "claw hammer" effect. If your line is tight when you are lying alongside the ship, the leverage of the tug's hull may increase the line load as you swing the stern out to get into position. This added strain can part lines, chocks, and bitts (fig. 17-9B).

Fig. 17-8
Minimizing the effect of the tug's
propeller wash
A: Wash affecting ship
B: Coning to angle wash
C: Tipping stern "up"
D: Adjusting azimuth to prevent
engine overload

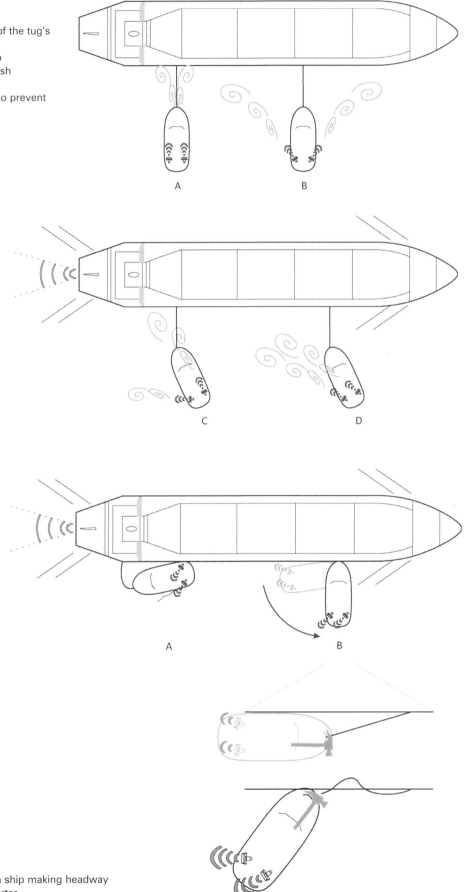

Fig. 17-9
Pushing positions with ship making headway
A: Using the tug's quarter
B: Rolling out with the "claw hammer" effect

## Holding Position

### Z-TPP

A common command while alongside the ship is to hold the tug in a neutral position—ready to quickly push or pull, but exerting minimal force on the ship. The key to finding this position is to minimize the effect of the tug's propeller wash and avoid pulling or pushing on the ship too much. If the ship is moving, some operators will walk to keep pace with the ship. Although this method facilitates keeping the line slack and the tug's 90° aspect, it can produce quite a bit of detrimental propeller wash against the ship (fig. 17-10A).

At slower ship speeds, some operators use the headline to stabilize the bow and thrust sideways to keep the stern in step with the ship's advance (fig. 17-10B). This method has the advantages of eliminating the propeller wash effect and enabling the operator to easily keep the tug at the desired 90° aspect. The disadvantage is that the weight and drag of the tug will load the tug's working line. This drawback can be minimized by adjusting the amount of pressure that the tug's bow has on the ship's side. There will be a balance point between drag and push that cancels each other out.

At higher speeds, it may be appropriate to fold in alongside the ship and run with it either bow first, or stern first with a slackline (fig. 17-10C). Because the ASD is so maneuverable, it can quickly roll out to the optimal 90° angle and pull or push.

Your choice of method will depend on ship speed and swing, and the pilot's maneuvering sequence.

### Casting Off and Breaking Away

If the ship is moving, go through the same process to break away as you did to come alongside—run parallel to the ship, hold position under the chock, lower the line down, then break away. Note that there are a lot of "what-ifs" to think of in these circumstances:

- The ship's speed is increasing.
- The ship is turning.
- The ship's crew drops your line in the water.
- The line fouls on the tug's winch.
- The line fouls the drive unit's propellers.
- The suction along the ship's hull is much greater than expected.

When you break away, always try to have the upstream end of the tug break away first. Use the techniques you practiced with a small pace vessel. If stern first, thrust in the direction you want to take the tug's stern away from the ship. If bow first, turn the outboard unit to thrust 90° toward the ship at an idle. Once the bow has lifted off the ship, come ahead on the inboard drive unit with it angled slightly away from the ship. If done correctly, you will start to walk away from the ship. Once the stern has lifted off and cleared the ship, you can come ahead on both engines.

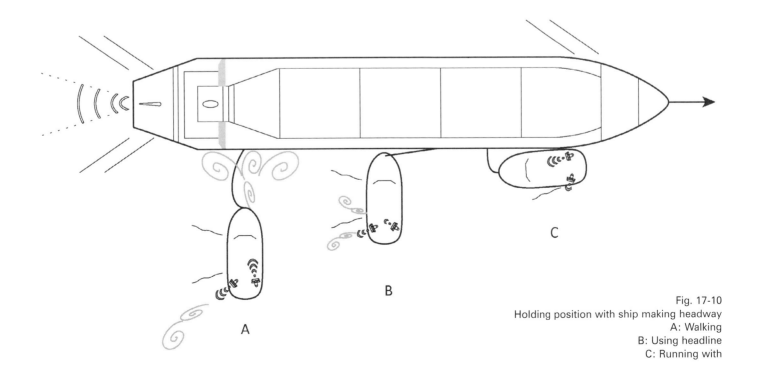

Fig. 17-10
Holding position with ship making headway
A: Walking
B: Using headline
C: Running with

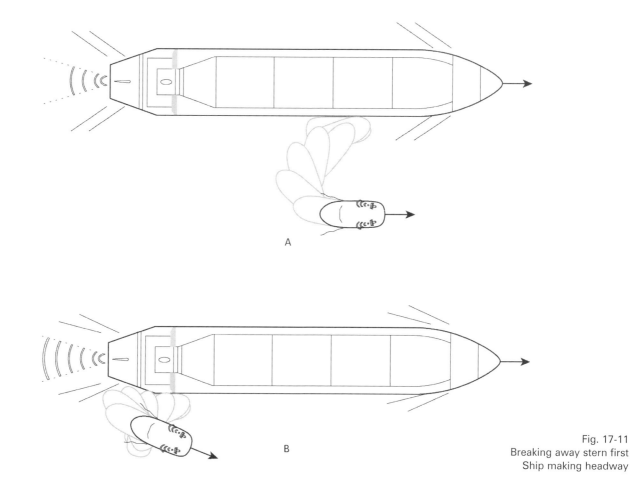

Fig. 17-11
Breaking away stern first
Ship making headway

### Z-TPP

There may be times when you will be tempted to break the stern away first when running bow first alongside a ship. Resist this temptation unless it is absolutely necessary. It may look reasonable on paper (fig. 17-11A), but in practice it may be filled with peril. Use this maneuver only if you must.

One experienced ASD captain relayed a story of his successful but less than graceful application of this technique. In his situation the tug was bow first, working a line on the ship's quarter while assisting it off the dock and to sea. Once clear of the dock, the master ordered an increase in ship speed. Lack of communication between ship and tug left the tug alongside the ship longer than usual. By the time the ship's deck crew came to let the tug go, the ship was moving at a good clip and accelerating. The tug's line was let go, but the suction on the ship's quarter kept the tug stuck. The ASD operator tried to get the bow to lift off, but two factors quashed that plan. The first was that the ship's suction was too strong; the second was that the stern of the tug was far enough aft that it would easily go under the ship's stern overhang if the tug's stern was angled in to get its bow to go out (fig. 17-11B). In addition, the tug was having trouble keeping up with the ship's speed of advance and was starting to slide aft on the ship. At this juncture the ASD operator had no choice—there was not enough time to wait for the ship to slow down, and the tug was inching down the side of the ship, heading for its stern and propeller. Do something or go under the stern rake—that was his choice. The operator made a split-second decision. He worked the tug's stern out until he had managed to attain a slight angle and then thrust the stern away from the ship as hard as possible. At this point there was no question that the tug's stern would remain clear of the ship, but the outcome of the bow was doubtful. As the tug's stern came away from the ship, the tug's bow fender rubbed hard down the ship's side. The friction between the tug's bow pud and ship was so great that it left a trail of black marks and smoke. Fortunately the tug's bow gained an extra few inches as it swept down under the overhang of the ship's stern. Once free of the bow-to-ship contact, the tug pulled clear of the ship.

Breaking away from a ship in this manner can be done, but it is not recommended for general practice, is not for the fainthearted, and requires an experienced operator at the controls.

# Lead Tug Bow to Bow

Going bow to bow and putting up a working headline to a moving ship will quicken the heart rate of any ASD operator, whether new or experienced. The tug is in close proximity to the flair of the bow overhead, its bulbous bow below the waterline, and the deck crew is working in the shadow of the looming bow. All this takes place while the operator is facing the forward end of the tug but steering the tug backward. A tug-handling mistake in this position can have serious consequences. Tug design and ship speed play a large role in the performance of an ASD tug working bow to bow. What works safely for one ASD tug design may be dangerously close or over the limit of another. In particular, older ASD tug designs may have problems sailing astern at speeds greater than 4 knots. More than ever, it is important to know your tug's capability before working bow to bow.

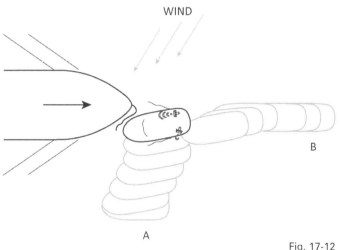

Fig. 17-12
Bow to bow, passing a headline

### Getting into Position

Generally the tug will spot its bow on one or the other side of the ship's bow to tuck in far enough to grab the ship's tagline and avoid contact with its bulbous bow (if so equipped). Many times, the choice of side is dictated by the location of the tag line's bitter end, since it tends to get set off to one side or another by the wind.

Once you have chosen your side, plan your approach. Some operators prefer to begin their approach off to the side of the ship's bow (fig. 17-12A), while others choose to begin in front of it (fig. 17-12B). The choice is dictated by personal preference,

regional practice, and navigation or environmental conditions that are present. In either position, it is important to pace the ship and give yourself time to determine the method (canting, coning, or tiller) that is best suited for you, the tug, and the ship's speed. It also allows you to get dialed in and connected to the tug before you move into position.

Before you begin to move into position, be sure to consider the "what-ifs":

- The ship's pressure wave at the bow is stronger than expected.
- Debris fouls a propeller and stalls one drive unit.
- The tagline comes loose as your line is being hauled up to the ship and the line fouls on the ship's anchor.

Even though you have practiced this maneuver with a small pace vessel, it is different when attempted with a ship. The pressure wave at the bow of a large ship is much stronger than the one associated with a small pace vessel. It will push the bow of the tug one way or another, and you will have to adjust your drive unit configuration to accommodate the effects. Once you are in the right spot to pass the working line, hold position.

### Z-TPP

When you are in position to pass up your line, you may end up with a slightly unfamiliar drive unit configuration, and the tug may be canted one way or the other (fig. 17-12). The angled aspect of the tug may look strange, but if it is holding position, do not try to fix it. If it works, keep on going.

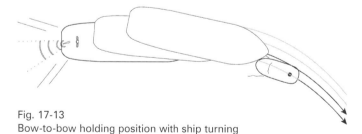

Fig. 17-13
Bow-to-bow holding position with ship turning

Remember, the stern leads the bow. Focus on locating the stern in a position that tracks where you want the bow to be. The tug's pivot point on its stern should be tracking parallel to the ship's course. Imagine a series of lines that run parallel to the ship's course. For the tug's bow to remain in position relative to the ship, the tug's pivot point near the stern needs to track parallel to those lines (fig. 17-13).

### Pulling on Your Line

Once your line is up to the ship, back up and pay out line, but be careful to regulate the amount of slack so the line does not foul on the ship's bow. Continue to open the distance between you and the ship until you are in line and a sufficient distance away from the ship to have a proper vertical angle on the line and minimize the effect of the tug's propeller wash. As you pull away from the ship, you will go through two transitions that affect the tug's steering.

The first is when you leave the influence of the pressure wave at the ship's bow. As you transition through this pressure wave, it may push the tug's bow or stern one way or the other. At this point in your learning sequence, your hands should be capable of instinctively making the necessary adjustments. The potential pitfall is not that your hands will not know what to do; it is that they may be occupied with other activities. They may leave the controls to operate the winch, radio, search light, alarms, etc. Be aware that every time your hand leaves the controls, the connection it has with the tug is interrupted. It may take a critical second or two to reconnect once it returns to the controls. These valuable seconds may be just the opportunity the tug needs to begin driving itself, and you along with it.

Having your hands leave the controls may be unavoidable in these situations, but you can proactively manage the timing. For instance, it may be more prudent to delay answering the radio if the call comes in while you are in the midst of transitioning through the ship's pressure zone.

The second transition is when you first take a strain on your line. When you are maneuvering in front of the ship, putting up and paying your line out, the tug is handling like a light tug. As soon as you take a strain on your line, you have established a towing point that changes the location of the tug's pivot point. The tug will behave a little differently and requires a steering adjustment. Again, your hands should be capable of instinctively making the necessary fine tuning, but they must be present on the controls and dedicated to the task.

### Tug Safety

The interrelationship between tug safety and applying assisting force to the ship is readily apparent when pulling on a line bow to bow with a moving ship. A mistake in judgment either by the pilot or tug operator can result in the tug being overrun by the ship, pinned underneath the bow, slammed against the side of the ship, or worse. The ASD operator follows the pilot's directives but must always be mindful of the tug's limits. This question is always in the back of the operator's mind: "How close to the edge can I get and still recover?"

### Ship Speed

The speed of the ship is a critical factor in the effectiveness of an ASD tug in the bow-to-bow position. As ship speed increases, the tug's effectiveness decreases. The faster the ship advances, the greater portion of the tug's thrust must be allotted to keeping pace with the ship. This leaves a diminished amount that can be applied as a pulling force to the ship.

### Z-TPP

When you are learning to operate the tug in this configuration, you should be attentive to ship speed. The more the ship's speed increases, the more vigilance you must exercise in limiting the amount you allow the tug to get offset from the ship's centerline. Subtly but constantly test your ability to recover from positions that are offset from the ship's centerline. When you are in position, pulling off to one side or the other, adjust the drive unit configuration to see what it takes to get the tug moving back toward a position in line with the ship.

### Angle of the Line versus Angle of the Tug

The direction of force transferred through the tug's headline is dependent on the horizontal angle the line makes with the ship, not the angle of the tug to the ship. The force on the line may differ with different angled aspects of the tug, but the direction of pull remains the same.

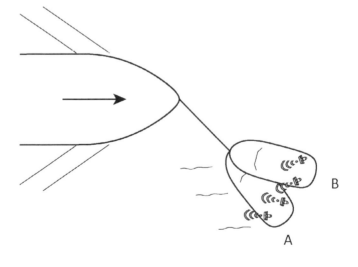

Fig. 17-14
Angle of line versus angle of tug

### Z-TPP

Knowledge of the relationship between tug angle and line angle gives the ASD operator a tool to manage risk. While having the tug pull in line with the line lead from the ship is possible (fig. 17-17A), a position where the tug's stern is tipped upstream may be a more recoverable position (fig. 17-17B). The horizontal line angle to the ship remains the same, but the tug's stern is in a better position to move quickly back in line with the ship.

### Combination Mode

Some of the newer ASD tug designs have a pronounced skeg forward. When this skeg is angled to the oncoming water flow, it can provide hydrodynamic lift that increases the bollard pull of the tug. This angle is created by tipping the tug's stern upstream in the bow-to-bow configuration (fig. 17-14B). Tugs with this capability offer the operator an additional option to apply force to the line safely.

### Casting Off

Casting off has the same operational considerations as getting into position: ship/tug interaction, holding position underneath the bow, and transferring the line without getting it fouled on the ship's anchor or bow. Ship speed should not be higher than the safe speed designated for connecting the towline. That being said, many times the ship's pilot or master will be anxious to get up to sea speed upon departure and will be building speed as you let go. In addition, you may have connected your towline while the ship was berthed, and only upon casting off are you first experiencing the specific effects of the ship's bow wave. When casting off, follow the five principles of conventional tug wisdom to keep your hands instinctively driving the tug with the finesse required to safely cast off and break away. Have a plan, consider the "what-ifs," make a good approach, stay in your comfort zone, and always leave an "out."

## Tail Tug-Tethered

### Getting into Position

Tethering to the ship's stern, especially at higher ship speeds, means working in disturbed water. Even though you have practiced this maneuver with a small pace vessel, it will be different when attempted with a ship. The effects of the suction and pressure zones, as well as the propeller wash you encounter at a ship's stern, will be much more pronounced than those associated with a small pace vessel. As in the previous assist positions, pace the ship at first and get a feel for the method best suited for the conditions at hand.

### Z-TPP

Many experienced ASD operators prefer the coning method when approaching a ship's stern. It is common to encounter an area of low pressure right behind the ship's stern that rapidly draws the tug the last few feet toward the ship. In addition, if the tug is working in an open roadstead, the swell may cause the tug to surge toward the ship. The ASD operator must have the ability to constantly steer and immediately put on the brakes. This precise control is created by starting out in the coning configuration with constant power and increasing or decreasing the drive unit azimuths as needed.

### Working Your Line

Your hold position while passing the line will be determined in large part by the shape and draft of the ship's stern. You may be able to push on the stern if the ship is deeply laden and has a flat transom. This is an optimal position, since it reduces the likelihood of a dropped line going into the water and fouling either the ship's or tug's propeller. This may not be an option with ships in ballast, since they may be so light that the rudder is partially exposed, requiring you to hold off the stern a few feet.

As you continue your on-the-job training in the tethered position, you will become familiar with six (6) basic maneuvers associated with being tethered to the ship's stern:

1. Transverse arrest
2. Reverse arrest
3. Direct towing
4. Indirect towing
5. Powered-indirect towing
6. Jackknife maneuver

### Transverse Arrest and Reverse Arrest

Both a transverse and reverse arrest are used to retard or stop a ship's forward advance. The drive unit configuration for a transverse arrest is the feathered position: both drive units thrusting toward each other at 90° to the tug's centerline (fig. 17-15A). The amount of thrust on each side is adjusted to provide the desired amount of braking force and keep the tug in line with the ship. Reverse arrest is when both drive units are thrusting in reverse (fig. 17-15B).

Although simple in concept, there are some nuances in applying these techniques.

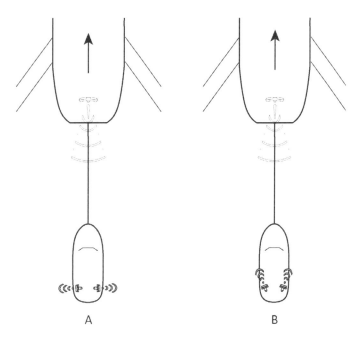

Fig. 17-15
A: Transverse
B: Reverse arrest

## Z-TPPs

• When initiating either arrest technique, ease into the line, letting the weight of the tug stretch the line first before loading the line from the tug's thrust.
• In typical arrest applications you will find yourself applying retarding force by first going to the transverse-arrest configuration.
• Modify the force applied to the line by increasing or decreasing the drive unit power or angle.
• Be attentive to engine and clutch loads. At higher ship speeds, one of the risks of going into the reverse-arrest or feathered-back position prematurely is that the tug's engine and clutch system may become overloaded. As the drive unit rotates from a transverse-toward a reverse-arrest position, the tug's propeller turns more and more against the direction of the water flowing by the tug's hull. This places the propeller in negative flow conditions, which considerably increases the torque loadings on the propeller and engine. In extreme cases the increased load may stall the engine or cause the clutch to slip and fail.

## Terminology

The expanding use of omnidirectional tugs has required the introduction of new terms used to describe the position of the tug and the type of assisting force applied to the ship. Although the dialogue between pilot and tug may vary from region to region, those conversations include three commonly used terms: direct, indirect, and powered-indirect towing.

• Direct towing: The tug pulls on the line in the desired direction (fig. 17-16A).
• Indirect towing: Pulling force is applied to the line by turning the tug at an angle to the oncoming water flowing by its hull (fig. 17-16B). The increased lateral resistance of the tug's hull creates lift and drag forces that add to the force applied to the ship.
• Powered-indirect towing: In this technique, the tug operator adds to indirect towline forces by creating a large towline angle (up to 90°) and applying the tug's power to add to the effect of the tug's lift and drag (fig. 17-16C).

Both in indirect and powered-indirect towing, the direction of the applied force can be varied by positioning the tug bow first, off to one side or the other of the ship.

Direct towing can be done with the ship stopped, or advancing with slow to moderate headway. Both indirect and powered-indirect towing require a higher ship speed to be effective. The definition of a slow to moderate or a higher speed is dependent on ASD design. A rate of 4 to 5 knots may be a moderate speed for older ASD designs, while 6 to 7 knots may be more applicable to new designs. This is where the role of the trainer or mentor is critical—in his knowledge of a specific tug's performance limits and passing that on to the trainee.

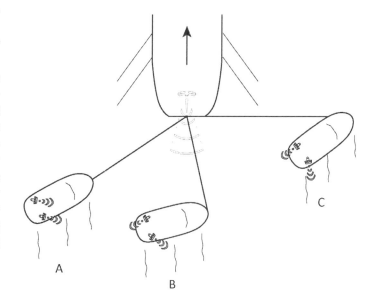

Fig. 17-16
Direct, indirect, and powered-indirect modes

Direct Towing                    Indirect Towing

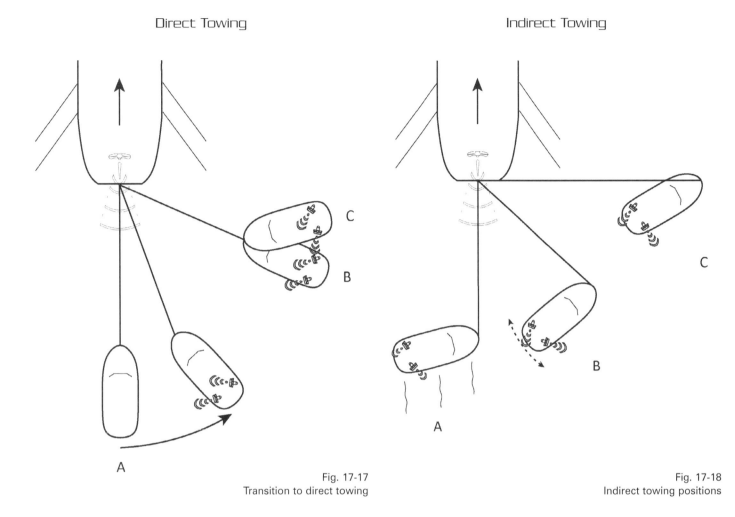

Fig. 17-17
Transition to direct towing

Fig. 17-18
Indirect towing positions

Direct towing is used at slower ship speeds to steer and retard the ship. Like the arrest position, there are some tips that will help you master this towing mode.

### Z-TPPs
- Stretch your line prior to swinging into position (fig. 17-17A).
- Keep a strain on the headline to help stabilize the tug's bow.
- Remember, it is the horizontal line angle from the ship, not the angle of the tug, that determines the direction of force applied to the ship.
- Be mindful of engine and clutch loads, especially on the upstream unit if you are using a split drive unit configuration.
- It may be better to use the drive units in unison, rather than to split them (fig. 17-17B).
- The combination mode may be effective in this position, if your tug has that capability (fig. 17-17C).

In the hands of a skilled operator, indirect towing is one of the most powerful maneuvering tools in the ASD operator's toolbox, but it must be used carefully and in appropriate circumstances. Applied incorrectly, this maneuver carries high risk to equipment and personnel.

Indirect towing is sometimes used for its braking effect (fig. 17-18A). In this case you will twist the stern upstream, pivoting it around the tug's staple but keeping the line pull in line with the ship's centerline. If the pilot requests "take my stern to starboard indirect," you would increase your line angle to approximately 45° and manipulate the angle of the tug to the water to regulate the amount of pull on the line (fig. 17-18B). At higher ship speeds you may be asked to go powered indirect, in which case you increase your line angle to 90° and power into the line. The drive unit configurations in indirect towing are determined by feel. The configurations illustrated in fig. 17-18 are some of the many possibilities at the disposal of ASD operators. Take them as a guide, but trust your hands to find the right combinations for your tug and your skill level.

Properly applying indirect towing relies on the operator's feel for the tug and the load on the line. Some tug operators refer to this feeling as being similar to the sensation of a waterskier at the end of a towline. The two prime sensory cues are the heeling angle and the sensation of "digging into the water." This is similar to a waterskier shooting off to the side of a ski boat's wake. As the waterskier turns and increases the angle of his skis to the water flow, the ski edge digs in, causing more hydrodynamic resistance and lift. This results in more pull on the towline. The more he moves off to the side, the greater these forces become.

In indirect towing, a tug operator may experience similar sensations. As he steers the tug to greater angles of water flow, the tug's resistance and subsequent strain on the tug's line increases. At some point, whether a tugboat or a waterskier, the combination of hydrodynamic resistance and towline pull will surpass the capability of either to resist. The waterskier will not have enough body weight and physical strength, and the tug will not have enough stability and buoyancy to counter the heeling action.

At this crossroads, both entities have three options. The first is to steer back toward the pulling force (ski boat or ship). This immediately reduces the angle to water flow and reduces hydrodynamic resistance. The second is to reduce power (ski boat or ship slows down). This immediately reduces the pulling force of the towline. The third is to release the towline altogether. If the skier or tugboat is heeling excessively and does not exercise one of these options, the skier may fall over and the tug may founder or capsize.

While these abort options may sound simple, they may prove difficult to execute in actual practice. It is possible for an operator to allow the tug to get beyond a recoverable position. The most recognizable sign of the tug's capability limit in indirect towing is the point of deck edge immersion. Once the deck edge begins to submerge in indirect towing, designed stability and buoyancy calculations become moot. At this point, it is possible for the tug to be pinned in a vulnerable position; it will lack the power or maneuverability to counter the sudden exponential increase in heeling force. Under these circumstances the tug may founder or capsize unless the towline can be released.

As a tug operator, it is important that you fully appreciate how little time it takes to transition from being on the edge to over the edge of an ASD's safe operating limit. While engaged in indirect towing it can be almost instantaneous.

## Jackknife

The jackknife maneuver is used to transition from indirect towing to direct towing, or to quickly reposition the tug from a position astern of the ship to direct towing to one side. Typically this is used when the ship's speed has slowed to the point that the tug is overrunning its line in the indirect mode and would be more effective in the direct towing mode. The maneuver requires that you simultaneously rotate the drive units and haul in the slack in the headline as the tug flips around. ASD operators employ two drive unit transitions: one splits the units and has one drive unit push the stern around to the new position, while the other unit rotates at a lesser RPM in the opposite direction to the new direct towing position (fig. 17-19A). The second method rotates

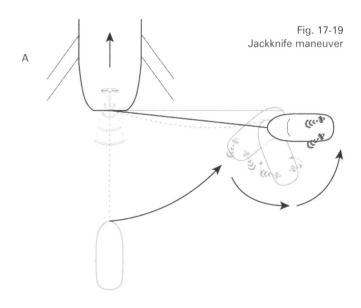

Fig. 17-19
Jackknife maneuver

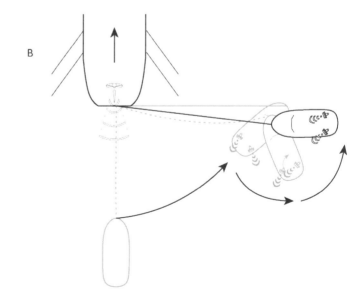

both drive units in unison in the direction required to swing the stern to the direct towing position (fig. 17-19B). The choice of technique depends on the ship speed and the design, the performance parameters of the ASD tug, and the type of winch technology on the tug (render-recover versus static brake). The objective is to make the transition quickly, keep some tension on the headline, and end up at approximately the same horizontal towline angle as when the maneuver started.

### Z-TPP

- At faster ship speeds, splitting the units may cause the engine powering the upstream propeller to stall due to the load induced by the negative water flow.
- This maneuver requires a deft touch both on Z-drive and winch controls.
- A good learning sequence is to first maneuver the tug while someone else operates the winch and regulates strain on your line.
- Once you feel comfortable jackknifing the tug, add the winch operation to your task.

## Summary

Handling an ASD tug engaged in shipwork is one of the high arts of the profession. Competence in the art requires skill and experience acquired over long periods of time. The on-the-job training described in these pages does not stop at book's end; it is a process that continues throughout one's career as a professional mariner. As you gain expertise you become both trainee and trainer to yourself. Each ship job is always a little different and has nuggets of wisdom embedded in the experience. Dig for those nuggets. They will enrich your skill and capability as a professional ASD tug operator.

# *Chapter Eighteen*
## Continuous Learning

## Overview

Operating a Z-drive tug or towboat is a continuous learning process. Whether you are a novice or a veteran operator, there is always new knowledge to be gained and skills to be acquired or refined. Even the most experienced operator will tell you, "I learn something every day." Sometimes this knowledge transfer occurs in a formal training environment with a trainer and a specified training agenda. However, there will be a time when formal training evolves into a continuous learning process of self-taught skills learned while on the job.

There is no secret to the learning process on the job: it involves repetition and taking advantage of "learning moments" as they come your way. Sometimes the learning moment comes from external sources, such as an equipment failure or environmental conditions (wind, sea, and visibility), or sometimes from internal sources, such as lapses in the operator's focus or judgment, or sometimes simply from a knowledge gap. Regardless of the source, you have ways to make the learning process safe and less likely to result in damage to personnel or property. A good day is when a few learning moments are thrown your way; you harvest a few nuggets of knowledge and finish the day with no dents, scratches, or bruises.

Many times these learning moments occur when a mentor or trainer is not present. In these cases, you must take on a dual role as a professional mariner learning his trade and as your training supervisor. You must have the ability to recognize your skill level, create a controlled learning environment, and manage yourself as would a competent trainer. You must have self-awareness and self-discipline to take advantage of opportunities to safely polish your existing Z-drive skills or learn new ones. The opportunities to learn may be known in advance or may turn up suddenly. It may be your first time working tethered to a ship's stern, downstreaming on a tow, or experiencing an unexpected Z-drive failure that creates these moments. Regardless of the source, these times can be managed productively and safely by following a few simple guidelines.

- Know thyself
- Define a box of learning
- Utilize trainer's tips
- Recognize signs of trouble
- Know how to get out of trouble
- Polish

## Know Thyself

An honest and clear self-assessment of your Z-drive skills is the first step in safely walking the path of continual improvement. You will not know your limits unless you measure your performance. There are four levels of tug or towboat handling competence:

1. Trainee: Understands maneuvering principles but cannot consistently apply them or complete basic maneuvers.

2. Apprentice: Able to complete basic maneuvers, but not consistently; requires an experienced operator or trainer present in the wheelhouse at all times; verbal coaching or physical intervention is required at times.

3. Functional: Able to complete maneuvers consistently; does not require a trainer present in wheelhouse; can take self-corrective action when required; able to apply maneuvering principles and experience to new situations.

4. Proficient: Able to complete maneuvers consistently and efficiently; takes minimal time to complete maneuvers; smoothly transitions from one maneuver to another; utilizes Z-drive propulsion to full potential.

The self-teaching process begins when you have reached level 3]—functionally competent in basic maneuvers. Continuous learning is all about acquiring new skills and expanding and polishing existing skill sets. These all require that you operate at the boundary of your ability, walking the narrow ledge between challenging yourself and falling off the cliff into incompetence and an accident.

There are four common performance measures you can use to rate your competence.

- Replication
- Time
- Precision
- Thinking mode

# Replication

The first measure of competence is the number of times you can successfully repeat a specific maneuver. You should be able to successfully demonstrate a specified maneuver at least five [5] times consecutively to consider yourself competent at that skill set. If not, then more practice is required in a controlled learning environment.

"Successful" is a self-defined standard. Keep a high standard. Consider the example of nosing up to a moored ship or barge to push perpendicular to the side shell. A self-imposed high performance standard would be defined as making a soft landing, touching down within a foot of the designated push point, and landing perpendicular to the side shell, ready to push. Landing 5 feet off the mark or coming in at an acute angle and then rolling out to 90° would not.

# Time

The second performance measure is time. During a training session we always emphasize "take your time," "don't be in a hurry," "speed kills," etc. These axioms are absolutely correct in a training context. However, there is always a time element in real-world applications of Z-drive boat-handling skills. Take the previous example of nosing up to a moored barge or ship. No one would consider an operator competent if it took him ten minutes from the time he was five [5] boat lengths off the ship or barge to the time he touched up. That is well in excess of an industry standard. So how do you establish a time standard in self-assessment? A good place to start is by comparing your time to an experienced operator's time to complete the same maneuver. An industry-accepted benchmark of functional competence is if your time is not over 30 percent in excess of the

time an experienced operator takes to complete a specific maneuver. In other words, if an experienced operator completes the maneuver in ninety seconds you can consider yourself functionally competent if you perform it in 120 seconds or less.

# Precision

A Z-drive has an inherent paradox. On the one hand, its maneuverability enables the skilled operator to execute maneuvers quickly with consistent precision. Touching down softly within inches of the designated push point, coming into a headline at precisely the right angle of pull, or producing consistent line tension while indirect towing all are examples of the performance perfection attainable with a Z-drive.

On the other hand, this same maneuverability can create a tolerance for sloppy tug handling. Rather than touching down within inches of a push point, the operator can miss by a few feet and easily recover by walking over to the designated spot. Or he can come into a headline at too shallow an angle and rapidly swing the stern to shift into the correct position. The ability to recover from a maneuvering mistake is an important skill set. When assessing yourself, you should use a high standard of precision. If you do not hold yourself to a high standard when you practice, you will not reach a high standard when you perform, and you may overestimate your degree of competence.

A simple example is assessing yourself docking the light tug or towboat to a dock. If your self-assessment tolerates deviating from the approach line and landing short of the berth (fig. 18-1A), you may assume erroneously that you are competent for executing the same maneuver with restricted space (fig. 18-2B).

# Thinking Mode: Head versus Hands

The last measure of functional competence is whether you are completing the maneuver by thinking in your head or thinking with your hands. Functional competency requires that you think with your hands. The reason is simple. Any time you take on a new maneuvering challenge, there will always be a conscious thinking element—you have to have the mental bandwidth to think through the new maneuver with your head. If you are already thinking through the basic steps of a specific maneuver, there simply is not enough brain bandwidth left to solve a more complex evolution of that same maneuver.

Take the example of turning the tug 180° from bow first to stern first (fig. 18-2A). If you cannot complete that maneuver intuitively in open water, just letting your hands do the thinking, it would be inappropriate to attempt the same maneuver in the

The first example involves no time or space restrictions. The second example includes the added variables of relative speed, heading, and position to the barge, as well as restricted time parameters. It is a much more complex maneuver, even though the tug's primary motion is the same.

Your awareness of whether you are thinking with your hands or thinking with your head is a key indicator of your readiness to take on a new challenge with a particular maneuver.

Once you have attained a functional level of competence, you are ready to take on the challenge of learning and practicing on the job.

Intended Position

Intended Track

B

Intended Position

Intended Track

Actual Position

A

Fig. 18-1
Precision
Pitfall of training without precision

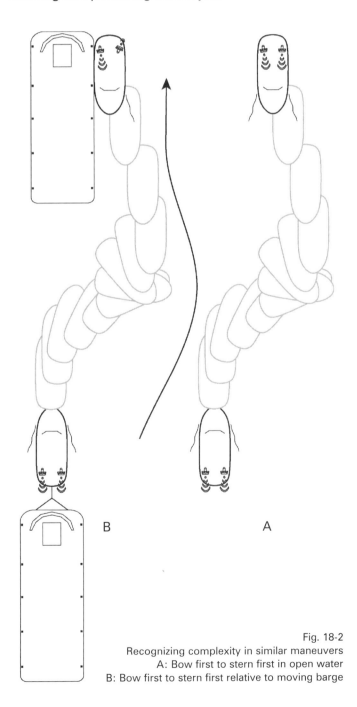

context of transitioning from towing astern to towing alongside (fig. 18-2B).

Fig. 18-2
Recognizing complexity in similar maneuvers
A: Bow first to stern first in open water
B: Bow first to stern first relative to moving barge

# Create a Box of Learning

It is important that you put your trainer hat on before you allow yourself to assume the role of trainee. The first step as a trainer of yourself is to create training boundaries (fig. 18-3). Training boundaries define a box of learning—a learning environment in which there is enough time and space to allow you to make, recover, and learn from a mistake. It also defines the "hard stop" of when it is time to abort the maneuver, rather than press on. Four [4] elements define the box:

1. Prerequisite skill sets
2. Safety gates
3. Limiting environmental factors
4. Abort criteria

## Prerequisite Skill Sets

Most advanced maneuvers consist of a series of basic maneuvers strung together in a rapid, specific sequence. Unless you are at least functionally competent in the basic maneuvers that form the building blocks of the complex maneuver, you can't expect to be able to safely practice a complex maneuver.

A good example of this is walking or sidestepping laterally into a restricted berth for the first time (fig. 18-4). You should not attempt this maneuver until you are at a functional level walking. This means being able to complete the drills in chapter 11 successfully, and also completing the maneuver without space restrictions. In this case, it would mean being able to walk laterally and land gently with precision in an unrestricted space (fig. 18-4A) before practicing in a restricted space (fig. 18-4B).

Fig. 18-3
Box of learning

Prerequisite
Skills

Environmental
Factors

Safety Gates

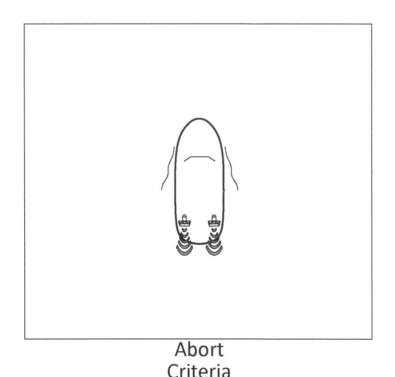

Abort
Criteria

Fig. 18-4
Prerequisite
Master basic skill before practicing more-challenging scenarios

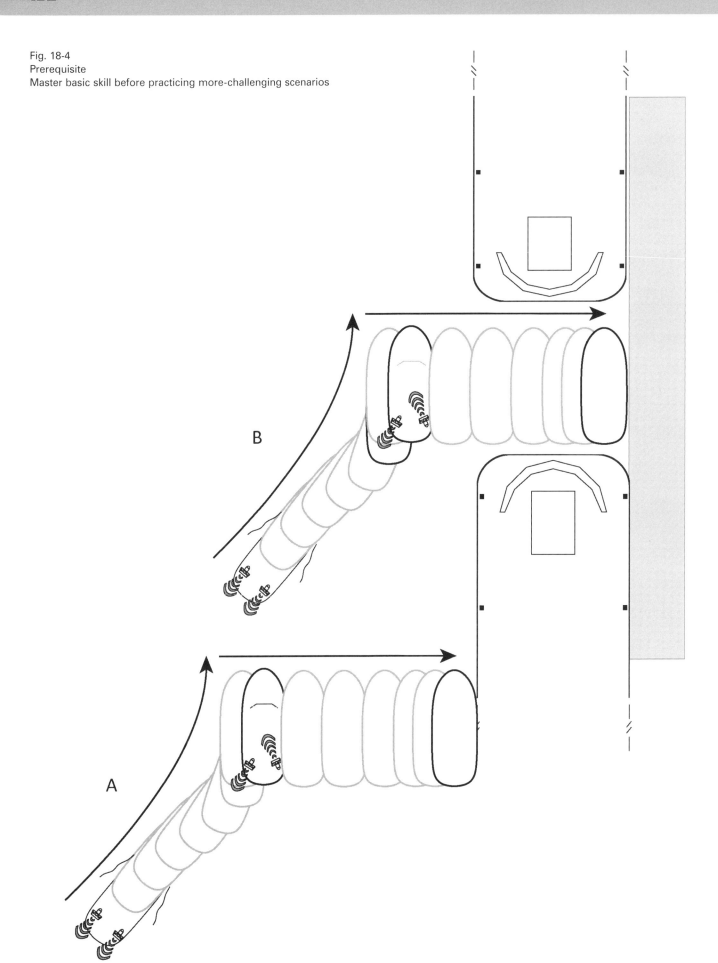

## Safety Gates

The second leg of the box is defined by safety gates. Safety gates are checkpoints in a maneuvering sequence in which there is an opportunity to self-assess whether to proceed or to safely exit the maneuvering sequence. They are also points at which you must confirm you have control of the tug to continue the maneuver to the next safety gate, or to completion.

In our walking into a restricted berth, typical safety gates would be at the initial lineup (fig. 18-5A), passing the outer boundary of the restricted space (fig. 18-5B), and approximately 5 feet off the dock (fig. 18-5C). You should not pass these figurative gates unless you are in control: drive units configured in the sweet spot, hands moving intuitively in small increments, and your mind out several tug widths ahead of the tug's lateral track.

## Environmental Factors

The third leg of the box of learning is defined by limiting environmental factors. These could be conditions such as water depth, visibility, current, wind, and sea state that preclude attempting a maneuver when in a learning situation.

As an example, restricted visibility would be a limiting environmental factor in practicing walking into a restricted berth. You would not want to attempt to walk into a restricted berth the first time if fog, rain, snow, or darkness prevented you from seeing the visual references needed to gauge your speed, aspect to the dock, and surrounding obstructions.

## Abort Criteria

The abort criteria are directly related to the risk of damage to personnel or equipment. It is a simple formula: Risk of damage + lack of positive control = abort the maneuver. Fig. 18-6 illustrates a common example that occurs in walking into a restricted berth. The operator has just passed the second safety gate and is continuing to walk toward the dock, but the bow is beginning to tip in toward the dock faster than the stern. The operator makes a correction—more azimuth and power—but overcorrects, and the tug gains headway toward the bow rake of the barge ahead of him. The operator tries to correct again but has lost the sweet spot, and the tug gains headway and starts to rotate. This is the time to bail out and regroup, rather than force the maneuver past a point of no return.

Fig. 18-5
Safety gates

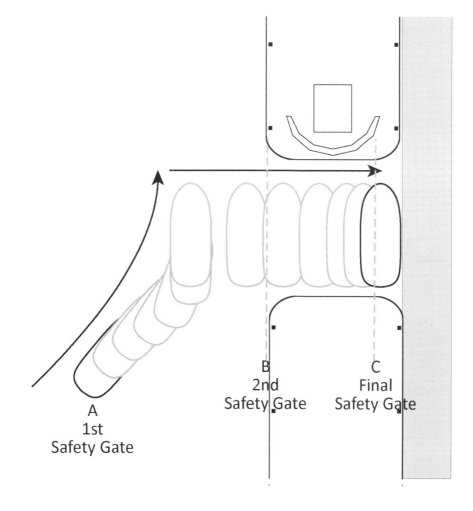

A
1st
Safety Gate

B
2nd
Safety Gate

C
Final
Safety Gate

Fig. 18-6
Time to abort

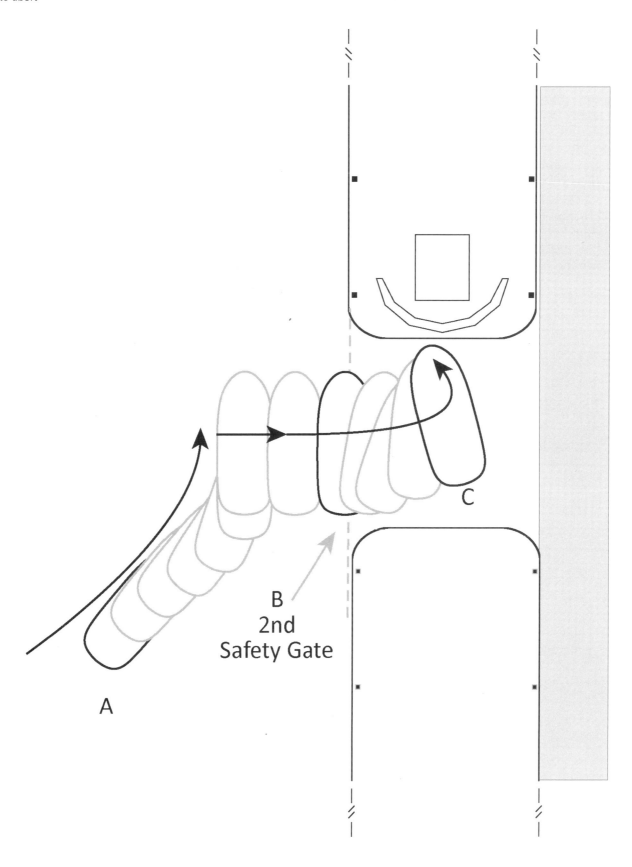

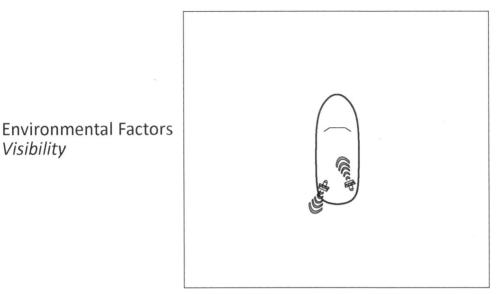

Prerequisite Skills
*Walking*

Environmental Factors
*Visibility*

Safety Gates
*1) Approach*
*2) Entry*
*3) 5'*

Abort Criteria
*Risk of Damage*
*Lack of Control*

Fig. 18-7
Box of learning
Walking into restricted space

The box of learning in this case is defined by four boundaries (fig. 18-7):

• Prerequisite (Walking drill competence)
• Safety gates (initial approach, entry, and final approach)
• Environmental factors—visibility
• Abort criteria: Risk of damage, lack of control

# Trainer's Tips

Here are a few tips you can use when assuming the role of instructing yourself:

• Find the sweet spot.
• Make small hand movements.
• Be aware of your maneuvering bubble.
• Match speeds.
• Be aware of caution zones.

## Find the Sweet Spot First!

Z-drive tugs and towboats have a common characteristic: either you drive the boat or it will drive you. There is no middle ground. The starting point of driving a Z-drive is to find the sweet spot—the balance of thrust that makes you feel that you have pinpoint control of every maneuvering aspect of the tug or towboat. If you do not have that feeling when you begin a new maneuver, you certainly will not find it as you near a dock, barge, ship, or other obstruction. You must have positive control before attempting any maneuver or allowing yourself to go into the next phase of the maneuver. That is the purpose of the safety gates—to provide opportunities to make sure you are in command and control before taking the next steps in the sequence of a new maneuver.

### Hand Movements

The role of the hands in driving a Z-drive is multipurpose. They should be your azimuth indicators, your physical connection to the tug or towboat and its machinery, and the maneuvering command center for ordering changes to the timing and amount of azimuth and power changes to the balance of thrust. They are the conduit for feeling "one with the boat," as well as sending control signals to the engine and Z-drive room.

It is extremely important that the hands do not lose those connections. The most common way to lose that connection is by making large hand movements (e.g., gross changes in azimuth or RPM).

• Small hand movements = small mistakes
• Large hand movement = large mistakes

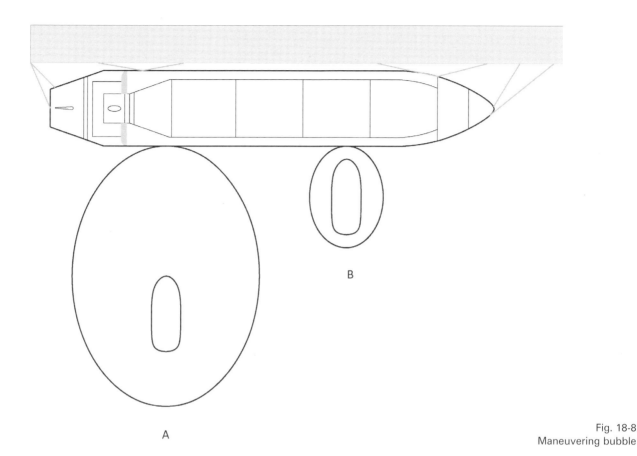

A

B

Fig. 18-8
Maneuvering bubble

When you are taking on a new maneuver or polishing existing ones, remind yourself to move your hands in small increments to maintain a positive connection to the tug or towboat and in firm control.

### Maneuvering Bubble

The maneuvering bubble is the space surrounding the tug or towboat that enables you to make a mistake, problem solve, and take corrective action before damaging property or equipment. The key is to be aware of how the bubble may expand or shrink in relation to the complexity and phase of the maneuver. Take the example of touching up the bow to a ship (fig. 18-8). The bubble is quite large in approaching from open water (fig. 18-8A) but shrinks rapidly as the distance closes to the ship—there is less room to make and recover from a mistake (fig. 18-8B). Regardless of the size of the bubble, the operator can remain in the bubble by managing speed. Whether a routine or new maneuver, an operator needs time as well as space to recover from mistakes.

Time is created by managing speed; the slower the speed, the more time within the bubble. This may seem obvious, but speed in a Z-drive is more than just vessel speed through the water or over the ground. An operator must manage multiple speed relationships to stay within the safety of the maneuvering bubble.

### Matching Speeds

Three speed-time relationships must be managed to create sufficient time for an operator to remain in control of the tug or towboat in any given maneuver:

- Hand speed to brain speed
- Hand speed to drive unit rotation speed
- Vessel speed to vessel response time

### Hand Speed to Brain Speed

The hands should not move the control handles any faster than the time required for the brain to keep up. If you do, you are shifting from precise, calculated hand movements with predictable results to random azimuth and power experiments. When the hands outpace the mind, it is a feeling similar to driving down a road so fast you miss your exit. The car is moving faster than your brain can pick up the letters and words of the sign, read and interpret them, and then send the signal to your hands to turn and exit. A Z-drive is no different. If you move your hands faster than your brain can interpret the cause and effect of the control changes, you will deviate from the intended path of your maneuver.

The tolerance for hand speed is directly related to whether you are maneuvering by "thinking with your hands" or consciously thinking your way through a maneuver.

Consciously thinking your way through a maneuver requires more time, and thus a slower hand speed. Your mind will be consumed with perceiving the sensory data of the tug's or towboat's movement, problem-solving drive unit configurations, and reconciling the effect of drive unit changes to the boat's motion. That process takes time. If your hands make control changes faster than your mind can consciously track the picture in your head, you will lose your train of thought, hurtle down the tracks, and most likely derail the maneuver.

If you are "thinking with your hands," you can tolerate quicker hand movements on the controls because you are bypassing the time it takes for conscious thought. However, you are still dependent on your brain's ability to gather and process sensory input and transmit the correct signals to your hands to adjust the controls. Whether thinking with your mind or thinking with your hands, the speed and rapidity of your control changes should not exceed the processing speed of your brain.

### Hand Speed to Drive Unit Rotation Speed

Drive units have a maximum rotation speed. If you rotate the control handle faster than the drive unit rotation speed, the actual azimuth of the drive unit lags behind. You may change the control handle azimuth 90° instantly, but it will most likely take the drive unit five to nine seconds to make the same change. When this happens you are vulnerable to losing your positive connection to the tug or towboat. Your hands will no longer be accurate azimuth indicators, and you may lose the feel for the sweet spot.

Remind yourself to manipulate the control handles in a manner that minimizes the lag time between what your hand position conveys to your mind and the actual azimuth position of the Z-drive unit.

### Vessel Speed to Vessel Response Time

Different vessels have different power-to-weight ratios, displacement, and underwater hull designs. These and other factors affect the vessel's response time to changes in azimuth or power. Some will react almost instantly; others may have some lag time. You must choose a maneuvering speed that allows enough time for the tug or towboat to react to your control changes within the context of the specific maneuver.

Your management of these three speed relationships is essential to keeping the tug or towboat within the confines of your maneuvering bubble and successfully practicing the intended maneuver. Sometimes this translates into a maneuvering speed that is no faster than a leaf drifting on a pond. Other times it may be as quick as a Formula 1 race car taking chicane turns. Either way, speed must match your level of proficiency
.

### Caution Zones

Caution areas are the times during a maneuver when the greatest probability arises of making either an unrecoverable mistake, or one that has only one brief chance to make an appropriate correction. There are two caution areas that are common to most maneuvers:

• Transitions
• The three foot zone

### Transitions

Transitions are when the tug or towboat is required to shift from one primary maneuvering direction to another. This change requires the operator to transition from one sweet spot and quickly find another. It is common for new Z-drive operators to lose positive control during the transition and take time finding the new, required sweet spot. This is part of the learning process. As the operator gains more experience and skill, the transitions will become smoother and seamless. During the learning process it is critical that you identify transition points and build in enough time and space to allow you to make and recover from mistakes during the transitions.

### The Three-Foot (1-Meter) Zone

The three-foot zone is that space between the tug or towboat and the desired touchdown point. Once the vessel enters this zone, the operator must quickly perceive, process, and execute the subtle control changes necessary to bring the tug or towboat gently to its destination. This usually occurs in a compressed time frame with limited space and can be challenging to the new Z-drive operator. If you are attempting a new maneuver, pay particular attention to the safety gate in the three foot caution zone. You must have the self-discipline not to enter the three-foot zone unless you yourself are "in the zone"—in the sweet spot and moving your hands calmly with precise, small movements.

# Signs of Trouble

The transition between your comfort zone and the "I've lost it" zone may not always be clear. The first key is to recognize the signs that indicate you are no longer driving the tug—the tug is driving you. There are some classic symptoms that may appear:

- Rapid hand movement
- Gyrating vessel
- Twin-screw twilight zone
- Escalating arms race
- Holding your breath
- Tunnel vision

### Rapid Hand Movement
Be wary if you find yourself turning the control handles back and forth rapidly through large arcs. This is called "hand hunting" and is a common indication that you are "searching with your hands." You have lost the mental picture of the drive unit cause and effect, and you are no longer connected to the tug or towboat. Instead, you are conducting a series of rapid trial-and-error experiments with your hands in an attempt to get both your hands and mind in sync with the vessel's motion.

This typically occurs when the vessel is maneuvering in close quarters, and the maneuvering sequence is evolving faster than your hands or mind can process. Your hand moves one way, but the tug or towboat does not respond the way you want, so you immediately move it in another, more exaggerated direction. Meanwhile, the vessel has already moved on to the next step in the maneuvering sequence. You feel like you can't keep up and your hope lies in moving the handles faster than the vessel's unpredictable motion. Your hands hunt for a solution, conducting random experiments. These experiments rarely work.

### Gyrating Vessel
If you are rapidly moving the controls and searching with your hands, the tug or towboat may begin to gyrate or corkscrew from side to side. This is similar to the effect of oversteering on a conventional tug. However, the stern of an ASD tug is more lively and skittish than a conventional tug or towboat, and the results of overcorrecting with thrust are much more pronounced. The tug or towboat turns and heels over one way or the other as the drive units are worked back and forth. It may feel like the vessel is in a beam sea, yet the sea is not creating this effect; it is the operator's attempts to hang on to control of the vessel.

### Twin-Screw Twilight Zone
The classic symptom of being lost in the twin-screw twilight zone is applying more power and moving the control handles in large increments when the tug or towboat is out of control. This may be an effective response in a conventionally propelled tug or towboat, but it makes the situation exponentially worse in most Z-drive cases. In a conventionally propelled tug or towboat, the hands typically make large motions: swinging the steering lever, holding the jog stick over, or pushing the throttle handles forward or aft. These are precisely the wrong type of hand motions to apply to an out-of-control Z-drive. It is an instinctual reaction for experienced conventional tug or towboat operators, and we all tend to default to our instincts in stressful maneuvering situations. Operators with experience in conventionally propelled vessels have to fight their instincts to get out of the twin-screw twilight zone and apply the Z-drive axiom of less is more.

### Escalating Arms Race
Another common symptom is an escalating arms race between the hands. This typically occurs when one drive unit is set to counter the effect of the other, and the operator is trying to maneuver the vessel by finely manipulating the balance between the two. One hand increases thrust to induce the desired vessel motion, and the second hand increases to counter but overcompensates. The first hand then responds with an additional increase in throttle. This initiates a continuous chain of ever-increasing thrust from the two drive units. The result is a lot of propeller wash and quite a bit of fuss in the water, but the tug or towboat goes nowhere.

### Holding Your Breath
Holding your breath is a natural reaction to a rise in anxiety. It is also the way your body braces itself when it anticipates a collision. If the operator's sense of control wanes, his anxiety rises. Holding your breath may be an early warning from your body, signaling that it anticipates the worst and is unsure whether you have real control of the tug or towboat.

### Tunnel Vision
Tunnel vision is a common side effect of the mental effort to regain the cause-and-effect picture of the tug's or towboat's motion. Most operators in their comfort zone will be relaxed and have expansive vision. When pushed out of their comfort zone, some operators try to concentrate harder by narrowing their focus. This can result in tunnel vision. A common example of tunnel vision is when an operator stares intently at the

azimuth indicator. It is as if by staring laser-like at the azimuth dial the operator can command the incongruity between the hand motion, vessel motion, and azimuth to clear up. You may feel like you are singularly focused on the one critical element, but what is really happening is you have lost the big picture of the interaction among your hands, your mind, and the tug or towboat.

These five symptoms may present themselves individually or in combination. Their sudden onset may be just the warning you need to call on one of the response techniques below to prevent losing control of the tug or towboat.

# Getting out of Trouble

If the tug is getting out of hand, what should be your response? One word: SIMPLIFY!

### Simplify, Simplify, Simplify

Losing control of the tug or towboat usually means that the maneuvering tasks have exceeded the ability of your hands and mind to anticipate, process, and react to the tug's or towboat's motions. To regain control, you must manipulate the situation to build in the time and space that enables you to recover. This time-and-space cushion is created by simplifying the tasks and mental juggling at hand. There are four common means that Z-drive operators use singularly or in combination to simplify a maneuver:

• Slow down.
• Go to your happy place.
• Clutch out.
• Reboot your hands.
• Eliminate variables.

### Slow Down

Excessive speed is the main contributing factor in many Z-drive accidents. If your mind and hands can't keep up with the tug or towboat, an easy way to immediately build in time and space is to *slow down*. Slowing down applies to more than just vessel speed; it also applies to your hands. Slow down your hand movements and avoid making rapid and large control changes. Calm hands calm the boat.

Slowing down simplifies a maneuver by building in space and time, enabling you to resolve a sequence of mistakes one by one rather than simultaneously. As an example, if your maneuver requires you to steer and manage speed, slow down to the point you can manage one aspect, then the other. Slowing down is an operator's primary tool to return to the safety of the maneuvering bubble.

### Go to Your Happy Place

The happy place is the drive unit configuration that stabilizes the tug's or towboat's heading and slows its advance. For most ASD operators this is the feathered position: both drive units aligned at 90° to the vessel's centerline and thrusting equally toward each other. This tried-and-true method has been used to extricate Z-drive tugs or towboats from many maneuvers that have gone awry. It works because it takes the guesswork away from the operator; he does not have to invent a new drive unit configuration—he knows where to go. Sometimes just beginning to go into the feathered position calms the tug or towboat enough that the operator regains control. It is the closest thing a Z-drive has to an abort button.

Clearly, it does not have universal application. If the tug were working bow to bow with a ship, you would not want to come to a stop in front of it. However, the principle of finding a mechanism to stabilize the tug and its speed to regain control has widespread application.

### Clutch Out

There may be circumstances in which taking both drive units out of gear and letting the tug or towboat drift may be the best alternative. Rather than trying to power your way out of a mistake and making a bad situation worse, it may be better to drift, allowing you to take your hands off the controls and reboot your hands.

### Reboot Your Hands

If you think of your hands and mind as processors, times will occur when they get overloaded and need to reboot. You can quickly reboot the connection between your brain and your hands by declutching both drive units and then clutch each one in and out individually. This cleans the slate in your brain and allows you to reestablish the correlation between each hand's position, drive unit azimuth, and the vessel's response. Once your mind sees the reaction of the vessel to each drive units' separate thrust, it can start piecing back the puzzle of how the interrelation between the two affects the tug or towboat.

### Eliminate Variables

When the tug's or towboat's speed surpasses the ability of your mind and hands to assess, process, and react, there are two ways to manipulate the maneuvering situation. The most obvious is to slow down; the other is to speed up your processing and reaction time relative to the most important task at hand. Many times a loss of control is the result of an operator making a maneuvering situation more complex than it needs to be. A good example is coming alongside, bow first, to a ship underway. This example also applies to a towboat coming alongside a moored barge in a head current. The objective is to control the tug's or towboat's speed of advance, to steer, and to land gently on the side of the ship or barge. If the operator attempts to meet these objectives by manipulating the RPM and azimuth of both drive units simultaneously, he is juggling the thrust variables of each drive unit, creating an almost infinite number of combinations. If he begins to lose control because he can't process all the thrust variables, it will help if he eliminates some variables. One means of reducing variables would be to match RPM and use azimuth changes as the primary maneuvering method. Now his mind and hands process the combination of azimuth changes in each hand without having to factor in RPM changes.

Eliminating the RPM variable enables the operator to devote more brain "bandwidth" to focus on the critical tasks at hand—steering the tug or towboat and managing speed. It is not that he sped up his processing and reaction time, it is that he eliminated some variables so his capability was more efficiently focused on the critical tasks at hand. An operator can eliminate thrust variables by

• using only RPM and leaving the azimuth fixed,
• using only azimuth and leaving the RPM fixed,
• using only one drive unit and leaving the other static, or
• taking one unit out of gear.

Find the technique that comes to you most naturally. Use it when you feel your mind beginning to seize up and your hands hunting for control solutions.

# Summary

Proficiency in handling a Z-drive requires a continuous learning process. There are times when that process is within a formal training context, and times when it occurs on the job. Either way, managing risk goes hand in hand with learning to drive a Z-drive. The tools for managing that risk lie in taking appropriate preventive measures, being aware of the signs of trouble, and being well versed in a few basic techniques to take back control of the tug or towboat. With those tools in hand, you can safely learn on the job with minimal risk to personnel, equipment, and property and attain a high level of proficiency.

# Notes

# *Chapter Nineteen*
## Conclusion

Let's face it—the draw of driving an ASD tug is the challenge of harnessing its power and maneuverability and getting maximum performance both out of the tug or towboat and you. Everyone who steps on an ASD tug or towboat wants to get his hands on the controls. He wants to experience the excitement of having this sophisticated and powerful machine come alive under his hands. More and more mariners in the towing industry are getting this experience. ASD tugs and towboats have dominated the number of new builds in recent years, and their numbers continue to expand worldwide in harbor, inland, river, and coastwise towing applications. As a result, more and more mariners will be handling the controls, learning how to drive this high-performance machine.

The propulsion technology may be new, but the basic learning process is not. That process is the traditional learning path of the professional mariner: hands-on practice and repetition under the guidance of a mentor or trainer. The process can be made more efficient by practicing skill sets in a systematic and sequential order that introduce and reinforce these basic principles of driving an ASD tug or towboat:

• Know your tug.
• The stern drives the tug.
• Steering and propulsion are linked.
• Hands in the present, head in front of the tug.
• Know yourself.

## Know Your Tug

ASD tug and towboat designs vary widely, and so do their performance capabilities and mechanical setups. Before you ask your ASD vessel to perform at its peak, you should know and respect its limits. Become just as familiar with your tug's or towboat's mechanical systems and hull design as with the control handles in the wheelhouse. We tend to focus on which way to twist the control handles to make the tug or towboat work for us. Of equal importance is knowing why the vessel responds to a turn of the control handle. Know how to make it work, but also know why it works.

## The Stern Drives the Tug

No matter which way the tug is moving, or you are facing, the stern drives the tug. The stern of an ASD tug or towboat reacts almost immediately to any changes in thrust, whether that thrust was correctly or incorrectly applied. Lose track or control of the stern and you have lost control of the tug or towboat. Master the art of controlling the stern and you have mastered the vessel.

## Steering and Propulsion Are Always Linked

Much more than in a conventional tug, steering and propulsion are inextricably linked together in an ASD. You can't change one aspect without affecting the other. Tracking the constantly changing steering-propulsion relationship is a task that should be in the back of your mind, but in the forefront of your hands. The ongoing equation between steering and propulsion is one to be solved by your hands as they learn to quickly and intuitively react to changes in the vessel's speed and direction.

## The Balance of Thrust

Regardless of the drive units' configuration, the two units create one resultant force that affects the tug or towboat. This means that your hands are always working together, directing the vessel's motion by constantly manipulating the balance between the two drive units. You can't move one hand without affecting the other and the resultant force on the tug or towboat. Remember the 1 = 2 and 2 = 1 axiom. One control change will always have two maneuvering effects. It takes two control changes to create one maneuvering effect. An expert ASD operator understands the balance of thrust and this axiom in his mind and retains an ongoing sensitivity to it in his hands.

# Hands in the Present, Head in Front of the Tug

Competence in ASD tug or towboat handling requires that you engage both your hands and mind in the task. You must have a "feel" for the vessel, sensitivity to its motion, awareness of its response to the controls, and a sense of command in your hands. The conduit for this intuitive connection is your hands resting on the controls, instinctively reacting to the tug's or towboat's subtle changes in direction and speed, while at the same time retaining command of the vessel. Your mind must be the lookout—pacing the tug or towboat two to three boat lengths ahead, assessing the maneuvering sequence, and anticipating the drive unit configurations that will be required.

## Know Yourself

Handling an ASD tug or towboat is all about knowing your capabilities, as well as your vessel's. The tug's or towboat's maximum performance may be fixed, but yours will change as you acquire new skills, experience, and expertise. Not all ASD tugs, towboats, and operators are created equal. That is a fact, not a judgment. Respecting your limits and those of your vessel are keys to a productive and safe day at the controls. It can be tricky learning how far you can push your personal envelope without breaking it. Managing this risk requires taking appropriate preventive measures and being aware of signs of trouble. You should also be well versed in a few basic techniques to take back control of the tug or towboat should the vessel get out of hand. Equipped with those tools, you can safely and continuously refine your ASD tug- or towboat-handling skills and acquire new ones.

Maneuvering an ASD in the hands of an expert looks effortless and seamless—smoothly spinning around, nimbly shifting position, and having pinpoint control, all the while instinctively and naturally moving the control handles. The expert is in a state of oneness with his vessel, sensitive to its motion and always in command. Many aspire to this state, and it is one that can be attained, but only through continuous learning and persistent, systematic practice.

There are no shortcuts on the path to Z-drive enlightenment. It takes commitment, self-discipline, patience, and a steady, continuous walk up the mountain of learning. The hike to the top will take time and effort, but the reward is the expansive view in your mind and the confidence in your hands that you have taken tug or towboat performance to a new level.

# *Glossary*

arc of transition: The arc and distance scribed by a tug when changing the horizontal angle of pull on a working headline.

ASD: Azimuthing stern drive; a vessel that has two Z-drive units positioned athwartships near the stern of the vessel.

ATD tug: Azimuthing-tractor-drive tug; a vessel that has two Z-drive units positioned athwartships, forward of amidships of the vessel.

azimuth: The angle the drive unit is positioned in reference to a horizontal plane.

balance of thrust: The propelling force applied to the tug as a result of the combination of the two drive units' thrust components.

bite: The feeling associated with a transverse arrest as the braking force takes hold in the water.

bow to bow: The towing-assist mode in which the lead tug's bow faces the bow of the vessel being assisted.

box of learning: Training boundaries that are set to manage the risks of onboard training.

canting: The drive unit configuration in which the propeller wash of each drive unit is angled slightly toward the vessel's keel.

comfort zone: The combination of maneuvering speed, drive unit configuration, and amount of engine power that enables the operator to feel in complete control of his vessel.

coning: The drive unit configuration in which the propeller wash of each drive unit is angled slightly outboard of the vessel's keel.

direct towing mode: The towing-assist mode in which the tug is pulling on a line and the tug's centerline is closely aligned with the angle of force applied to the ship.

downstreaming: A towboat maneuver in which the towboat is working in current and facing up to the up-current end of a barge.

drive unit: Generally refers to the lower leg of the Z-drive propulsor, which can rotate 360°.

facing up: The maneuver in which a towboat positions its push knees at one end of a tow to put up the necessary ropes and wires for the push towing mode.

feathered: When both drive units' azimuths are at approximately 90°, thrusting toward each other, propeller wash going outboard.

fighting yourself: When a Z-drive operator utilizes a drive unit configuration that has the thrust of one drive unit countering the thrust of the other unnecessarily.

flanking: A towboat maneuver in which the towboat is rounding a bend going down current and holds the tug stationary to the ground, allowing the current to swing the head end of the tow around the bend. Also a colloquial term to describe lateral motion in a towboat.

flopping: The maneuver required when a tug transitions from towing astern mode to towing alongside.

hand orientation system: A consistent, systematic way of placing the hands on the Z-drive controls so that hand position is an accurate indicator of drive unit azimuth.

happy place: A feathered position with equal RPM.

hipping up: Getting the tug or towboat in position to handle a tow alongside.

hover: Holding the tug or towboat in position with no fore and aft, lateral, or rotational movement.

indirect towing mode: Applying force to the head line by turning the tug at an angle to the oncoming water flowing by its hull. The increased lateral resistance of the tug's hull creates lift and drag forces that add to the force applied to the ship.

inertia: A characteristic of an object that resists changes to its state of motion.

jackknife maneuver: The maneuver when a tug transitions from indirect towing to direct towing.

kinesthetic learner: A person who learns by feel.

less is more: The Z-drive axiom that by making smaller control changes, moving the hands less, or using less thrust, you can maneuver more effectively.

long way around: When the operator purposely chooses to transition from one azimuth angle to another by rotating the drive unit through the longer rather than the shorter angular arc.

maneuvering bubble: The space surrounding the tug or towboat that allows an operator to make, recognize, and correct a mistake before damaging equipment, property, or personnel.

maneuvering maxim: A maneuvering technique that is based on one or more accepted maneuvering principles.

momentum: The resistance of an object to a change in its state of motion, or in simple terms the "amount of motion."

one equals two: One control change (azimuth or RPM) resulting in two effects on the vessel.

one to many: One Z-drive configuration linked to multiple responses from the vessel.

powered-indirect towing mode: Adds to indirect towline forces by creating a large towline angle (up to 90°) and applying the tug's power.

propeller wash: The direction and magnitude of the water flow created by the rotating propeller.

radial scan: A technique used to make an organized, visual assessment of an instrument panel. The scan begins at the primary instrument and moves to the secondary supportive dials and switches, depending on the purpose.

reboot the hands: A technique to clear the hand-brain connection by declutching both drive units and then clutching each side in and out separately and individually.

reverse arrest: Creating a braking effect by having both drive units thrusting directly aft.

Rotortug®: A vessel that has three Z-drive units, with two Z-drive units forward—similar to a tractor configuration—and one Z-drive unit aft.

safety gates: Checkpoints in a maneuvering sequence in which there is an opportunity to assess whether to proceed or to safely exit the maneuvering sequence.

short way around: When the operator purposely chooses to transition from one azimuth angle to another by rotating the drive unit through the shorter rather than the longer angular arc.

sidestepping: Another term for moving the vessel laterally, with no fore or aft movement or change in heading.

slide: Lateral motion induced by momentum created in a turn.

stick: When a tug or towboat is in stationary contact relative to another vessel, as in facing up or coming alongside a barge.

sweet spot: The feeling associated with the drive unit control position in which you can control the tug with very small, subtle hand movements and have it respond instantly.

tail up: The stern of the vessel is the up-current end.

think with your hands: Solving maneuvering challenges through the intuitive movement of your hands.

thrust: The directional effect of the propeller wash. The direction of thrust is opposite the direction of the propeller wash.

tiller steering: Using the azimuth and RPM of one drive unit to maneuver the vessel.

towboat: A towing vessel that operates primarily on inland rivers in a push towing mode.

tractor tug: A vessel that has its propulsion system forward of amidships. The term refers to the location of the propulsion units in a vessel, not the type of propulsion.

transition: The point in a maneuver when the vessel is changing from one primary direction of motion to another.

transverse arrest: The Z-drive configuration in which the two drive units are aligned at 90° to the vessel's keel and thrusting in opposition to each other.

tug: A towing vessel that operates primarily in harbors, coastwise, and in ocean towing and may operate towing astern, alongside, or pushing ahead, or in shipwork.

twin-screw twilight zone: The confusing mental state between thinking like a Z-drive operator and thinking like an operator who is used to conventionally propelled tugs or towboats.

two equals one: Two control changes (azimuth or RPM) resulting in one effect on the vessel.

visual learner: A person who learns by creating a clear picture in his mind.

walking: Moving the tug or towboat laterally, with no fore and aft movement or change in heading

what-ifs: The potential circumstances that could negatively affect the planned maneuver.

Z-TPPs: Tricks of the trade contributed by experienced and knowledgeable Z-drive operators.

# *References*

Hensen, Henk, FNI. *Tug Use in Port*. 2nd ed. London: Nautical Institute, 2003.

Hensen, Henk, FNI. *Bow Tug Operations*. London: Nautical Institute, 2006.

Slesinger, Jeffrey. *Shiphandling with Tugs*. Centerville, MD: Cornell Maritime Press, 2008.

# *Index*

# *About the Author*

Capt. Slesinger's maritime career has spanned over 40 years both at sea and ashore. He has served as captain of oceangoing and harbor tugs, port captain, safety director, marine surveyor, and auditor. Capt. Slesinger created his own company, Delphi Maritime, in 2008 to create innovative maritime business, safety, and training solutions. The company develops and implements onboard and shoreside continuing professional-development programs and conducts audits and surveys. Capt. Slesinger is committed to promoting the professionalism of the brown- and blue-water mariner and has collaborated with individual companies, maritime training institutions, and national organizations to develop recruitment, training, and retention programs to achieve that goal.